T0274929

KIDNAPPED AT SEA

The Battle of the USS "Kearsarge" and the CSS "Alabama."
Édouard Manet, 1864.
The John G. Johnson Collection, Philadelphia Museum of Art, Cat. 1027.

KIDNAPPED AT SEA

The Civil War Voyage of
David Henry White

ANDREW SILLEN

Johns Hopkins University Press

BALTIMORE

Johns Hopkins University Press
2715 North Charles Street
Baltimore, Maryland 21218
www.press.jhu.edu

Library of Congress Cataloging-in-Publication Data

Names: Sillen, Andrew, author.
Title: Kidnapped at sea : the Civil War voyage of David Henry White /
Andrew Sillen.
Description: Baltimore : Johns Hopkins University Press, 2024. | Includes
bibliographical references and index.
Identifiers: LCCN 2023057495 | ISBN 9781421449517 (hardcover) | ISBN
9781421449524 (ebook)
Subjects: LCSH: White, David Henry, 1845–1864. | Prisoners of war—
Confederate States of America—Biography. | Confederate States of America.
Navy Navy—Biography. | United States—History—Civil War, 1861–1865—
Prisoners and prisons, Confederate—Biography. | Impressment—Confederate
States of America. | African American sailors—Delaware—Biography. |
Semmes, Raphael, 1809–1877. | Privateering—Confederate States of
America. | United States—History—Civil War, 1861–1865—Naval operations,
Confederate. | Lost Cause mythology.
Classification: LCC E599.A3 W457 2024 | DDC 973.7/57092
[B]—dc23/eng/20240227
LC record available at https://lccn.loc.gov/2023057495

A catalog record for this book is available from the British Library.

Material in chapter 4 was previously published in Andrew Sillen, "The Cope
Line Voyages of David Henry White: Evidence from the Cope Family Archive,"
Pennsylvania Magazine of History and Biography 148 (January 2024). Figures 8.1, 8.2,
and 8.3 are reproduced from Charles Greyson Sommersell, *CSS* Alabama*: Builder,
Captain, and Plans* (Tuscaloosa: University of Alabama Press, 1985).

*Special discounts are available for bulk purchases of this book.
For more information, please contact Special Sales at specialsales@jh.edu.*

For my mother and father

ESTELLE SILLEN FUCHS (1922–2015)

WILLIAM FUCHS (1917–1998)

Contents

Part III. Aftermath

Author's Note

At the outset, it is necessary to consider how best to refer to the lost teenage sailor David Henry White. This is a challenge because we don't know his preference, and we are certainly unable to ask. "David" would convey a familiarity I do not have, and besides, it seems diminutive, especially since I will refer to his kidnapper, Raphael Semmes, as "Semmes." Since I can't ask, I will use his last name. It might not have been White's preference, but at least it does not assume familiarity or diminish him when compared to others in this account.

In turn, this decision creates its own complication since it is confusing to use the same term, "White," to refer both to an individual and to a group identity different from his own. In this case, the solution is in the orthography—to not capitalize "white" when referring to the identity. This requires some further explanation.

Almost one hundred years ago, W. E. B. Du Bois initiated a letter-writing campaign asking publications, including the *New York Times*, to capitalize the "N" in "Negro" (a term long since fallen into disuse).[1] The *Times* at first demurred but came around in 1930, recognizing such usage as "not merely a typographical change but an act of recognition of racial self-respect."[2] Ninety years later—in July 2020—the *Times* began capitalizing the term "Black" when describing people and cultures of African origin.

While recognizing the need to capitalize "Black," the *Times* retained the lowercase form for "white." In rejecting the need for parallelism, rightly or wrongly, the editors suggested that "white doesn't represent a shared culture and history in the way Black does, and also has long been capitalized by hate groups."[3] On the other hand, historian Nell Irvin Painter has persuasively argued that retaining the lowercase "w" allows white people to avoid having to see themselves in racial terms. "We should capitalize 'White,'" she wrote, "to situate 'Whiteness' within the American ideology of race, within which 'Black,' but not 'White,' has been hyper visible as a group identity."[4] This, she argued, outweighed any association of the capital letter with white supremacists. Subsequently, the *Washington Post* adopted the capital "W."

Since, at the time of this writing, both positions are defensible and in use, as a matter of narrative clarity in this instance, I have chosen to use the uppercase "White" to refer to David Henry White and the lowercase "white" to refer to the racial identity.

Preface

❧

Growing up in Brooklyn, New York, I had never heard of the Confederate commerce raiders, let alone the Confederate States Ship (CSS) *Alabama*, or the teenage sailor David Henry White. Rather, my three-decade fascination—with the vessel, its officers, crew, and White—began with a somewhat random and unlikely encounter.

It was the late 1980s, and I was walking down Strand Street in Cape Town, South Africa, where I had taken a position in the Archaeology Department at the University of Cape Town (UCT). I was going downtown for a haircut and happened to pass the Koopmans–De Wet house. At the time, this graceful old Dutch-styled building housed the South African Cultural History Museum. A signboard outside announced free admission. On a whim, I stepped inside and came upon a glass case displaying a Confederate battle ensign. My immediate reaction was that this was strange and ahistorical. As an archaeologist, I had been trained to look at artifacts in their context, and it struck me that the ensign was obviously out of place, like a European stone tool in an African cave, or a Neolithic carving in a Paleolithic sediment. I had to know more.

I learned that in August 1863, midway through its world cruise, the Confederate commerce raider *Alabama* sailed into Table Bay and captured an American merchant ship, the *Sea Bride*, in full view of the entire city. The British population of the Cape of Good Hope was quite sympathetic to the Confederate cause, and in one of the numerous parties and celebrations in which the *Alabama*'s captain, Raphael Semmes, was welcomed, he presented the battle ensign to a local ship chandler, and the ensign eventually found its way into the South African national collections.

While relatively few people in the United States (other than Civil War naval enthusiasts) have learned about the *Alabama*, it has remained famous in South Africa. It even entered folklore in an Afrikaans folksong—"*Daar kom die Alibama*"—much loved by both the white Afrikaners and the Cape Colored population.[1] There was something poignant about this—that a distant community on another continent would for 150 years musically enshrine the memory of a vessel that connected it to US history, while America itself mainly forgot about it.

Only a fraction of what I subsequently learned about the *Alabama* concerns South Africa, but my sixteen years there from 1985 to 2001, during which I witnessed the transition from Apartheid to democracy, shaped my interest and approach to the historical record—especially the memoirs of the *Alabama*'s officers. Nobody could live in South Africa during the transition from Apartheid to democracy and not take note of the profound intellectual, social, and institutional changes that accompanied the political revolution. Many Americans who lived in and visited South Africa in the post-Apartheid years understood that the country was a crucible in which attention to systemic racism—relatively diffused in the American consciousness at the time—was concentrated and intensified. And the reason was obvious: racism was a blight that affected the majority, not the minority, and now there was democracy.

Collectively, these changes became known as "transformation," a term that connotes meaningful change as a corrective to structural racism.   In the South African context, transformation included adopting a human rights–based constitution, corporate South Africa steadily engaging with Black Economic Empowerment, and the Johannesburg Stock Exchange (JSE) becoming the first in the world to launch a social responsibility index.[2] A key feature of the early transformational period was the Truth and Reconciliation Commission (TRC), cochaired by Archbishop Desmond Tutu, which sought to disclose the country's fraught Apartheid past and provide accountability.[3] (This is not to say that the South Africa of today has achieved the dreams and expectations of the immediate transformational era.)[4]

On my return to the United States in 2001, I noticed that racism, always central to an understanding of American history, was, at the time, relatively peripheral to the American conversation. In the era before Black Lives Matter, with the possible exception of the civil rights period of the 1960s, voting rights in America had to compete with many other events and narratives, notably 9/11 and the subsequent wars in Iraq and Afghanistan. In my experience of late-twentieth-century South Africa on the other hand, racism was not one subject of conversation among many; in many ways, it was the only subject.

To be sure, powerful voices in the American Black community and in the political and cultural spheres have long demanded attention to historical and current injustices, and a recent generation of historians has deeply interrogated the tragic history of American racism. The Black experience has also increasingly been explored and celebrated in both the scholarly and popular realms for some thirty years now, and South African and American scholars and public intellectuals have long engaged in robust interchange. For instance, the South African Black Consciousness Movement (BCM), whose most famous cofounder was Steve Biko (along with cofounders Mamphela Ramphele and Barney Pityana), was influenced not only by African intellectual traditions but also by American ones, notably W. E. B. Du Bois's concept of "double identity," Pan-Africanism, and the Black Power movement of the sixties.[5] Within the realm of the law, the

South African Legal Resources Center, founded in 1979 to challenge the legal structures of apartheid, was inspired partly by the NAACP Legal Defense Fund.

Continuing with the theme of transnational influence, the recent reckoning with Confederate statuary is an extension of a global movement that began on the steps of UCT, where the student-driven "Rhodes Must Fall" campaign resulted in the removal in April 2015 of Cecil John Rhodes's statue, which had somewhat defined the campus since 1934. The new energy to remove colonialist iconography quickly jumped the Atlantic to Oxford, Cambridge, Edinburgh, and, notably, Harvard Law School, where the "Royall Must Fall" movement emerged. By 2017, long-standing attempts to remove the Confederate memorial "Silent Sam" at the University of North Carolina (UNC) finally overcame opposition. In his notable book *The False Cause*, historian Adam Domby, reflecting on the moment the statue was finally removed, rhetorically asks, "What changed?"[6] The answer has to do not only with developments at UNC but also with social change in the rest of the world: the table had been set. Eventually, the movement caught up with the *Alabama*'s captain, Raphael Semmes; on June 5, 2020, his statue was unceremoniously removed from a downtown street in Mobile, Alabama.

In addition to addressing the immediate past, a key part of South African transformation was a scrutiny of the historical record and a deliberate effort to recover a narrative that reflected the experience of the majority (and in some cases, the exterminated). Biko himself had written that Black Consciousness "has to be directed to the past."[7] For South African scholars, it was no longer possible to study the Dutch without reckoning with slavery, the British without reckoning with colonialism, or the Afrikaners without reckoning with Apartheid. Well before political Apartheid ended, colleagues at UCT and other South African universities across the many disciplines in the humanities were deeply engaged in research scrutinizing conventional historical narratives and recovering the history of the disempowered.

While their work reflected a broad intellectual reformulation of South African identity taking place across the entire academic community, this transformation was much more than just an academic exercise. It played out in the public sphere as museums focused on slavery, racism, and oppression, so that these issues became more central to the country's public understanding of its history.[8] The complexities of race relations were examined through the literature of ethnically and culturally diverse authors, such as Andre Brink, Achmat Dangor, Athol Fugard, Nadine Gordimer, Zakes Mda, Njabulo Ndebele, and Miriam Tlali, among others.

The South African interrogation of history through literature influenced me when I read the memoirs of the *Alabama*'s officers. A colleague on the faculty at UCT was the novelist and subsequent Booker and Nobel Prize winner J. M. Coetzee, and so I had read one of his earliest novels, *Dusklands*, in the late 1980s.[9] In this book's second part, "The Narrative of Jacobus Coetzee," the author relates the private journal of a fictional Dutch ancestor who travels to Namaqualand in 1760. It is a horrific tale of early cultural contact permeated with deception, treachery, torture, and vengeance. After offering this graphic, private narrative, Coetzee presents Jacobus's official report to the authorities: a bland, minimalist description of the country traversed, the distance traveled, and the interesting flora and fauna. Literally and figuratively, the private account was drained of its blood. I was primed to read official war memoirs with skepticism, especially those dwelling on flora and fauna and written with an eye toward posterity.

As South African identity and its associated history became transformed, the racially fraught past did not become a new addendum to the country's history; rather, it continued as a central theme and necessary predicate, among many, for reconciliation. And in creating a new democratic national identity that recognized diversity and complexity, it became not passively acceptable, but actively imperative to recover the experience of the disempowered, who had been edited out of the Apartheid history books. In telling David Henry White's story, I am applying that perspective to the American past.

In doing so, I have sought to reference the relevant historiography, craft a narrative that keeps White as the central focus, and provide a substantive synthesis. To this end, the material is organized into three parts: Context, Voyage, and Aftermath. Although White does not feature in all of the chapters, throughout I describe key global, national, and local circumstances that help to understand his experience. As it happens, White's life spans the fifteen-year run-up to the Civil War, often understood to have begun with the annexation of Texas in 1845.[10] Therefore, the year 1845 provides a convenient benchmark for much of the context.

Part I

CONTEXT

Chapter 1

❦

David Henry White and
the False Cause

On permanent exhibition at the Philadelphia Museum of Art is Manet's masterpiece painting of one of the most famous naval battles of the American Civil War—between the USS *Kearsarge* and the CSS *Alabama*—on June 19, 1864, in the English Channel, seven miles off Cherbourg. Although the encounter is little known by most Americans today, the word "famous" is appropriate because, for the generation that survived the Civil War, this battle was as recognized as Gettysburg; the ships involved were as noted as the *Monitor* and *Merrimack*; and the captains, Raphael Semmes of the *Alabama* and John Ancrum Winslow of the *Kearsarge*, were as renowned as Admiral David Farragut.[1]

Manet's painting is but one manifestation of the international and domestic attention the battle received in its day and the universal recognition of its importance. At a moment when the outcome of the Civil War was still in doubt, and with Abraham Lincoln in a tough campaign against George McClellan, the *Alabama*'s timely demise enhanced his chances of reelection.[2] It also delivered a much-needed lift to Northern morale, and a corresponding gut punch to the South.

By further seeding international doubt about the South's viability, the outcome helped to keep England, which had failed to prevent the *Alabama* being constructed in Liverpool, from recognizing the Confederacy. Not unlike the Russian-Ukrainian conflict that began in 2022, the Civil War had become a conflict of attrition, and much of the world was hedging its bets. When news of the battle arrived in Washington on July 5, Secretary of the Navy Gideon Welles recorded in his diary: "There is great rejoicing throughout the country over this success, which is universally and justly conceded a triumph over England as well as over the Rebels."[3]

What made this battle, fought more than 3,000 miles from the nearest American shore, worthy of such attention? Over a twenty-two-month voyage, from 1862 to 1864, the *Alabama* had cruised the North Atlantic, South Atlantic, and Indian oceans and captured or burned sixty-four US merchant vessels and a US Navy warship. Along with other raiders, such as the CSS *Sumter*, CSS *Georgia*, CSS *Florida*, and later the CSS *Shenandoah*, it was part of the Confederacy's plan to disrupt Union commerce in retaliation for the North's blockade of Southern ports. In an increasingly desperate effort to end the highly effective assault, US agents in foreign ports and numerous US Navy vessels kept a vigilant lookout. By January 1863, the *New York Times* reported that the United States had no fewer than eighteen ships scouring the high seas.[4]

Conquests, sightings, and port visits were eagerly reported and shared among newspapers around the world, from the *Cape Argus* to the *Singapore Free Press*. By the end of the *Alabama*'s cruise, these Confederate raider ships helped drive nearly half of the remaining US merchant fleet to find foreign flags and caused more than a 500 percent increase in maritime insurance rates. In an important 1940 review, maritime lawyer George W. Dalzell argued that the robust pre–Civil War US merchant fleet had never really recovered from the disaster.[5]

Global news coverage and subsequent historical accounts have focused on the *Alabama*'s cruise, seizures, officers, and maritime law, but little attention has yet been given to the cost in human life. A case in point is the subject of this book: David Henry White, a free Black teenage sailor from the coastal village of Lewes, Delaware. White was kidnapped by Raphael Semmes on the high seas from the *Tonawanda*, a Philadelphia-based packet ship. He was subsequently enslaved on the *Alabama* for more than six hundred days, and lost his life during the battle impressionistically depicted in the Manet painting.

It will be shown that Semmes and Winslow were polar opposites in their ideology, politics, and approach to warfare. In addition to their group identity, however, they also had in common their literacy and therefore their capacity to become subjects of history. While both were famous in their day, Semmes actively advanced his own fame in a popular memoir that also articulated a revisionist history of the entire Civil War. In this book, Semmes not only heavily distorted White's life but claimed that, in snatching White from the *Tonawanda*, he did him a favor.

David Henry White—aka David Henry, Henry White, little David H. White, Dave, "poor little Dave," or simply "the slave"— was born in 1845 in Sussex County, Delaware, in or near the seaside town of Lewes. Delaware's counties are subdivided into "hundreds," a designation going back centuries and variously explained as originally an area containing 100 families, an area containing 100 people, or an area that could raise 100 soldiers. White's existence was first recorded in the census of 1850, which listed the "Free Inhabitants of Lewis and Rehoboth Hundred, Sussex, Delaware," with his name, David H. White, and his age, five.

Although White spent more than 600 days on the *Alabama*'s cruise, and even though he was lost in the final battle, as an illiterate Black teenager, White had a legacy that was entirely subject to the disinformation provided to us by his captors. As a result, the real David Henry White—a free, hardworking teenager seeking to escape poverty and forge a career—completely disappeared and was replaced instead by Semmes's invented, racist caricature.

If the historical voices that speak to us tend to be only those of the empowered and the literate, it is no surprise that information about White is scant, and that historical accounts of the *Alabama* have focused primarily on Semmes and his officers.[6] In the case of the *Alabama*'s captain and officers, there is much material from which to draw, because they were highly conscious of the need to frame their stories for posterity. Indeed, the postwar books published by Semmes; his first lieutenant and executive officer, John McIntosh Kell; and his fifth lieutenant, Arthur Sinclair, are classic examples of Lost Cause literature—a determined postwar effort by Confederate veterans to define the rebellion as a legal and just war. In these texts, secession and Southern wartime activity were generally characterized by honor, civility, and virtue. This pseudo-historical Lost Cause narrative sought to reframe the Confederate secession as part of an honorable crusade waged to protect the "Southern way of life" against Northern aggression, and thereby minimize the human cost of slavery while defending it as an economic necessity.[7]

Historians studying the Lost Cause have identified its key elements, including a revisionist denial that the defense of slavery was the principal cause of Southern secession, and a new, replacement rationale holding that the war was fought over a constitutional disagreement.[8] An enduring trope, inherited from the antebellum era, is that of the contented servant, as described by historians Frank J. Wetta and Martin A. Novelli: "In 1946 . . . it was perfectly acceptable to continue to present on film that plank of the Lost Cause platform that emphasized the contented lives of Black people in the postwar South and the affectionate relationship between white and Black

Southerners—an extension of the antebellum master-servant relationship and their mutual sense of community."[9]

Semmes articulates this trope explicitly in his Mexican-American War memoir, published in 1851: "the master . . . (bestowing . . .) upon his slave the kindly feeling which is naturally inspired by those who are dependent upon us, and the slave, in return, regarding himself as a member of his master's family, and more or less identified with his interest."[10] By 1939 the trope had been most vividly expressed in the deeply flawed film extravaganza *Gone With the Wind*, based on Margaret Mitchell's 1936 novel. It will be shown that this "affectionate relationship" between master and servant is exactly how Semmes described his relationship to White. Not surprisingly, given the whole weight of twenty-first-century historiography, which has methodically sought to recover the stories and experiences of the enslaved and disempowered, this description will not survive scrutiny.

The historian Gaines M. Foster explored in detail how the Lost Cause could be viewed as an effort by postwar white Southerners to reconcile deeply held notions of honor with a corresponding principle that defeat was itself a dishonorable transgression.[11] Foster noted that "honor" was a critical part of the value system of the Old South, and the code of honor had made personal bravery and oath taking central to men's status. Historian Paul Quigley has further expanded on the Southern concept of virtue by explaining that the word connoted a close dependency of national cause with personal morality.[12] In the context of war, this ideology had the effect of intensifying the importance of either personal glory or shame, depending on the outcome of the relevant conflict. One Confederate veteran wrote:

Look not for hope or pity now,
Nor joy, nor pleasure evermore
Shall shine on your dishonored brow
Dishonored aye, and in the dust laid low . . .

Who forever struggling to be free
Were crushed beneath the oppressors might
And made such things of shame as we.[13]

At a societal level, the response to such emotional distress was not so much contrition as revision: a determined effort to glorify and sentimentalize the Old South, secession, and the conduct of the war. In turn, this enabled white Southerners to accept participation in the Union, thereby giving up slavery while continuing to adhere to white supremacist ideology. (As discussed in a later chapter, this code of honor, in which glory was celebrated and defeat without glory was accompanied by personal shame, was a feature not only of the Old South but also of the antebellum US Navy, in which Semmes had served.)

Historian Caroline E. Janney identified Semmes as one of fifty-four prominent Confederate veterans who participated in the 1873 Southern Historical Society (SHS) meeting to promote the Lost Cause.[14] However, his determined intellectual contribution to the narrative has yet to be fully explored. Specifically, Semmes helped to frame the Lost Cause in his best-selling *Memoirs of Service Afloat During the War Between the States*, written during 1868 from his last home in Mobile, Alabama. In this memoir, White is described in the form of a stereotype of the loyal slave contented in his natural role as servant. The memoir was published in the critical post–Civil War period when the Lost Cause narrative was actively under construction—notably bookended on the one hand by Edward Pollard's *The Lost Cause: A New Southern History of the War of the Confederates* (1866) and on the other by former Confederacy vice-president Alexander H. Stephens's two-volume *Constitutional View of the Late War* (1877).[15]

At the time, Semmes's memoir was viewed by white Southerners as a cogent defense of the Confederacy, but to understand it as a post hoc reinvention of the war's purpose, one needs to trace the evolution of Semmes's postwar rhetoric by comparing it to that in his earlier, 1851 memoir, *Service Afloat and Ashore during the Mexican War*, as well as his Civil War letters.[16] In his pre–Civil War book, Semmes offered both a frank defense of slavery and an open assertion of white supremacy.[17] In comparing Southern slavery to the Mexican peons, Semmes wrote, "The well-fed and well-cared-for dependent of a southern estate . . . is infinitely superior," and he refers to both with the biblical epithet "hewers of wood and drawers of water."[18] In a thorough biography of Semmes, historian Stephen Fox noted that Semmes wrote during the war that "we were fighting the first battle in favor of slavery" and "the true issue of the war" was "an abolition crusade against our slave property."[19] This analysis comports with long-standing historiography placing slavery squarely at the center of the South's motivation to secede.[20]

The subsequent evolution of Semmes's rhetoric closely mirrors the shared sense of victimhood that became a powerful animating force in both Confederate nationalism and subsequent Lost Cause ideology.[21] In the aftermath of a crushing defeat and in seeking to salvage some kind of moral high ground, Semmes's narrative changed.

In his postwar memoir, he devotes seventy pages to a dense, legalistic defense of "States Rights" and the Constitution. He invokes Patrick Henry. He conveys a litany of grievances the South held against the North, and further derides the North for pursuing a war for economic dominance masquerading as a moral crusade, while only obliquely conceding that the South seceded for the explicit purpose of defending and expanding slavery.[22] Using heroic rhetoric, he dedicates the book to those "Sailors and Soldiers of the Southern States, who lost their lives . . . in defense of the liberties which had been bequeathed to them by their fathers."[23] Without a trace of reflection or irony, he writes, "We . . . have struggled to preserve our liberties, and the liberties of those who are to come after us; and the history of that struggle must not perish. . . . A final separation of these States must come, or the South will be permanently enslaved."[24]

With this deft trick, Semmes takes more than two centuries of authentic American carnage—inflicted primarily on Black, Brown, and indigenous peoples—stands it on its head, and expresses it as a white grievance! This had been common rhetoric among white Southerners for decades; as Lincoln had once noted, "The perfect liberty they sigh for is the liberty of making slaves of other people."[25]

If the Lost Cause narrative may be seen as a disingenuous construction that downplayed the cost of racism for generations of Black lives, the appropriation of White's life is a vivid example, one that can be tied directly to one of the Lost Cause's founding architects.

In the *False Cause*, Adam Domby makes a convincing case that the historical memory of the Civil War embodied in the Lost Cause was in fact a construction based on deliberate falsehoods. Domby focuses on the developing language and literature of Confederate veterans in North Carolina, especially in the period following Reconstruction. He also argues that, in exposing such falsehoods, it is appropriate to use the word "lie," since a less provocative term "might obscure the purposeful creation and use of these constructions, and thereby render them innocuous."[26] The research in this book extends Domby's approach by applying it to the earlier period when the Lost Cause was actively under construction, and demonstrates that by 1869, such lies and distortions were propagated at a national level.

In *Digging through Darkness*, the historical archaeologist Carmel Schrire reflected on the relationship between literate Dutch colonial masters in South Africa and the illiterate indigenous peoples— a relationship that applies just as well to the relationship between enslavers and the enslaved in North America. "Natives had plenty to say," she noted, "but they were for the most part illiterate. . . . For all the anger, argument, and confusion that must have attended every exchange . . . colonial masters were hardly obliged to record whatever the other side said. Indeed, as they saw it, for the most part the other side was better left unsaid."[27]

The perspective (if not the methodology) of an archaeologist is perhaps appropriate in telling White's story, since archaeologists are used to studying those in the past who left no written record of their existence. Sometimes we can see great economic and societal shifts, and other times we can see how these developments affected individuals. "A single event," Schrire noted, "may be viewed as part of the political history of a great chartered company, and at the same time it may be seen through the eyes of a hunter-forager girl, spurned for dalliance with drunken soldiers."[28] So too, the *Alabama*'s voyage, and for that matter the Lost Cause itself, frequently has been viewed through the prism of a great ideological and military conflict, whereas it may also be viewed through the eyes and experiences of an illiterate Black teenager, kidnapped on the high seas and abandoned to drown in the English Channel.

It is impossible, however, to write the biography of a ghost. It is one thing to write about Semmes, or any of the *Alabama*'s officers, but quite another to write about an illiterate sailor with no descendants, no property, few records, and no voice. Here the challenge is more like that encountered by Saidiya V. Hartman in her book *Scenes of Subjection*, in which she reflected on the vast gaps in written materials relating to the lives and perspectives of enslaved Black women in numerous everyday situations.[29] Subsequently, Marisa J. Fuentes researched the life stories of enslaved Caribbean women in Bridgetown, Barbados. In her book *Dispossessed Lives*, she discusses the "methodological challenges produced by the near erasure of enslaved women's own perspectives, in spite of and because of the superabundance of words white Europeans wrote about them."[30]

In this way, telling White's story must differ from many other important recovered stories of the enslaved, such as that of Robert

Smalls in Cate Lineberry's *Be Free or Die.*[31] Smalls was an experienced pilot who escaped slavery by commandeering a Confederate vessel and eventually served in the US House of Representatives during Reconstruction. The life story of this literate, well-known historical figure can be told from letters and contemporaneous journalism. Nor is it a simple matter to infer White's shipboard experience from the memoirs of peers. Of the thousands of Black seamen who sailed in the pre–Civil War merchant marine, much has been written, but not by them. There are precious few relevant firsthand written accounts, no less from the Confederate Navy.[32]

The French historian Ivan Jablonka has likened the historical study of the disempowered to "staring into a well."[33] The metaphor is apt. We know that the waters are deep and precious, but all we can see is a murky blur interrupted with a few key facts like ripples on the surface. What's down there? There are so many things unknown about White, but we know this: his life did not follow the "heroes journey"—the mythic structure based on the scholarship of Joseph Campbell, in which the protagonist leaves his home; undertakes a journey while encountering and overcoming a series of obstacles and trials; and returns triumphant.[34] In fact, like so many sailors who drowned on the high seas in the days before radio or telegraph, White never returned at all.[35]

Indeed, White's story—to the extent it is recoverable—is fundamentally tragic, and the difficulty is that real life just does not cooperate with formulaic media-driven memes or with conventional understandings of heroism. As Fuentes notes in *Dispossessed Lives*, conventional understandings of heroism cannot apply to those whose circumstances were severely constrained by the ongoing threat of violence.[36]

While the gaps in White's life story may seem frustrating, the fragments that remain provide something just as important: evidence that whatever his story was, he never got to tell us, and what Semmes conveyed about him years after his death were, by any standard, deliberate lies. This limited demonstration requires in the first instance a forensic approach.[37] Therefore, in this book I have sought to adhere to the limited documentary record and squeeze every last ounce of juice from it in order to expose the lies through which White's short life was appropriated and used to construct a False Cause narrative. In telling his story, beyond the documentary record specific to White, only information generally applicable to young Black sailors of his time and place was used to provide the necessary context. And while there is no way to know what White thought, there is much to say about what he experienced, and so the key places he lived and visited are described, as well as the people he most certainly encountered. Along the way, some key incidents and accounts from American history help us understand the forces amassed against him.[38] Perhaps the closest we can come to knowing him is to imagine ourselves in his situation.

As current US politics resonates with the increasingly polarized pre–Civil War era, historians such as David Blight have noted echoes of the Lost Cause narrative in the 2020 "Stolen Election" narrative.[39] Both the Lost Cause and the "Stolen Election" are fictional narratives consciously and deliberately constructed as weapons to animate reactionary forces. Just as investigators and journalists have sought to identify every conceivable lie about the 2020 election, so too must we question the Lost Cause and expose its invented foundation. It will be shown that White's actual life belies the racist narrative his captors sought to construct.

Chapter 2

Time and Place

The world of the 1840s was one of transition, precariously balanced between the colonial ideological legacy of the seventeenth and eighteenth centuries and the increasingly cosmopolitan and idealistic impulses of the nineteenth and twentieth ones. This chapter describes the global, national, and local forces at play at the time of White's birth and childhood.

The transitional world of 1845 can be described in a variety of ways. Indications of things to come were as profound as the first use of anesthesia, and as mundane as the invention of rubber bands and adhesive tape. The most significant technological developments of this era were the rapid advance of railroads and the electric telegraph. Only two years earlier, the US Congress had appropriated funds for Samuel Morse to lay the first telegraph line from Washington, DC, to Baltimore. There was not even a cable across the English Channel yet. With no transatlantic cables, communication between America and Europe remained as slow as the fastest boat—about two weeks. Although relatively isolated, Delaware was on its way in April 1846 with the opening of the first telegraph line from Philadelphia to Wilmington.

From a global perspective, the 1840s was a decade of incessant colonial expansion and domestic conflicts. Although England had lost the thirteen American colonies in the previous century, its determined empire-building continued elsewhere. With Queen Victoria at the helm, it remained the world's most formidable global power. Britain, acting through the East India Company, significantly consolidated its power in India with the hard-fought Anglo-Sikh War. The Treaty of Lahore which ended the war in 1846, forced the Sikh Empire to cede Kashmir to the East India Company and surrender the Koh-I-Noor diamond to Queen Victoria.[1]

Britain had started the First Anglo-Afghan War in 1838 to defend India from the Russian Empire's expansion into Central Asia; thus the British began the series of moves and countermoves known as the Great Game. In an uncanny precursor to the present century, the British sought to impose a friendly government in Afghanistan, but the regime was short-lived and proved unsustainable without British military support. By 1842, the British garrison was forced to abandon Kabul due to constant civilian attacks, and it eventually withdrew from Afghanistan altogether. In the process of retreating, the British lost about 4,500 troops, along with some 12,000 civilians who had supported them.

Still, the British continued to enjoy some success in East Asia, with the first of the two Opium Wars with China ending in the cession of modern-day Hong Kong Island to the British. Although Singapore had been a British possession since 1824, Japan remained firmly closed to outsiders. The decade also saw significant consolidation of British hegemony in Australia and New Zealand.

While most of Africa remained largely unknown to Europeans, the coasts were of strategic importance as markets for enslaved persons, as potential resettlement areas for Black Americans (Liberia was formally constituted in 1847), but also as victualling stations for ships bound for the East. By this time, the British also controlled the Cape of Good Hope, which in the days before the Suez Canal, was perhaps the most essential victualling station for ships traveling between the West and East. A map of Africa drawn in 1845 was geographically accurate in its outlines, with more than a hundred towns identified on the coasts; but most of the African interior on the map, from modern-day Chad in the north to Botswana in the south, and from Cameroon in the west to Kenya in the east, was empty. Of course, it wasn't empty—just unknown to Westerners. Stanley Livingstone reached Lake Ngami only in 1849 and finally Victoria Falls in 1855. The colonial "scramble for Africa" by Belgium, France, Germany, and England belongs to later decades.

In Europe, the decade was characterized by incessant domestic turmoil. Perhaps the greatest disaster of the age was the Irish potato famine, which caused the deaths of more than one million Irish from 1845 until the early 1850s and spurred the emigration of more than 780,000 to the United States, many on packet ships such as the ones on which White would later sail. This was more than three times the immigration number of the previous decade, and the 1850s would see nearly a million more.[2]

In the United States, an intensifying vision of American expansionism became crystallized in John O'Sullivan's coinage "manifest destiny."[3] With a simple majority vote in each house, Congress annexed Texas, thereby setting the stage for the coming Mexican-American War (discussed further in chapters 5 and 6). Earlier, in May 1845, *Narrative of the Life of Frederick Douglass* was published in Boston. Although slave narratives had been published previously, few carried the authenticity and vivid descriptions of inhumanity of Douglass's account. He begins by explaining that he cannot be sure of his age, because "by far the larger part of the slaves know as little of their ages as horses know of theirs, as it is the wish of most masters within my knowledge to keep their slaves thus ignorant."[4] He then makes clear that he was fathered by a white man and describes chattel slavery whereby his bondage was inherited from his mother. He discusses the system in Maryland, which generally separated enslaved children from their mothers before they reached twelve months of age. He tells how he was purposefully denied literacy and nourishment and was forced into egregious manual labor at the point of a whip. Most importantly, he emphasizes that the horrific experiences he endured—families torn asunder, torture, forced labor and denial of human dignity—were not the exception but the rule.

The import of this narrative is fully recognized in two preceding introductory essays, one by William Lloyd Garrison and the other by Wendell Phillips, an important member of the Boston Anti-Slavery Society who would go on to become a prominent advocate for voting rights, suffrage, and Native American rights after the war. "No one can say that we have unfairly picked out some rare specimens of cruelty," Phillips writes in his letter to Douglass. "We know that the bitter drops, which even you have drained from the cup, are no incidental aggravations, no individual ills, but such as must mingle always and necessarily in the lot of every slave. They are the essential ingredients, not the occasional results of the system."[5]

By graphically describing the cruel inhumanity of slavery in practice and making evident that his testimony was not anomalous, Douglass's *Narrative* resonates with the Eric Garner and George Floyd videos of 2014 and 2020, respectively. Among other forces compelling abolition, it was becoming ever more difficult for northern populations to accept the story of the benign master, and to make believe that slavery was anything less than moral anathema.

Indeed, perhaps the most portentous idea of the age, ultimately leading to the century's most deadly conflict, was the growing international and domestic sentiment to abolish slavery. In 1774, John Wesley, founder of the Methodist Church, had denounced slavery as "the execrable sum of all villainies."[6] A group of Evangelical English Protestants allied with the Quakers formed the Committee for the Abolition of the Slave Trade in 1787. France abolished slavery in

1794 in its colonies. By the end of the century, abolitionist sentiment in Britain, led by Thomas Clarkson and William Wilberforce, sought global abolition of the trade in enslaved people, if not slavery itself. By 1807, the British Parliament passed the Slave Trade Act, followed by the Slave Trade Felony Act in 1811, which made the overseas slave trade a felony throughout the empire. Further, the Royal Navy established the West Africa Squadron to suppress the Atlantic slave trade by patrolling the coast of West Africa. With the Webster-Ashburton Treaty of 1842, the United States formally, if ineffectually, began contributing to the patrol.

As much as, if not more than, any other US state, Delaware has traveled the full distance from an eighteenth-century plantocracy to a twenty-first-century pluralistic democracy. In the mid-nineteenth century Delaware of White's youth, one could find vestiges of the old colonial world, along with glimpses of the democratic world to come; these vestiges and glimpses are manifested in the varied lived experiences of Delaware's rural Black population.

As a mid-Atlantic state precariously situated between slave state Maryland to the south and free-state Pennsylvania to the north, Delaware occupied what historians describe as the "middle ground," in historian Barbara Fields's words a "misty and elusive terrain."[7] Delaware was one of the few slave states that remained loyal to the Union; as a result, Delaware's enslaved were not covered by the Emancipation Proclamation, and remained in bondage until the passage of the Thirteenth Amendment.[8]

In many ways, Sussex County resembled neighboring Maryland, though it was much smaller, and by the early nineteenth century, slavery was becoming uneconomical for both states.[9] Also, New Castle and Kent counties, in northern Delaware, were heavily influenced by their proximity to Philadelphia-based Quaker and Methodist abolitionism. Eventually, Wilmington would become a nexus of the Underground Railroad.[10] Delaware's 1776 constitution included an explicit clause prohibiting the import of African enslaved persons, and in 1830 a member of the legislature introduced a bill to abolish slavery, which failed. A similar bill in 1847 failed to abolish slavery by just one vote.[11] The abolitionists came close but were never successful and until the passage of the Thirteenth Amendment in 1865, the situation remained metastable.[12]

Of Delaware's three counties, Sussex retained the largest number of enslaved people and the lowest number of free Blacks. Even so, by 1840, two-thirds of Sussex County Blacks were free, an extraordinarily high proportion for the times—a result of both economic and ideological factors that distinguished it from the Deep South.[13]

Unlike the middle-ground states of Maryland and Delaware, the South's economy was inexorably tied to cotton and the enslaved labor on which it depended. It had not been this way for long. Cotton had been grown, spun, and made into textiles for centuries on small holdings in India and exported to global markets. In 1791, US cotton production was only around two thousand pounds, and almost all of that was exported to Britain.

A number of factors had conspired to radically alter the US economy, expand the global cotton trade, and inexorably link the South to both the British and French economies. These deep commercial linkages set the stage for the friendly reception the *Alabama* would ultimately receive in the various ports it visited, and this contributed to the isolation and entrapment that White may have experienced during his long voyage.

Among these conspiring factors were the technological developments of the cotton gin, which made it possible to efficiently separate cotton seeds from fiber; and the spinning jenny, spinning mule, and power loom, all of which—coupled with the new motive power of steam—made the manufacture of cotton textiles both inexpensive and efficient. With seemingly limitless demand, the global cotton market continued to explode. In fact, by 1850, the five main cotton-growing states—South Carolina, Georgia, Alabama, Mississippi, and Louisiana—produced nearly 2 million bales, or well over 500 million pounds of Petit Gulf for export.[14] Cotton thus came to command the lion's share of the entire US export market, exceeding the value of all other US exports combined.[15] At that stage, almost one-fifth of Britain's 21 million inhabitants depended on cotton textile manu-facturing, and nearly 40 percent of Britain's manufactured exports were cotton textiles. Vast fortunes were made in the United States, not only among southern plantation owners and shippers but also among the Philadelphia-, New York-, and Boston-based financial, insurance, and shipping houses, all of which reaped some 40 percent of the total cotton revenues.

Although slavery had existed in Delaware since the days of to-bacco farming, Delaware was unsuitable for cotton, and thus the re-gion's small-scale farmers did not benefit from the boom. From the 1630s until 1664, Delaware had been governed by the Dutch, with Peter Stuyvesant at the helm in New Amsterdam. The chief problem for the Dutch, as for the Swedes who briefly preceded them, was the difficulty in obtaining labor to make farming practicable. In contrast to the Swedes, however, the Dutch were crackerjack slave traders. In fact, they controlled a global mercantile empire and oceangoing fleet that enabled them to conquer the slave-trading centers along the West African coast previously controlled by the Portuguese.

Stuyvesant had previously been a governor of Curaçao, a key Dutch slave entrepot, and so he had the necessary contacts. In 1660, he petitioned the Dutch East India Company to import African enslaved people.[16] Until 1664, when the colony was transferred to

British control, the number of Blacks enslaved in Delaware was absolutely small but relatively high. By one estimate, at least 125 enslaved Blacks lived in Delaware, representing approximately 20 percent of the total population, in contrast with 9 percent for Maryland and 5 percent for Virginia.[17]

The British takeover of New Amsterdam brought with it the liberal land grant policies of the Duke of York and the development of tobacco as a cash crop. Tobacco was hard on the soil; it could be grown profitably only for about five years and then required a fallow period of up to twenty years. The prospect of cheap virgin soil, therefore, made Delaware attractive to small-scale tobacco planters from Maryland who migrated north and brought their enslaved laborers with them. A decline in the tobacco market in the late seventeenth century had suppressed slavery-based farming, but the market recovered in the eighteenth century, resulting in a marked increase in enslaved people accompanying farmer-owners from Maryland's Eastern Shore and beyond. On the eve of the American Revolution, an estimated 12,800 people, or about 22 percent of the state's population, were enslaved in Delaware.[18]

By the middle of the eighteenth century, Delaware tobacco was perceived to be inferior, and growing wheat and corn became more profitable. Tobacco required continual attention, from sowing seeds and hand cleaning plants of worms to constant pruning, topping, and harvesting. In contrast, once planted, wheat and barley required little further care. Since Sussex County was less suited to grain than the rest of the state, corn was favored. This situation closely mirrored neighboring Maryland, as described by Fields in *Slavery and Freedom on the Middle Ground.*

Sussex County has a total area of 1,196 square miles, of which 936 square miles is land and 260 square miles water; it is by far the largest county in Delaware by area. The eastern portion of Sussex County is home to Delaware's beaches and seaside resorts, including

Lewes. Of Sussex's eleven Hundreds, Lewes is situated in Lewes & Rehoboth Hundred, and it is in this 1850 census designation that we first encounter the White family in the following chapter.

By the early nineteenth century, even corn and grain were exhausting the soil, and Sussex County's farmers struggled. A typical antebellum farm was described by diarist Mary Parker Welch, whose ancestors arrived in Delaware around 1670 and who grew up midway between Milton and Millsboro, less than ten miles from Lewes. Welch detailed how a nearby farm struggled against the increasingly low yields, "as the unfertilized fields became more and more sterile."[19] She also described instances of harsh servitude in terms strikingly similar to Frederick Douglass's description of his enslavement in Maryland.

In reaction to declining agricultural yields, Sussex County farmers were prone to agricultural fads, notably an interest in raising mulberry trees for silk cocoons in the 1830s and 1840s. The antebellum farmer, William Morgan, left a detailed memoir in which he thought he might find economic salvation in silk, but ultimately became disillusioned and came to call the fad "a humbug."[20]

Where farming became unprofitable, white farmers often found it unsustainable to support enslaved people with food, clothing, and shelter for an entire year. Given the local agricultural conditions, it made more economic sense for them to hire free (that is, unenslaved) labor for the few weeks of planting and harvesting. The result was a dramatic increase in manumissions and sales of enslaved people to interregional traders over the course of the early nineteenth century. As manumissions increased, there was a concomitant increase in house and garden lease labor agreements between white farmers and Black tenants.[21]

Just as the Black experience of midcentury Delaware varied widely, so did white farmers' adjustments to the new economic and ideological realities in the region. With Delaware, it is impossible to

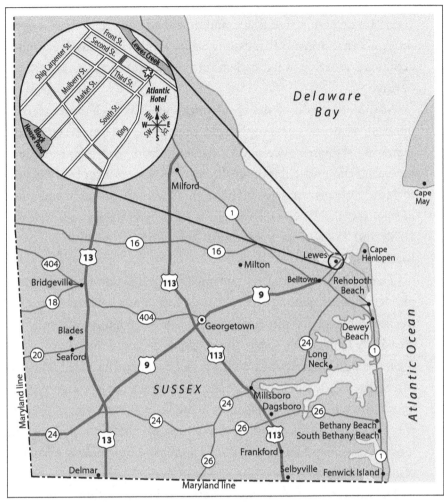

MAP 1. Sussex County, Delaware. The inset detail shows the location of the Atlantic Hotel in Lewes, Delaware. *Cartography by Jade Myers.*

generalize.[22] Probate records indicate that many white families were concerned about the livelihoods of the manumitted and made material accommodation accordingly.[23] In her memoir, Welch describes the burden her parents experienced supporting the enslaved people they had inherited and their seemingly well meaning, if befuddled, efforts to help them.[24] Not only had the antebellum economics of

Delaware created a free Black underclass, but chattel slavery was so insidious that even well-meaning white families, themselves under economic pressure, were sucked into the moral vortex they had inherited.

At the other end of the spectrum, when slavery became uneconomical, some whites simply sold their enslaved south. Historian Jennie K. Williams developed a database from ship manifests documenting the mid-Atlantic enslaved who were transported by ship to New Orleans for sale.[25] Although Williams's research does not pertain specifically to Delaware, it is clear from the records that the 1820s and 1830s were peak traffic years for mid-Atlantic enslaved Blacks sold south.[26]

Those freed families that remained in rural Delaware faced complex challenges; among them a deep fear among whites that free Blacks would incite the enslaved to seek freedom. As a result, increasingly harsh Black Codes limited mobility and residency, making it exceedingly difficult for free Blacks who stepped outside Delaware to return. While such restrictions were practiced throughout the South, the phenomenon was most acute in Delaware, where over 90 percent of the Black population was free by 1860.[27] In contrast, in most of the Deep South, free Blacks were generally below 5 percent of the Black population.[28]

Describing the free Black experience in antebellum Delaware, historians William H. Williams and Patience Essah have explored the persistence of various forms of legally sanctioned bondage and limited mobility during a period in which both the perceived economic benefit of slavery and formal legal enslavement were in steep decline.[29] Writing about neighboring Maryland, Barbara Fields notes that "it was characteristic of the middle ground's perverseness that free Black people paid heavily both for their closeness to slavery and for their detachment from it."[30] The profusion of legal restrictions ensnared many of Delaware's rural free Blacks of the period in intractable poverty. In 1837, William Yates, a minister who visited the state on behalf of the American Anti-Slavery Society, observed, "They enjoy but a mongrel liberty, a mere mock freedom. They are truly neither slaves nor free; being subject to many of the disabilities and disadvantages of both conditions; and enjoying few of the benefits of either."[31]

Yates further observed that the presence of so many free Blacks raised an "extensive and moral fear" among whites that served to fuel further racism.[32] As early as 1740, the colonial legislature was openly concerned that the increasing number of free Blacks would have a corrupting influence on enslaved ones. Thus began a decades-long effort by Delaware legislatures to increasingly limit the rights of free Black people, notably by limiting movement, political rights, and education.[33] The laws that, correctly or incorrectly, pertained to White, included the 1797 Act that, "found by experience, that free Negroes and Mulattoes are idle and slothful, often prove burthensome to the neighborhood wherein they live, and are evil example to slaves."[34] The law made it illegal for free Black children to be indigent; instead children of indigent free Black parents were made to serve indenture (the males until the age of twenty-one, the females until age eighteen). Although indenture was a form of forced labor, it differed from chattel slavery in that the term of servitude was limited contractually and was not heritable.

In 1807, the Delaware legislature sought to curb growth in the number of free Blacks in the state due to manumission and "emigration" from other states. To address this, it passed "An Act for the Better Regulation of Free Negroes and Free Mulattoes." Nonresident Blacks entering the state were to be fined "not exceeding thirty dollars, with all costs of prosecution"; if those convicted could not pay, "then said free negro or free mulatto, shall be adjudged to be sold by the Sheriff of the county as a servant, for any term, not exceeding seven years, to any person or persons whatever, residing in this state, willing to purchase him or her."[35]

The 1831 Nat Turner rebellion, together with the Baptist War slave rebellion in Jamacia, had severe consequences for both Delaware's enslaved and its free Blacks. The explicit intent and impact of the laws passed later in the 1830s were to ensure an ample supply of cheap labor by further curtailing mobility. In 1849, the legislature continued to make it illegal for free Blacks to be unemployed and poor, bluntly stating the law's rationale in its preamble: "Whereas the emigration into this State of free negroes or free mulattoes from the other States is injurious and corrupting to the resident negroes or mulattoes: And whereas, large numbers of resident free negroes and free mulattoes are in the habit of leaving the State during the most important working seasons, when their labor is most necessary to the white populations."[36] The 1807 Act had also imposed fines on free Blacks who left the state for more than two years. However, given the importance of maritime trade and the need for labor, the legislature made an important exception—later utilized by White—for any "sea-faring person or persons of color, who may be following his or their occupation."[37]

Apart from limiting mobility, a central aspect of the antebellum power dynamic was the denial of literacy to Delaware's rural Black population. Yates derided "the dreadful state of destitution" in regard to schools, noting that there was "but a single school in the whole state for the instruction of Black children during the week, and perhaps two or three Sabbath schools."[38]

A special challenge was that free Blacks of Sussex County lived with the constant threat of kidnapping. They were especially vulnerable because of the state's geographic position on the border with Maryland and the south beyond. In his 1837 letter, Yates attested to this constant threat of kidnapping experienced both by enslaved and free Black citizens. Historian Carol Wilson has reported: "Lawyer and anti-slavery pamphleteer Jesse Torrey declared in 1818 that it would take a book to record all the incidences of kidnapping that had occurred in Delaware."[39] Sussex County historian Harold B. Hancock described a ring operated by the notorious Patty Cannon, which operated from Bridgeville, forty miles west of Lewes. In a contemporaneous memoir, Cannon was described as "one of the most cruel, profane, avaricious and notorious women of any age or place . . . her name struck terror to the hearts of slaves and free people of color."[40] Eventually the law caught up with her, and she died in jail in 1829 of self-inflicted poison.

Notwithstanding the challenging economic and social circumstances of the 1820s, free Blacks began to organize in small communities, and by 1870, there were at least forty such enclaves in the state, in which individuals found employment, organized churches, and owned property. While disenfranchised politically, many free Blacks, both in the region and specifically in Lewes, earned wages, paid taxes, and otherwise participated in their local economy.

In his letters, Yates celebrated those Black individuals who had become successful, among them farmers, mechanics, merchants, and builders. "Having so often alluded to the unpleasant side of the picture in the condition of the free people of color," he wrote, "it would be unjust where [*sic*] I to say nothing of the opposite."[41] We will meet some of those successful individuals in the following chapter. While many of Delaware's rural free Blacks emigrated to Philadelphia, and others remained behind and were successful, many, like White's family, remained trapped in rural poverty and illiteracy.[42]

Chapter 3

≈

Childhood in Lewes

In the twenty-first century, historians have systematically explored and recovered the stories, challenges, and achievements of Delaware's antebellum free Black population.[1] An exhibition at the Lewes History Museum entitled "17 Men: Portraits of Black Civil War Soldiers" featured important photographs and illustrations by artist Shayne Davidson, who had stumbled on a miniature album of eighteen photographic portraits of Black men from the United States Colored Troops (USCT). The exhibit highlighted six enslaved and free Black men, mainly from Delaware's Sussex and Kent counties, some of whom White may have encountered while growing up and all of whom eventually served in the Union army.[2]

Among them was George H. Mitchell, born in 1844 in nearby Georgetown, Delaware. He was just nineteen years old in January 1864 when Caleb Layton, his enslaver, enlisted him in the USCT. In return for this enlistment, Mitchell received his freedom, and Layton a $300 bounty. Another was Theodore Tennant, born free around 1829 in Sussex County. Married with children, he was recorded as a "farmer" with "black hair, eyes and complexion, and standing five feet, nine-inches tall."[3]

When the Civil War came, the communities of Milford, Lewes,

Seaford, and Laurel contributed at least 75 free Black sailors to the war effort.[4] The occupations of the approximately 300 Black men from Delaware who enlisted in the US Navy included laborers, waiters, farmers, tanners, shoemakers, axle makers, blacksmiths, stove makers, barbers, butchers, carpenters, brickmakers, painters, and firemen; 32 of the enlisted were identified as sailors, seamen, mariners, and watermen.[5]

While growing up in the small community of Lewes, White may have known a number of exceptional Black individuals who were indeed successful. Cato Lewis, for one, learned the art of shipbuilding while enslaved and, once freed, opened a shipbuilding yard in Lewes, employing his sons and other formerly enslaved men.[6] Another, Mingo Tilghman, worked as a house carpenter, contracting his skills to white farmers and employing a free assistant. A comprehensive review by the University of Delaware's Center for Historic Architecture found free Blacks of the region to be artisans, including shoemakers, butchers, tanners, and blacksmiths, who served both whites and Blacks in the community.[7]

By 1850, 26 free Blacks living in Lewes were listed as carpenters, 3 in the "Maritime" category, and 19 under "Day Labor."[8] The local fishing industry also provided employment for free Black men to harvest turtles, oysters, shad, and sturgeon. Five of the 11 free Black households in Lewes owned their homes in 1840, and by 1850, 7 of the of 28 free Black households lived in their own dwellings. As the University of Delaware's study makes clear, "For those free blacks fortunate to find skilled or semi-skilled labor in the town of Lewes, there was significant room for economic growth and the improvement of one's quality of life."[9]

As historian Hilda Norwood has recounted, the free Black settlement of Belltown arose just west of Lewes. According to local legend, Jacob Bell paid poll taxes in 1822 and 1833 and by 1836 had acquired a house and land. Bell then sold some of his parcel to other free Black families, forming the basis for the Belltown settlement. Further, he donated land for what became the first John Wesley United Methodist Church.[10] Prior to the Civil War, free Blacks had organized churches in nearby Georgetown and Milford, as well.[11]

White did not come from a literate family—neither he nor his parents could read or write—so there are as yet no known memoirs or family letters to provide insight into his personality or decision-making. There are also no draft cards, bank statements, or probate or tax records—not just because he was illiterate but also because he neither inherited, owned, nor left behind anything of much material value.[12] Direct information about his childhood comes mainly from the US censuses of 1850 and 1860, supplemented with a few tax records for his family.

Both censuses clearly document that White was free. In fact, he is recorded in both 1850 and 1860 censuses under the category "Free Inhabitants in Lewes & Rehoboth Hundred in the County of Sussex,

Table 3.1. White Family in the 1850 Census (Dwelling 875, Family 875)

Name of every person whose usual place of abode on the first day of June 1850 was to this family	Age	Sex	Color	Profession: Description of such male persons over 15 years of age
John White	34	M	B	Laborer
Sarah	25	F	B	
Daniel	11	M	B	
Jacob	10	M	B	
William	6	M	B	
David H.	5	M	B	
Hannah	2	F	B	
Edward W.	0/12	M	B	
Hannah Bailey	65	F	B	

Source: US Census Bureau, Lewis & Rehoboth Hundred, Sussex County, Delaware, Dwelling 875, Family 875, John White household (1850), 44B, http://www.ancestry.com.

State of Delaware."[13] In 1850, the census taker enumerated the members of John White's household as shown in table 3.1. The 1860 census again recorded David White in the schedule of "Free Inhabitants in Lewes & Rehoboth Hundred," but this time twice—once with his family unit and a second time at the Atlantic Hotel, a Lewes public house, where he worked as a servant.[14] Table 3.2 presents information in the first 1860 entry.

In both censuses, the White family was recorded as having no real estate or personal estate of value; as the father, John White was a landless "laborer." In a tax assessment document from 1860, under the category of "Negroes," a John White is recorded as owning one yoke of oxen worth $40 and personal possessions worth $150.[15]

Table 3.2. White Family in the 1860 Census (Dwelling 174, Family 167)

Name of every person whose usual place of abode on the first day of June 1860 was to this family	Age	Sex	Color	Profession: Description of such male persons over 15 years of age
John White	43	M	B	Laborer
Sarah	37	F	B	
Daniel	21	M	B	Farm Hand
Jacob	19	M	B	Sailor
William	16	M	B	
Henry	14	M	B	
Edward	10	M	B	
Hannah	12	F	B	
George	7	M	B	
Wesley	2	M	B	
Patience A.	3	F	B	
Joseph	1	M	B	
Hannah Baley	70	F	B	Wash Woman

Source: US Census Bureau, Lewis & Rehoboth Hundred, Sussex County, Delaware, Dwelling 174, Family 167, John White household (1860), 26, http://www.ancestry.com.

If one assumes that Sarah White was the mother of all of these children, she had her first child at the age of sixteen and, by the age of thirty-seven, had borne nine more. Ages, however, were often inaccurate and inconsistent in census and other records. If Sarah was not the mother of all the children (if John had a previous wife, for example), she is likely to have married John between about 1840 and 1844, the largest gap in the children's ages (that is, four years between Jacob and William). The two older brothers, Daniel and Jacob, found work by 1860, one as a farm hand, the other as a sailor. The name of a younger brother, Wesley, suggests that, like many Black families in the county, they were Methodist. An older woman, Hannah Bailey, perhaps Sarah's mother, lived with them and worked as a "Wash Woman."[16]

David Henry White's paternal grandparents, Daniel and Hannah White, were free, but details about the White family's manumission are scant. John and Sarah named their firstborn son Daniel, after John's father, and their firstborn girl, Hannah, after his mother.

No doubt the White home was modest; whatever possessions they had are likely to have been meager; free rural Black families typically owned cooking utensils, some hand tools, and perhaps some furniture, such as pine beds, tables, chests, stools, and chairs.[17]

Like many other free Black families, John and Sarah ultimately left the area. In the 1880 census, they are listed as living in the North District of Pilesgrove in Salem County, New Jersey, across the Delaware River and some two-thirds of the way from Lewes to Philadelphia. The census taker found that John "works on farm" and noted that he suffered from rheumatism, while identifying Sarah as "keeping house." Both were identified as illiterate.[18]

By age fourteen, White was working for a Mr. Edward Watson at the Atlantic Hotel, a short distance from his family home, to which in all likelihood, he returned frequently, thereby accounting for the double entry in the census. Data in the second 1860 census entry are presented in table 3.3.

Table 3.3. 1860 Census Entry for Watson Public House (Dwelling 195, Family 187)

Name of every person whose usual place of abode on the first day of June 1860 was to this family	Age	Sex	Color	Profession: Description of such male persons over 15 years of age
Edward Watson, public house	49	M		
Caroline	43	F		
William E.	16	M		
George	13	M		
Isabella	9	F		
Laura	7	F		
Joseph Lafretta	25	M		Carpenter
David J. Murry	24	M		Bar Keeper
David H. White	15	M	B	Servant
Kitturah Burton	25	F	B	Servant
Mary A. Paynter	19	F	B	Servant
John W. White	25	M	B	Ostler

Source: US Census Bureau, Lewis & Rehoboth Hundred, Sussex County, Delaware, Dwelling 195, Family 187, Edward Watson, public house (1860), http://www.ancestry.com.

The records make clear that White was not and had never been indentured. Delaware kept excellent records of indentures and there is no such record for White. In October 1847, Watson had purchased, for $2,000, a "lot of ground with tavern house in Lewes, adjoining South and Front Streets," along with an additional lot across Front Street, on which he built a stable. From this information, the hotel can be located on the corner of what is now Front Street and Savannah Road (formally South Street). In the 1848–52 tax list, the property is noted as a "tavern house and lots," and the 1852–56 list identifies it for the first time as the "Atlantic Hotel."[19] The spot was drawn by the German lithographer Augustus Köllner in 1841 (fig. 3.1).

FIGURE 3.1. *Breakwater, Delaware Bay,* 1841, by Augustus Köllner (1813–1906). Ink with wash on paper, composition: 9⅜₆ × 11⅟₁₆ inches; sheet: 11 × 12¾ inches. The view from the Atlantic Hotel (previously known as the Eagle Hotel) in 1841, as depicted by Augustus Köllner. Beyond the Lewes Canal is a marsh and Lewes Beach. In the distance, ships can be seen in the harbor protected by the historic breakwater at Cape Henlopen. *Delaware Art Museum, Samuel and Mary R. Bancroft Memorial, 1935.*

Watson accumulated several unpaid debts through the 1850s, and in 1855 and 1859 also incurred Superior Court judgments. The outbreak of the war then restricted vacationers who might otherwise have traveled to Lewes, and by April 1862, a suit threatened the loss of the property. The court instructed the Sussex County sheriff to collect the debt by October 13, 1862, or proceed to a sheriff's sale.[20]

Of all the professional and amateur historians who mentioned White, only one correctly identified him as a free inhabitant of Lewes:

Dr. E. D. Bryan of Lewes, who became interested in the *Alabama* because one of his ancestors, a great-great-grandfather, had signed onto the vessel when it anchored in Cape Town. Bryan deserves credit for being the first writer in more than a hundred years to debunk the fiction that White was enslaved. Yet in his otherwise excellent 2001 article, Bryan accepted Semmes's account that White was traveling "in the company of his master, a Delaware businessman," and further speculated that the businessman was Watson, fleeing creditors.[21] Bryan noted that Watson's debt was due on October 13, 1862, and inferred incorrectly from this that Watson fled the country on September 30 on the *Tonawanda*.

There is no evidence, however, that Watson ever fled the country. He does not appear in the Philadelphia port records, nor does he appear on the *Tonawanda*'s passenger manifest in any class (see chapter 4). Indeed, there is unequivocal evidence that White traveled not as the servant of a white "master" but as part of a galley crew with two experienced, perhaps related Black sailors, and that this was at least his second such voyage. Possibly he left for Philadelphia either with his father or with the ostler, John W. White, who, according to 1860 census, was a fellow Black employee of Watson. It is likely that White sought work as a sailor for the simple reason that Watson was intending to close his hotel.

White was perhaps further impelled by the deteriorating political climate, both across the nation and in Lewes. Historians point to 1862 as the year the war turned serious.[22] The time and place presented a special danger for the teenager. It is no accident that Lewes was colonized early, as it was a strategic gateway to Delaware Bay and Philadelphia beyond. There was a well-understood concern that if the South's advance continued, Lewes would become an obvious target. In March in Hampton Roads, Virginia, the USS *Monitor* and CSS *Virginia* battled each other to a draw. That same April brought news of a series of horrific battles—notably Shiloh, with more than 20,000

Union and Confederate casualties. In June, following the Battle of
Seven Pines, Confederate general Robert E. Lee was given command
of the Army of Northern Virginia.

At this point, the war's outcome was far from clear, and in the
border states, in the middle ground, it was possibly unsafe. Hancock
relates that the region's population became increasingly militarized
in the run-up to, and during the outbreak of the Civil War—part
of a national phenomenon discussed further in chapter 7. Because
of its central location between the North and the South, the region
held many stops on the Underground Railroad, though specific loca-
tions are difficult to identify.[23] Seaford became an important station
on the "underground railroad in reverse"—that is, the forwarding of
Northern recruits to the Confederacy.[24] By the summer of 1862, Sussex County was like an armed camp, with militias drilling in every
town. Milford, Georgetown, Lewes, and Seaford each organized
both Union and Confederate companies. There is no way of knowing whether White might have joined these men in either the army
or the navy. Black individuals as young as fifteen years are well documented in the US Army, but the legal age restriction was eighteen.[25]
In 1862, White would have been at most seventeen years of age.

For White, June 1862 might have been a good time to leave town;
there is no reason or evidence to suppose that he accompanied Watson. In fact, it appears that he left Lewes at least two months before
the Atlantic Hotel closed in August. Facing uncertainty and privation in Delaware, and a bit young for the military, White made the
sensible decision to pursue one job that would provide an escape
from the rural poverty that had entrapped his father, and, presumably, from the widening military conflict. Like many free Delaware
Black men, and like his older brother before him, he secured a gig
on a sailing packet; this one heading from nearby Philadelphia to the
unimaginably exotic and distant city of Liverpool, England.

Chapter 4

⌘

Passenger Cook

White's decision to leave Lewes and join the crew of a Philadelphia packet ship made good sense, and along with his previous employment, showed a determination to avoid servitude. Furthermore, he was following a time-honored tradition of Delaware's free Black citizens who traveled to Philadelphia and Wilmington to join sailing crews. According to maritime records, by the 1820s, approximately 30 percent of Black mariners entering or leaving the port of Philadelphia came from Delaware and Maryland.[1] White's older brother Jacob, possibly five years older than him, is listed in the 1860 census as having the occupation "sailor."

Indeed, the law was such that enlistment on an ocean vessel provided one of the established means of escaping servitude. As discussed in chapter 2, Delaware law prohibited free Black men under the age of twenty-one from being destitute, and it otherwise ensnared many in annual cycles of poverty and indenture. The state legislature also made it exceedingly difficult for free Blacks to leave the state and return, but Delaware made an exception for those who went to sea.

The 1849 amendment to the 1807 act that governed free Black emigration had reduced the time allowed out of state from six months to sixty days, but still exempted any "sea-faring person or persons of colour, who may be following his or their occupation."[2] With this exemption, White could travel to Philadelphia, sign onto a merchant ship crew, earn a salary, save some money, and still return home.

By the early nineteenth century, sturdy and long-lived sailing ships, which carried both passengers and cargo, were already plying the Atlantic between Liverpool and East Coast American cities from Baltimore to Boston. Before this time, ships generally waited in port until they achieved maximum freight and it became profitable to sail. Well before the use of steam became normal, New York and Philadelphia shippers had made an important innovation. In 1818, the Black Ball Line of New York began to offer regular, packet service—ships that left port on a set day. Just two years later, Thomas P. Cope began regular packet service between Philadelphia and Liverpool, and by midcentury, the firm he founded dominated shipping between those ports.[3]

For the Philadelphia-Liverpool route, the Cope Line employed four ships: the *Wyoming, Tonawanda, Tuscarora,* and *Saranak,* one sailing from Liverpool on the twelfth day of every month, and another sailing monthly on the twenty-fifth from Philadelphia. The boats were reliable, but old and slow and, by this time, obsolete. As far back as 1840, the British company Cunard had begun steamer service from Liverpool. During the decades when a typical packet might take several weeks to cross the Atlantic, the Cunard steamer *Britannia* reached Halifax in just twelve days and ten hours, averaging eight and a half knots. Even by 1845, steamship lines led by Cunard carried more saloon (first class) passengers than the sailing packets.

White made his first known voyage on the Cope Line packet *Wyoming,* which left Philadelphia on Wednesday, June 25, 1862.[4] Historian W. Jeffrey Bolster has explored the motivations that lured Black men to seafaring in the age of sail, noting that embarking on such a voyage literally meant striking out anew. "Aesthetically . . . a well-navigated ship in the midst of the primal sea conveyed a powerful image of stability in flux—an image profoundly appealing to those with little control over their own lives."[5] White was getting away from the war, was ready to earn a living, and perhaps—like any other teenager—was looking forward to an adventure of a lifetime. At that point, he was lucky and, under the circumstances, may have felt that he had made the right decision.

Built in 1845, the *Wyoming* was coincidentally about the same age as White. At 912 tons, it was relatively small (compared to the *Tonawanda*, built in 1850 and weighing over 1,200 tons). Packet ships of the mid-nineteenth century remained the primary means of immigration from Europe, and there had long been abuses, including the notorious crossing of the *Elizabeth and Sarah*, which sailed from Ireland in July 1847, carrying 276 persons of which 42 perished on the voyage. In 1855, Congress passed the Carriage of Passengers Act, which specified the maximum number of passengers, mandated "clear space" of 18 square feet per passenger, and detailed the necessary provisions and ventilation.[6]

Against this background, the Cope Line had a reasonably good record and was known for choosing its captains carefully, including Capt. William Burton of the *Wyoming*. The *Wyoming* had been profitable for the Cope Line, and up until the war, the packet had shipped with full cargoes in both directions. Throughout the 1850s, the *Wyoming* carried thousands of Irish immigrants fleeing the Great Famine. Analysis of Cope Line manifests shows a dramatic increase in steerage passengers from Liverpool to Philadelphia after 1845, peaking in 1853.[7] By 1862, steerage passengers from Liverpool remained mainly Irish.

White's signing on with this particular company is noteworthy and, like his initial decision to leave Lewes, suggests a plan made with an eye toward safety and within the rules. Joining the *Wyoming* as part of a team is entirely consistent with what is known about how free Black sailors operated in the Philadelphia maritime labor market of the time.[8] Apart from the *Wyoming*'s track record of safety, its owners, the Cope family, were Quakers and abolitionists. Not all shippers were abolitionists; for years, Philadelphia merchants and shippers had benefited mightily from their proximity to the South.[9] Not all Quakers were abolitionists, but the Philadelphia Copes most certainly were. In fact, founder Thomas P. Cope himself had been a prominent member of the Pennsylvania Abolition Society and a benefactor of the Institute for Colored Youth.[10] White is recorded in the crew manifest shown in figure 4.1.

White replaced a William Davis, and his "place of abode or the sureties" is listed as 336 South Street, owned at the time by John O'Brian.[11] White stood for Davis at the last minute, as Davis's name appears in the papers submitted to the Philadelphia port authorities.[12] However, White's passage is confirmed by the *Wyoming*'s forty-

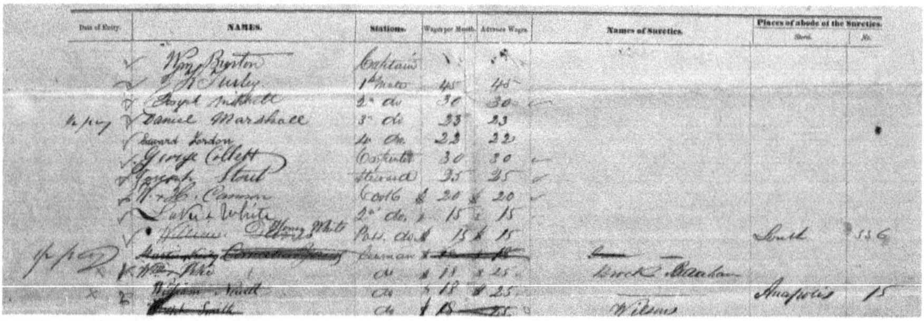
Date of Entry
NAMES.
Stations.
Wages per Month.
Advance Wages.
Names of Sureties.
Places of abode of the Sureties.
Street.
No.

Figure 4.1. White in the crew manifest of the *Wyoming*'s forty-eighth voyage, 1862 (see line 10). *Cope Family Papers, Collection 1486, Box 270, Historical Society of Pennsylvania.*

Table 4.1. From Crew Manifest of the *Wyoming*, Forty-Eighth Voyage

Names	Stations	Wages per month	Advance wages
W. H. Cannon	Cook	20	20
Luke White	2nd cook	15	15
Henry White	Pass. cook	15	15

eighth voyage bill of portage, which recorded his advances and wages (fig. 4.2). White earned $45.50, and after advance payments were subtracted, he actually received $32.45 on his return to Philadelphia. Unable to sign his name, he marked the receipt with an X (fig. 4.3).

The manifest records White's pay at $15 per month. It may not seem like much: $15 dollars in 1862 had the value of about $500 in today's market. Yet it was still higher than what the most junior members of the crew, "Boys," earned—$6 per month—and what landsman (novice) sailors were paid—typically $12 per month. In the Union navy, ordinary seamen in 1860 earned just $14 per month.[13]

On packets like the *Wyoming* and the *Tonawanda*, steerage passengers generally cooked their own meals, but forward cabin and cabin passengers would have the services of the ship's cooks, which in-

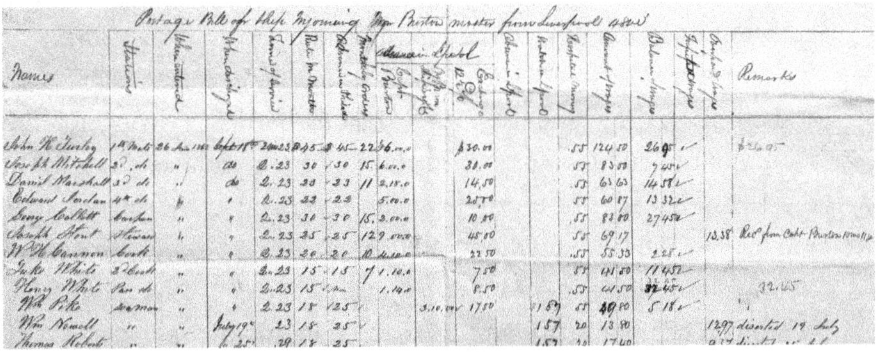

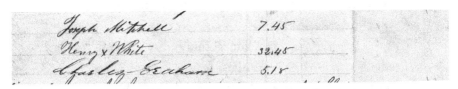

FIGURE 4.2. White in "Portage Bill of Ship *Tonawanda* from Liverpool, 36th Voyage of the *Tonawanda*" (see line 9). *Cope Family Papers, Collection 1486, Box 270, Historical Society of Pennsylvania.*

Joseph Mitchell 7.45
Henry x White 32.45
Charley Graham 5.18

FIGURE 4.3. Obverse of "Portage Bill of *Wyoming*'s Forty-Eighth Voyage." "Henry White" appears on line 9. *Cope Family Papers, Collection 1486, Box 270, Historical Society of Pennsylvania.*

cluded White.[14] His closest companions would have been the experienced cooks, William H. Cannon and Luke White, and he would have regularly interacted with the cabin and forward cabin passengers.[15]

That White sailed with Cannon and Luke White both on this voyage and subsequently on the *Tonawanda* is of interest because of these men's connection to an international network of deeply religious, temperance-advocating Black abolitionists. The names presented in table 4.1 appear together in sequence in the *Wyoming*'s manifest (fig. 4.1). William P. Powell, a founder of the New York Anti-Slavery Society, had created an international network of anti-slavery messengers and, as early as the 1830s, had established the Colored Seamen's Homes in both New Bedford, Massachusetts, and New York City. Long underappreciated as a key Black abolitionist figure, Powell was both unforgettable and forgotten, according to historian Philip S. Foner.[16]

Powell was the grandson of Elizabeth Barjona, a cook for the First Continental Congress, and the son of an enslaved father.[17] In the 1850s, in order to escape what he described as a declaration of war against the "free coloured population" and to secure an education for his children, Powell temporarily moved to Liverpool.[18] He continued to work actively to make the transatlantic sailor's network a conduit for anti-slavery materials, by forwarding goods to Boston for Maria Weston Chapman's annual anti-slavery bazaar, procuring British subscribers for American Anti-Slavery Society periodicals, and assisting British abolitionists in purchasing American abolitionist books and pamphlets.[19]

Well known in the maritime community, Powell regularly reported his work on behalf of Black seamen in *The Sailor's Magazine*. In a letter from Liverpool to abolitionist Samuel May Jr. in December 1859, Powell wrote:

The list of Anti-Slavery publications which I wrote for are for our mutual friend and co-adjutor Wilson Armistead of Leeds which I hope you will not fail to send. Now whilst I think of it, if you should fail to send by New York ship you can give instructions to Philadelphia Anti-Slavery office (for they have the same publication) to send the books by Mr. Fisher, Steward of the ship *Saranak* or Mr. Freeman, Steward of the ship *Tonawanda*, both Philadelphia packets running to L'pool, either gentleman will be glad to serve me.[20]

Powell was referring to Thomas C. Fisher, who throughout 1858 and 1859 was the *Saranak*'s steward.[21] Both Cannon and Luke White repeatedly sailed with Thomas C. Fisher on the *Saranak*, and their names are recorded together in the manifests of the *Saranak*'s forty-first, and forty-third through forty-ninth voyages.[22] In these voyages, Luke White is listed as "Pass. [Passenger] Cook," and by the time he joined the *Wyoming* and later the *Tonawanda* in 1862, he had been promoted to assistant cook. David Henry White took Luke White's entry-level position as passenger cook on the *Wyoming* and *Tonawanda*.

Both Cannon and Luke White also sailed with Mr. Freeman referenced by Powell in December 1859 on subsequent *Tonawanda* voyages. All these records document the deliberate care of White's decision. Not only was he escaping dangerous Lewes, but he had joined a team on a safe, abolitionist Quaker–owned ship that offered chances of regular long-term employment and promotion and whose owners expressed philanthropic concern for seamen of color. Further, he was connected to members of an international network of experienced Black sailors who acted as couriers for Black and white British and American abolitionists.

Such networks were likely to be connected to those active back in port. Journalist Keshler Thibert describes how Black seamen at the port of Philadelphia formed an important communication network that aided in freeing many enslaved people on vessels passing through the port.[23] Such communication was not limited to acting as couriers. William Brown, a retired Black steward from a Liverpool packet, founded the first professional Black theater company, the African Grove, in 1821 in New York. His main actor, James Hewlett, worked as a tailor and steward on the Liverpool packets. Through the medium of theater, Black sailors of the Atlantic packet era contributed to the movement of ideas across transnational ethnic communities.[24]

Sailing remained a difficult way to make a living, and much depended on the management style of individual ship captains. Powell wrote of sailors' "hard usage at sea, wholly at the mercy of tyrant captains and brutal officers (more especially the coloured sailor) subject as he is to the unholy prejudice, in consequence of the usage, customs and laws of his native country."[25] But this gig had its advantages. For one thing—unlike the *Alabama*'s endless cruise—the *Wyoming*'s had a beginning, middle, and end. After two weeks, White could expect to disembark in Liverpool and work for the Cope Line on a return voyage. The *Wyoming* was a safe ship and William Burton was a decent captain. Moreover, it was generally recognized that a cook's lot was better than that of an ordinary seaman, since cooks were not tasked with the dangerous work of climbing the masts and hauling the sails, or the drudgery of holystoning the decks and scraping paint.

It was a slow start, but nonetheless an exciting one. The steam tug *America* took the *Wyoming* down to the mouth of the Delaware, but after the tug turned back for Philadelphia, the *Wyoming* was briefly grounded for about two hours. Burton reported to the Cope Line that he was a few seamen short, including one who apparently changed his mind, jumped overboard, and swam nearly a half mile back to shore.[26] Otherwise, he was happy with his crew.

White's first few days at sea presumably would have been spent learning from William Cannon and Luke White how to prepare breakfast, lunch, and dinner for some forty passengers in the cabin and forward cabin classes. In a present-day ship's kitchen, we would accord him the status of *commis chef*. It would have been a small place—just enough room to contain a stove, of which the chimney pipe emerged on the upper deck, and some workspace hung round with pots and pans.[27]

Invoices and manifests tell us not only about the ship's main cargo—corn and wheat—but also the various foodstuffs and ingredients White would be working with in the galley. The cabin passengers appear to have eaten well: one invoice covers chocolate, rice, cheese, cloves, ginger, nutmeg, raisins, peaches, salt, lemons, apples, prunes, figs, currants, olives, sardines, cans of tomatoes, pickles, vermicelli, macaroni, herring, salmon packed in jars, sausages, and baking powder. Another includes fresh and roast beef, lard, hams, and mustard.[28]

At night, White would have rested and slept with the rest of the crew in the forecastle—the most forward part of the below deck. Here, under the bow, in the very "eyes of the ship," is where ordinary sailors slept on hammocks and gathered to smoke, tell stories (spin yarns), and play checkers and cards. By this time, Black sailors had long been integrated into both naval and merchant marine crews, and sailors were nothing if not a polyglot society. As Bolster relates in his book *Black Jacks*: "At sea Black and white sailors faced down the same captains, weathered the same gales, and pumped the same infernally leaking ships. . . . Work pulled them together."[29] Only a few days into the voyage, all this would be new to the landsman White.

And then there were the chanteys: work songs whose popularity and number reached their zenith from the 1840s to the 1860s on transatlantic packet ships. Recent scholarship has shown that such songs were heavily influenced by, if not an outgrowth of, Black work song traditions and were a kind of technology that made it possible to efficiently organize communal labor such as hauling and furling.[30] With the development of steam, the chanteys disappeared as work songs but survived as folklore.

On July 19, 1862, the *Wyoming* arrived in Liverpool and would not depart for Philadelphia until Wednesday, August 13. Here White would have had a three-week layover, perhaps with Cannon and Luke White as guides. By this time, Liverpool was a cosmopolitan city of some 400,000 that had experienced rapid growth through the early nineteenth century—by 1820, its population had more than doubled.[31] Due mainly to the cotton trade, there was passionate sympathy for the South; so strong were these connections that it was said that "more Confederate flags fluttered above Liverpool than over Richmond."[32] But the city also had possibly the oldest Black community in Europe, and many of its inhabitants were related to generations of sailors who had come through the port since the days of the triangular trade. This free community was also more integrated than what White might have experienced in Delaware, and there were plenty of Union supporters there as well. According to Herman Melville, "In Liverpool indeed the negro steps with a prouder pace, and holds his head like a man; for there no such exaggerated feeling exists in respect to him, as here in America. Three or four times, I encountered our black steward, dressed very handsomely and walking arm in arm with a good-looking English woman. In New York, such a couple would have been mobbed in three minutes; and the steward would have been lucky to escape with whole limbs."[33]

As noted previously, Powell himself had moved with his family to Liverpool temporarily in order to secure an education for his children.[34] Since White was traveling with experienced sailors, he would presumably have arranged accommodations in this Liverpool community. Perhaps during those three weeks, he slept aboard the *Wyoming* or perhaps at the Liverpool Sailors' Home. Founded in 1846, this extraordinary establishment accepted boarders and provided safe lodging for visiting sailors of all backgrounds. The building, on Canning Street, could hold five hundred men in wooden cabins, arranged on six floors overlooking a central hall. A devastating fire gutted the building in April 1860, but within two years, it was up and running again.[35] Unfortunately, the building was demolished in 1974 and the home's register is lost, so it may never be known whether White stayed there while in Liverpool.

Alternatively, there were the flophouses on Canning Street, which catered to transient sailors.[36] Charles Dickens visited Liverpool that year on a pub crawl and saw it differently than both Melville and Powell, perhaps reflecting a changed atmosphere during the Civil War. He described a drinking house in which the landlord and most of the clientele were Black. "They generally kept together these poor fellows . . . because they were at a disadvantage singly, and liable to slights in the neighboring streets." The clientele appeared to have fun, with the landlord presiding over a scene of "merriment and dancing."[37]

During this period, Captain Burton was busy maintaining the *Wyoming*. First, he had his chronometer serviced. A chronometer is a device for precisely keeping time at sea, an instrument essential for determining longitude. Although timepieces in the form of clocks and watches had long been manufactured, pendulums could not work on vessels rolling and pitching on the high seas, and conventional timepieces of the day were affected by magnetism and temperature. The technical challenge was significant since an error of only seconds a day, compounded over weeks or months, would add up to miles of uncertainty. In 1773, after some forty years of work, master clockmaker John Harrison was recognized by the British Parliament for designing the chronometer. With steady improvement, mid-nineteenth-century chronometers came to look like large watches set inside a gimbaled wooden box.[38]

Second, there was the management of the ship itself. Keeping a sixteen-year-old vessel in good trim was no easy matter, and Burton reported to the Cope Line from Liverpool that the ship "leeks [*sic*] about the same as usual," the pumps were "well attended to," and there was never enough water to "get at the cargo." Even so, a manageable leak appeared, and Burton saw to its repair.[39]

After just over three weeks in port, on Wednesday, August 13, 1862, the *Wyoming* left for the return journey with 150 passengers on board. It would be a long voyage. Heading west against the wind, it arrived back in Philadelphia only on Friday, September 19—a voyage of some thirty-seven days.

This first round trip seems to have gone well enough for White to remain sailing for the Cope Line. While not mentioning the cooks specifically, Burton reported that "I think I have a good crew of men."[40] On his return, White's homestay was relatively short, as the *Tonawanda* was scheduled to depart on September 25 (though in the event it was delayed until the 30th). With $32.50 in his pocket, that might have provided just enough time to catch a ride home and see his family before heading back to Philadelphia, or he may have returned to the South Street address listed for him on the *Wyoming* manifest.

What a week to return home! September 1862 was among the most difficult and pivotal months in US history. The Philadelphia newspapers were filled with incoming reports of the battle along Antietam Creek near Sharpsburg, Maryland. September 17 had been the bloodiest single day of the entire war, with casualties on both sides numbering more than 23,000. The battle was only a qualified success since Union General George B. McClellan allowed Lee's retreating army to escape, but at least the Confederate invasion of Maryland was stopped dead in its tracks.

This gave President Abraham Lincoln the opportunity to issue, on September 22, the provisional Emancipation Proclamation. Lincoln told his cabinet that he had made a covenant with God that if the Union drove the Confederacy out of Maryland, he would issue the proclamation. However, the executive order applied only to the states in insurrection, and it offered compensation for the enslaved only to former owners in loyal slave states, such as Delaware. For some, the draft was greeted with a bewilderment of joy, while for others it was either a feeble half measure or unconstitutional tyranny. The Philadelphia papers carried the news from September 23 to 29, and these issues would certainly have been in the *Tonawanda*'s mailbags when it eased down the Delaware on September 30.[41]

At 1,240 tons, the *Tonawanda* was a relatively large, twelve-year-old packet with three decks and a draft of twenty-one feet. Like the *Wyoming*, it was obsolete and slow, depending entirely on wind for propulsion. The ship had been constructed in 1850, but in spite of having no steam, it was reliable and was skippered by a superbly competent veteran, Capt. Theodore Julius.

The *Tonawanda* had arrived on September 1, bringing 130 passengers from Liverpool. In the days when newspapers eagerly reported the arrival of every vessel, the passage was described in the *Philadelphia Inquirer* as having been "very successful with the exception of the tediousness usual on long voyages" and having had "no sickness."[42] The "no sickness" notation was important and indicated a well-run vessel, since illness among packet passengers, particularly in steerage, was a serious problem for packets and a long-standing matter of public concern.[43] Captain Julius himself had fought a serious outbreak of cholera on board back in 1854—in an age before cholera was discovered to be caused by fecal bacteria—when returning from Liverpool. The details of that unfortunate voyage were reported in the Philadelphia-based *Transactions of the College of Physicians.* Even so, in that same report, the College of Physicians provided its seal of approval to the Cope Line in general and to Julius in particular.[44]

Captain Julius prepared the *Tonawanda* for its thirty-sixth voyage at Cope headquarters, at the wharf on Front Street. The bill of lading not only details the *Tonawanda*'s cargo but also documents Julius's precision in recording weights and values—down to the last sixtieth of a bushel. Like the *Wyoming*'s cargo, the *Tonawanda*'s reflected the existing export market for Pennsylvania and Delaware wheat shipped out of Philadelphia. There were 12,671 $^{56}\!/\!_{60}$ bushels of "Red Wheat" in the forward bin; 11,035 $^{40}\!/\!_{60}$ bushels of red wheat in the after bin; and 1,167 $^{35}\!/\!_{60}$ bushels in the middle bin; also 910 $^{33}\!/\!_{60}$ bushels of "White Wheat" were stowed in 255 ships bags, and 10,403 $^{27}\!/\!_{60}$ bushels of red wheat in 3,076 ships bags.

The passenger manifests further illuminate this particular voyage of the *Tonawanda*. They list 4 men who traveled as "Cabin Passengers" (first class); about 28 men, women, and children as "Forward Cabin Passengers" (second class); and another 37 men, women, and children in steerage: about 70 in total. There is no mention of White as a passenger, but just as tellingly, there is also no mention of Edward Watson, either in cabin, forward cabin, or steerage; so, in contradiction to later accounts and suggestions, White did not travel up to Philadelphia to board the *Tonawanda* as Watson's servant.

The rest of the documentary record is also definitive. First, the original records of the Port of Philadelphia from the 1860s no longer exist, but they were transcribed sometime in the 1930s, and the typescript is preserved in the archives of the Maritime History Museum of Philadelphia. The manifest contained the names of most of the crew and their age, place of birth, height, station, and residence. There were thirty-five entries, including one for Captain Julius. Twenty-six entries were complete, but the last nine entries were abbreviated. Among them is the following:

David Henry
Description: Not Given
Remarks: No protection

The phrase "no protection" is informative because it signified that, like most junior seamen, White had not yet obtained a Seaman's Certificate of Protection. Seasoned sailors had carried this document since Congress authorized it in 1796 in response to British impressment of US sailors. (Luke White and William Cannon had such certificates.)

Yet the most informative document is the crew manifest of the *Tonawanda*'s thirty-sixth voyage. Here White is once again recorded, this time under the name "David Henry," under a standard seaman's contract, and his station and pay are recorded as "Pass." (Passenger) cook and $15 per month (fig. 4.4).

Two entries below Joseph Fisher's is the name John White, but it is struck out. The tantalizing entry suggests that perhaps White's fa-

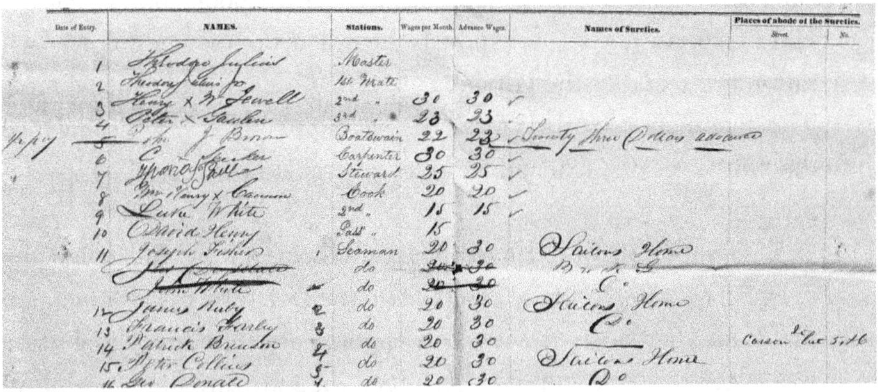

FIGURE 4.4. "Crew Manifest of the 36th Voyage of the *Tonawanda*." *Cope Family Papers, Collection 1486, Box 254, Historical Society of Pennsylvania.*

Table 4.2. From Crew Manifest of the *Tonawanda*, Thirty-Sixth Voyage

Names	Stations	Wages per month	Advance wages
Wm. Henry Cannon	Cook	20	20
Luke White	2nd cook	15	15
David Henry	Pass. cook	15	0

ther planned to accompany him, or that perhaps John W. White, the ostler at Edward Watson's hotel, had planned on making this voyage.

After a long enumeration of the crew's duties and responsibilities, a clause states "that for the due performance of each and every of the abovementioned articles and agreements, and acknowledgement of their being voluntary, and without compulsion, or any other clandestine means being used, [this contract is] agreed to and signed by us."[45] This document proves that White was gainfully employed and not indentured, and it dispels the notion that he came with his "master," "a Delaware businessman."[46] It makes clear that his responsibility was to prepare food for the passengers, for which he was paid a wage. It also implies that he joined the galley crew, as part of a team.[47]

A final poignant document in the Cope's family archive is the "Portage Bill of Ship Tonawanda from Liverpool 36th voyage."[48] Here Captain Julius meticulously recorded the money due to each sailor at the end of the voyage, based on advances and time worked. The document records White's time as eighteen days, with a balance due for wages of $4.80 and an indecipherable note regarding its dispensation.[49]

September 30 would have been another exciting day, when the delayed *Tonawanda* finally eased down the Delaware toward the open sea. White had been provided no opportunity for education, but he was eager to work and, by age fifteen, had already found employment. When the Atlantic Hotel faltered, he grabbed one opportunity Delaware offered to avoid indenture and rural poverty, and now he was boarding a Liverpool packet with two older peers—one perhaps a trusted relation—on the busy Philadelphia wharf. He was no longer a landsman, and his first voyage had gone well enough for him to immediately sign on again with the same team. White's story continues in chapter 10; but to fully appreciate his imminent predicament, it is first necessary to meet his kidnappers and the ship on which he would be enslaved.

Chapter 5

⌒⇋

Manifest Destiny

White's childhood experiences from birth to employment at the Atlantic Hotel remain largely unknown, but there is a great deal to relate of this period regarding the political and military environment that shaped the experience and behavior of his captors—especially Semmes. Just as it is not my intention to write a biography of White, neither will I provide a biography of Semmes. In contrast to White's life, this is not because there is insufficient information, but rather that the terrain has already been well and thoroughly explored.[1]

This chapter instead summarizes the essential circumstances of Semmes's background, character, and actions necessary to understand his eventual role in White's capture and demise. The following chapter explores, among other things, Semmes's experiences in the Mexican-American War, since the crucible of combat provides something of a portal into his character and subsequent actions.

Twentieth-century historians were generally kind to Semmes, and in truth, he was not without his redeeming features. Notwithstanding his explicit racism, it should not be forgotten that he was very much a product of his time and that his passionate defense of slavery was hardly exceptional. Further, it might be argued that it would be unfair to judge him for not meeting our twenty-first-century, or for that matter twentieth-century, standards of racial tolerance.[2] Moreover, he was a vivid chronicler who wrote passionately, if selectively, about his observations of the lands he visited during his early years in the navy. He seems at times to have been genuinely offended by the poor conditions and servitude of enslaved people and others subjected to peonage in the southern latitudes.[3] That said, there is a self-serving quality to almost everything he wrote, and when these writings are scrutinized, it becomes obvious that he regularly lied to protect his reputation and advance his prejudices; these flaws are timeless.

Just as the Civil War may be seen through the eyes and experience of a Black teenager, the trajectory of American racism from colonization to secession, and ultimately the construction of the Lost Cause narrative, may be seen through the history, experience, and rhetoric of a single family. It may be thought of as a strand—one of many—in the United States' founding ideological DNA.

Semmes was born in 1809 to an established Maryland family going back five generations in North America. His Maryland ancestors grew tobacco, owned slaves, and were prominent members of the local Catholic gentry. In fact, one of his ancestors, Benedict Joseph Semmes from Normandy, had accompanied Leonard Calvert in 1640 aboard the *Ark* to America.[4] On his maternal side, he was a direct descendent of Arthur Middleton, a signatory to the Declaration of Independence. His mother died when he was just three, and his father in 1823, leaving fourteen-year-old Raphael and his only brother, twelve-year-old Samuel, orphans. The boys were placed in the care of three successful uncles: Benedict, a prominent physician; Raphael, an established businessman who owned a Georgetown warehouse; and Alexander, who owned a fleet of merchant ships that sailed out of Georgetown, down the Potomac, and out to sea. Another close relative, Joseph Semmes, owned the popular City Tavern, on the corner of Wisconsin and M streets, which was an important meeting place for local businessmen and slave traders. When Joseph Semmes died in 1829, the establishment was sold to George McCandless—the same McCandless's Tavern referred to in *Twelve Years A Slave*.[5]

A notice published in the December 8, 1823, *Daily National Intelligencer* by Semmes's uncle Raphael, offering a reward for the capture of an escaped enslaved woman only identified as "Harriet," is perhaps an early indication that the relationship between the Semmes family and those they enslaved was probably not so affectionate.[6]

Semmes's formative years in Georgetown with his uncles were notable for exposing him to stories of seafaring and distant ports and for instilling in him an appreciation of reading and learning. For the rest of his life, he vacillated between parallel careers in the navy and the law. In between stretches of active naval duty he found time to study law, so that by 1835, at age twenty-six, he had not only obtained a midshipman's warrant but had also been admitted to the Maryland bar. Growing up on the banks of the Potomac, he also learned to swim, a factor in his survival in at least two of the three vessels eventually lost under his command.

The 1830s were an inauspicious time for junior naval officers. The nascent US Navy had undergone rapid growth and change while engaged in a series of local and international conflicts—most notably the Quasi-War with France, the War of 1812 with the British, and the two Barbary Wars in the Mediterranean. From the end of the Second Barbary War in 1815 to the beginning of the Mexican-American War in 1846, opportunities for commissioning and promotion were relatively few, and the competition became intense.

To obtain a midshipman's warrant, it was useful to have political connections. After attending Charlotte Hall Military Academy and with the help of his Uncle Benedict, Semmes obtained an appointment in 1826 from President John Quincy Adams. Six years later, having completed his land training, he achieved the credential of Passed Midshipman.

The navy was a deeply hierarchical culture with strict codes of honor and behavior. In his masterful *Six Frigates*, historian Ian Toll observes that the navy was a society even more rigid and deferential than that of the nation it served.[7] Other historians, too, have explored in detail the challenges and opportunities facing midshipmen.[8] In his novel *White Jacket*, Herman Melville describes the imperiousness and nearly absolute power that midshipmen held over common sailors, while showing craven submission to those of senior rank.

Semmes was now embedded in a deeply competitive culture in which, since the earliest days of the navy, a passion for glory in battle was highly coveted. In describing the character attributes desirable in a midshipman in the early US Navy, Robert Smith, the first secretary of the navy, identified "a high love of character and passion for glory."[9] "Does any man enter into naval service for the sake of subsistence?" he asked. "Are not glory and fame the grand incentives?" Toll describes the early American naval officer typical of the Mediterranean squadron as "done up in his high standing collar and gold lace . . . as testy and vain as a fighting gamecock. He prayed for war as a farmer would pray for rain and a lawyer would pray for lawsuits. War was his profession; it offered the most practical outlet for his aggression and the best hope for his advancement. For the junior officers of the Mediterranean squadron, there was not enough war to go around."[10]

In the intense competition for promotion, heroic deeds provided the consummate form of merit recognition. There was the example of John Roberts, who served on the *Constellation* in 1799 during the Quasi-War with France. After the *Constellation* captured the *L'Insurgent*, Roberts became a national hero by successfully navigating the prize to friendly St. Kitts through two storms, though his small crew was vastly outnumbered by the captured French sailors. He was immediately promoted to the rank of captain.

Among the most prominent lessons from that generation was the spectacular career of Stephen Decatur, perhaps the most celebrated of early American naval officers. The Marine Corps hymn, "The Shores of Tripoli," refers to the Barbary Wars, fought in the early nineteenth century against various North African fiefdoms that had exacted tributes from ships plying the Mediterranean coast and routinely seized American sailors for ransom or enslavement. Jefferson refused to pay these tributes and instead sent a fleet. When the USS *Philadelphia*, under Commodore William Bainbridge, ran aground in an uncharted reef near Tripoli harbor in October 1803, Bainbridge and his crew were captured and imprisoned. Bainbridge managed to warn the US fleet that Tripolitan crews would disguise themselves as Christian merchantmen. Deception—with regard to identity—was par for the course on both sides.

The loss of the *Philadelphia* was a potential disaster for the Americans. Commodore Edward Preble, acting while Bainbridge was imprisoned in Tripoli, now authorized a daring plan. Just before Christmas Eve, the *Constellation* had captured a 60 ton ketch of Turkish design, the *Mastico*, that had been sailing under Tripolitan colors. It wasn't worth much, but it had the advantage of looking like a thousand other merchant vessels that plied the North African coast. Under cover of darkness, Decatur slowly sailed the ketch, now renamed the *Intrepid*, into Tripoli harbor with the intent of boarding and recapturing the *Philadelphia*. A crewman who spoke Arabic called out to harbor guards with a story, while the crew, dressed as Arab seamen, remained below out of sight. When close enough, Decatur and some sixty seamen boarded and reclaimed the *Philadelphia*, killing twenty Tripolitans in the process with no American lives lost. Despite exhausting every possible exigency, it was impossible to refloat the *Philadelphia*. Rather than let the ship remain in Tripolitan hands, Decatur and his men set it on fire and successfully escaped on the *Intrepid*, all the while taking shots from the Tripolitans. Decatur had turned a bitter defeat into a victory and source of national pride and self-congratulation. He would be promoted to the rank of captain over seven other more senior lieutenants.

Another pertinent incident from the Barbary Wars reveals the importance of claiming victory in battle, even when the circumstances were equivocal. Following the burning of the *Philadelphia*, with the Tripolitans not inclined to surrender, Commodore Preble approved a plan to load the *Intrepid* with 5 tons of gunpowder, tightly packed, and some 150 mortar shells above the magazines. The idea was to sail the vessel close into Tripoli harbor, light fuses, and escape, but it was a suicide mission if the fuses didn't work properly or if the ketch took a shot. The plan went into effect on the night of September 4, 1804. The *Intrepid* was commanded by Lt. Richard Somers, who led another midshipman and eleven volunteers. For some unknown reason, the floating bomb detonated prematurely, with the loss of the entire crew and little damage to Tripoli harbor. The mission might have been thought a failure, but in dying gloriously, Somers became a national hero. As Toll relates in *Six Frigates*, "The official story was that, preferring death to capture, Somers put a match to the magazine. This version enabled family and friends to believe they [the crew] had died a glorious death and drew attention from the likelihood that 13 lives were thrown away to no good purpose."[11]

In 1836, during the Second Seminole War, Semmes was in command of a small steamer, the *Lt. Izard*, that fought to enforce the Indian Removal Act of 1830, which mandated the removal of indigenous people from north of Lake Okeechobee and their relocation west of the Mississippi River.[12] Semmes was ordered to supply the forces of Brig. Gen. Richard K. Call by transporting 150 Florida militiamen and towing a barge laden with provisions for Call's troops. Semmes's immediate mission was to determine whether the *Lt. Izard* could navigate the Withlacoochee River. During this complicated and delicate operation, the *Lt. Izard* ran aground, was wrecked, and had to be abandoned.[13] It was the first of three vessels lost under Semmes's command. Call believed the loss was due to the navy assigning officers like Semmes who had insufficient training for navigating narrow river channels. Semmes blamed the loss on the recently recruited, inexperienced crew. Charges and countercharges eventually led Semmes to request a court of inquiry, but the Navy Department didn't pursue it any further.[14]

The incident did not go unnoticed, however, and Semmes was roundly criticized in the *Pensacola Gazette* with the suggestion that the loss had harmed the military operation. In an early sign of his defensiveness, Semmes furiously replied to the *Gazette* story: "The public will see the undue importance which has been attached to the loss of this vessel . . . if there is blame to be attached to myself or my officers, this will be the proper subject for a Court of Enquiry and not for newspaper discussion."[15] Given the shame associated with failure, a furious defense of one's honor was normal and understandable in the US Navy of the 1830s.

A subsequent incident, in 1843, however, confirmed Semmes's reputation as a litigious and difficult officer, or in Fox's words a "sea lawyer," that is, someone overly inclined to question and quibble.[16] The commandant of the Pensacola Navy Yard, Alexander Dallas, whose brother George M. Dallas was US vice-president under Polk, declined Semmes's recommendation to appoint his brother-in-law, Frances Spencer, to the position of chief clerk. Instead, Dallas gave the position to one of his own friends. So began an escalating feud that culminated in Semmes's house arrest, a subsequent protest to the Navy Department, and a court martial of Dallas. Ultimately Dallas was cleared of all misconduct, but the feuding parties were separated, with Semmes remaining in Pensacola and Dallas appointed commodore of the Pacific Squadron. Referring to Semmes, one colleague later recalled, "As a controversialist . . . he was unequalled in the Navy."[17]

At this time, the United States was swept up in an expansionist project that came to be known as Manifest Destiny. The vision was based on a belief in the special virtues of America; and a mission embraced by Southerners to remake the West in the image of the agrarian, slaveholding East. The concept of replacement was reflected in the scientific racism of the time, expressed starkly in Herbert Spencer's 1851 *Social Statics*, in which he opined that imperialism had served civilization by clearing the earth of inferior races: "The forces which are working out the great scheme of perfect happiness, taking no account of incidental suffering, exterminate such sections of mankind as stand in their way. . . . Be he human or be he brute—the hindrance must be got rid of."[18] The ideology of such replacement itself evolved into the phrase "survival of the fittest," which Spencer coined after reading Charles Darwin in 1859; this ideology came to be known as Social Darwinism.[19] Although the phrase had not yet been coined, Semmes expressed the ideology perfectly in his 1851 Mexican-American War memoir:

> The passage of our race into Texas, New Mexico, and California, was but the first step in that great movement southward which forms part of our destiny. An all-wise Providence has placed us in juxtaposition with an inferior people, in order . . . that we may sweep over them, and remove them (as a people) and their worn-out institutions from the face of the earth. We are the northern hordes of the Alani, spreading ourselves over fairer and sunnier fields, and carrying along with us, besides the newness of life, and the energy and courage of our prototypes, letters, arts, and civilization.[20]

The national debate over the annexation of Texas and subsequent Mexican-American War, which Semmes enthusiastically supported, was closely linked to the fate of slavery. Having thrown off the yoke of Mexican suzerainty in 1836, the Lone Star State had ratified a constitution that not only allowed slavery but forbade any owner from freeing enslaved people without the consent of the Texas Congress. Further, it forbade Congress from making any law that restricted the slave trade or emancipated slaves. Much of the white population growth in the next decade originated in Mississippi, Louisiana, and Arkansas, and many of these immigrants kept laborers in bondage and brought them along. Slavery persisted in Texas after the Emancipation Proclamation until June 19, 1865,[21] which as of 2021, is celebrated as Juneteenth, the most recently declared US national holiday.

The abolition of slavery in Britain in 1833 and in Mexico in 1837, as well as formal adoption of slavery in Texas, convinced the South that Texas needed to be admitted to the Union as a slave state. Following the American Revolution and the War of 1812, distrust lingered between Great Britain and the United States, even into the 1840s. Moreover, Britain's concerns about American expansion, the Oregon question, and the British abolition of slavery under Prime Minister Charles Grey's Reformist administration, all contributed to a fraught environment far removed from the "special relationship" of modern times. Matters came to a head over Texas, as southerners feared British machinations to make the territory free.

South Carolina senator John C. Calhoun, who became secretary of state in 1844 under President John Tyler, made the case explicitly in a famous and consequential letter to Richard Pakenham, the British minister in Washington, DC. As historian Joel H. Silbey notes, Calhoun thought "the issue before the nation was the protection of southern slavery, threatened as it was by Britain's persistent intrigues and growing influence in Texas."[22]

Thus, the annexation of Texas in 1845—obtained without a formal treaty with either Mexico or Texas but requiring, as an act of Congress, only a simple majority in both chambers—was understood by contemporaries as a transparent effort to expand and protect the slave economy. President James K. Polk sought to further expand the United States, both in the Northwest by negotiating with Britain over Oregon and, more especially, in the South by ginning up a war with Mexico. Silbey describes Polk as willing to go to war to add potential slave territory to the Union.[23] On the other hand, Silbey writes, "the President . . . compromised away the just territorial claims of free-state expansionists in the areas where slavery was unlikely to go and could never prosper."[24] In a long speech on the House floor, a New York representative concluded, "The rule . . . is to . . . grasp in one direction all the territory within our reach, and to abandon that to which we are justly entitled in the other."[25]

In protest, Mexico broke off diplomatic relations with the United States and refused to receive John Slidell, Polk's minister to Mexico (who would later become the Confederacy's commissioner in Paris). A Mexican revolution in 1845 installed a strongly protectionist military government. Polk responded by baiting Mexico into war; he ordered Gen. Zachary Taylor south ostensibly to protect Texas. Taylor crossed the Nueces River at a point about 160 miles north of the Rio Grande, near Corpus Christi, then occupied the left bank of the Rio Grande in a transparent act of war. The Nueces had been considered the southern boundary of Texas for a century.[26]

While clothed in the language of American destiny and exceptionalism, the subsequent war was increasingly abhorrent to many northern Whigs who recognized that its true purpose was the expansion of slave territory. Understanding that Polk had in fact invaded Mexican territory, Abraham Lincoln, then representing Illinois in the House of Representatives, challenged President Polk to identify the particular "spot [of soil] . . . on which the blood of our citizens was . . . shed."[27]

Naturally, abolitionist sentiment was set fiercely against the war. Henry David Thoreau objected by refusing to pay his taxes and by later writing *Civil Disobedience*."[28] Summing up his outlook in the aftermath of the war in 1850, Unitarian minister Abiel Abbot Livermore wrote, "The reasons assigned for the war were but pretenses, covering ulterior designs, which it would not do at once to disclose but which have, in succession all come out, and now stand in their naked deformity before the world: conquest, dismemberment, annexation, the extension of slavery."[29]

The rhetorical flamethrower Jane Swisshelm, who later wrote for Horace Greeley's *New York Tribune*, and who in 1850 would become the first woman admitted to the Senate press gallery, wrote, "This great nation was engaged in the pusillanimous work of beating poor little Mexico—a giant whipping a cripple." To one soldier who had served in Mexico, she decried "the blood of women and children slain at their own altars, on their own hearthstones, [shed] that you might spread the glorious institution of woman-whipping and baby-stealing."[30]

If the Mexican-American War was a dubious project—designed and implemented for the purpose of expanding the slave economy—it can also be seen that there was fierce and vocal opposition to the war at the time. These objections, it will be shown, were also privately expressed by at least one officer—Winslow—in the very navy sent to strangle Mexico into submission.

Chapter 6

Gulf of Mexico

When the Mexican-American War broke out, Semmes, who by now had received his lieutenant's commission, joined Commodore David Conner's thirteen-ship squadron, sent to form a blockade off the coast of Vera Cruz. Initially he was assigned to Conner's flagship, the *Cumberland*. As boarding officer it was his duty to board enemy ships and neutral vessels to make sure no contraband reached Mexico.

Everyone hated blockade duty, and the reasons were manifold. The ships were small, and the accommodations cramped. The summers in the western Gulf of Mexico were unbearably hot and humid, and furious winter storms called northers pummeled the squadron. The navy rations were poor and often weevilly. Malaria, yellow fever, scurvy, and dysentery were constant threats, and the mosquitoes were torturous. For example, in May 1845, officers on board the USS *Potomac* reported "eleven- and one-half boxes of 'raisins,' one hundred and thirty-one pounds of 'cheese' and eighty-six pounds of 'butter' unfit to be served as part of the Navy rations. And therefore condemn them and recommend that said 'raisins' and 'cheese' be thrown overboard."[1] In April 1846, the officers aboard the *Cumberland* found 110 gallons of beans wholly unfit for consumption, "being worm eaten and smelling badly," and tossed them into the sea.[2] A similar, "strict and careful survey" in December 1846 condemned more than 4,000 pounds of bread, apples, beans, rice, and beef aboard the USS *Raritan*. That year, so many officers were ill with dysentery on the *Raritan* that a navy surgeon pleaded for help.[3]

In *Shifting Grounds*, Quigley observes that the glorification of death and sacrifice during the Mexican-American War were key components of nascent Confederate nationalism.[4] This is clearly evident in Semmes's 1851 memoir, in which he bemoans the "holocausts of the navy . . . untrumpeted of fame."[5] Blockade duty was exhausting, and while exhaustion might have been endurable, the real problem for Semmes was that the assignment provided no opportunity for glory. In another revealing passage, he wrote: "We looked forth from our ship, as from a prison, upon the glittering specks of sand . . . hither we resorted toward sunset every evening, when the weather was propitious, to stretch our cramped limbs, smoke an idle cigar, and talk over the events of the war; a war, for the navy, of toils and vigils, without the prospect of either excitement or glory."[6]

Semmes's yearning for glory fit perfectly with the navy's contemporaneous culture since self-distinction was the navy's substitute for wealth and, as previously noted, it was the best way to get promoted.[7] In this case, it would turn out to have dubious and fatal consequences.

In October 1846, Semmes was given command of the USS *Somers*, then on blockade duty off Vera Cruz. The *Somers* was already known as a bad-luck ship, if ever there was such a thing beyond superstition. Its name itself connoted trouble: she was named for the lieutenant who was lost when the *Intrepid* prematurely exploded in Tripoli harbor in 1804.

Launched in 1842, the *Somers* had departed New York for the west coast of Africa under the command of Alexander Slidell Mackenzie. On board was Midshipman Philip Spencer, the son of the secretary of war, John C. Spencer. Its mission was to carry dispatches to the frigate *Vandelia*, but by the time the *Somers* arrived in Monrovia, Liberia, the *Vandelia* had already departed. Mackenzie then headed for the Virgin Islands, hoping to meet the *Vandelia* at St. Thomas. During the voyage, the *Somers*'s officers noticed a worsening of morale, and an informant told 1st Lt. Guert Gansevoort that Spencer and two others were plotting a mutiny so that the *Somers* could become a pirate ship. A search of Spencer's locker found suspicious papers written in Greek. The officers reported that they had "come to a cool, decided, and unanimous opinion" that Spencer and the two others were "guilty of a full and determined intention to commit a mutiny." Despite Spencer's claim that they had only been pretending piracy as part of a game, the officers recommended that they be put to death.[8] The three were then hanged that day and buried at sea. Thus the *Somers* had been—and remains—notable for being the only US Navy ship to have court-marshalled purported mutineers at sea and hanged them from the yardarm. It was the kind of thing that could happen only in the days before telecommunication.

Not surprisingly, there was intense interest when the *Somers* returned to New York with the sensational news that the son of the secretary of war had been hanged at sea! A naval court of inquiry was convened—eagerly followed by the New York newspapers—and ultimately, Captain Mackenzie and his officers were exonerated. An important outcome of the incident was recognition that the existing midshipman training for navy officers was insufficient, leading to the founding of the US Naval Academy in Annapolis. Another was an authentic literary milestone: it happened that First Lieutenant Gansevoort was a cousin of Herman Melville, and his recounting of the story formed the early basis of *Billy Budd, Sailor*.

And then there was the awkward matter of a sexual predator among the crew. In a letter to Conner on June 2, 1845, Commander James Gerry reported: "It becomes my unpleasant duty to report one of my crew to you for frequently attempting to take beastly and unnatural liberties with one of my apprentice boys, and to request your order as to the disposal of the culprit."[9] The matter was settled with a court martial, which sentenced that the culprit be discharged from the service. Such matters were generally swept under the rug at the time.[10]

When, on October 23, 1846, Semmes was given command of the *Somers*, not everybody was pleased; at least one officer preferred not to serve with him. In a letter the very next day, October 24, Lt. M. G. L. Claiborne wrote to the Commodore: "I hear Ltnt. Semmes has been ordered to hold himself in readiness to take command of this vessel. Should it have been decided on to order him in Such capacity, I respectfully request to be detached from the squadron with permission to return to the U.S. Self-respect compels me to make this application. Naught else."[11]

If it were a matter of seniority, this request might simply have been an honorable expression of pique at not having landed the assignment. In this case, however, Semmes clearly had seniority: he had obtained his lieutenant's commission in February 1837, a year before Claiborne. Perhaps the request was an expression of lack of confidence or of a private conflict. In any event, the request was denied; Semmes assumed command and Claiborne continued to serve as first lieutenant.

As commanding officer, Semmes now had a starring role in two fiascos that resulted from an absent commodore and an eager commanding officer, both serving in an age when the lack of telegraph or radio provided plenty of leeway, if not encouragement, for officers on the front lines to act on their own initiative. This without any restraints that might, in later decades, be supplied by better communications and a functional chain of command.[12]

While Commodore Conner was away from Vera Cruz, the Mexican merchant brig *Creole* escaped the *Somers* and ran the blockade. Semmes decided that because the *Creole* had taken a huge risk in running the blockade, the cargo must be important and should be destroyed. Perhaps with the *Somers*'s namesake in mind, or channeling the great Decatur himself, a plan was devised to burn the *Creole* at its anchorage on a coral reef projecting from the city. In a distant echo of Decatur's Arabic hail in Tripoli harbor, Lt. James L. Parker duped the Vera Cruz port sentinels by hailing them in fluent Spanish. Under cover of darkness, the *Somers* ran close to the brig, then Parker, Passed Midshipman R. C. Roers, Passed Midshipman John R. Hynson, and five crewmen managed to set the *Creole* aflame and escape.[13] The only problem was that the *Creole* was a spy ship actively working for Conner. The commodore had neglected—or was unable—to inform Semmes, and Semmes was not one to sit idly on blockade duty and decline a chance at some action!

The next incident was more dubious and somewhat more deadly. On December 8, 1846, after forty-five days of boring blockade duty, Semmes ordered the *Somers* to chase a sail, which turned out to be the USS *John Adams*. Having been warned that the weather looked "Northerish" (both by Parker and by Claiborne), the *Somers* had returned to the safety of its anchorage off the eastern end of Green Island (Isla Verde) when another ship was sighted. Literally throwing caution to the wind, Semmes ordered the *Somers* back out into the channel under full sail to chase the mystery vessel.

A squall struck before the *Somers* could get close. Before they could furl all the sails, the ship was blown onto its beam ends and sank in less than ten minutes with heavy loss of life, including Midshipman Hynson; only 37 of the 76-member crew survived. The efforts to save the men were genuinely heroic: Midshipman Frances J. Clarke, manning the one available lifeboat, carried 17 men to Green Island, then with great effort returned to the site of the disaster and picked up more men, including Semmes and Parker. The whole incident was observed by Capt. George Robert Lambert of the HMS *Endymion,* who provided a minute-by-minute account in his log.[14]

One of the officers rescued by the *Endymion* was Claiborne, who, according to Semmes, had avoided drowning by holding onto a small piece of wreckage.[15] It turns out that the second mystery sail Semmes pursued was probably another American vessel, the US brig *Abrasia*.[16]

The very next week, on December 16, a naval court of inquiry was convened aboard the frigate *Potomac*, with Commodore Perry as president and Semmes acting in his own defense. Fortunately for Semmes, in this case the New York papers did not cover the inquiry and it lasted only one day. Among the key witnesses were Claiborne, Parker, Clarke, and the ship's doctor. All of the witnesses testified that Semmes had been warned that the weather was inclement, and all stated that the proximal cause of the disaster was not the wind, but rather the vessel being "light"—that is, having insufficient ballast, making it top-heavy or what sailors called "crank," or easily tipped.[17]

When asked the direct question, "Was the *Somers* very light, how much ballast water and provisions had she on board at the time of the accident?" Claiborne testified that "she was very light—lighter than I had ever seen her."[18] Parker testified that the vessel capsized because of "her being too light, and want of sufficient ballast, rather than to the influence of the wind."[19]

In spite of these frank observations, on direct cross-examination by Semmes, neither officer would doubt his judgment in chasing the second sail, and he was exonerated. The court concluded that "the accident may be fairly ascribed to the want of weight in the vessel, and her consequent loss of stability." As for rendering a verdict on Semmes's decision to pursue the second ship, the court simply declined to do so, preferring to focus on the heroism of the survivors. "Whatever precautions might have been taken previously to the gust which capsized her, it is in proof, that everything was subsequently done that skill could suggest, and the court cannot refrain from expressing its admiration of the conduct and bearing of every individual attached to the vessel on the occasion of the deplorable catastrophe."[20] Even so, Vice-President George M. Dallas, the brother of Semmes's old enemy from Pensacola, had a Senate resolution passed calling on the secretary of the navy for a full report. The resulting report included a cover letter from Commodore Perry, Semmes's own account, and a list of those officers and men lost and saved. The naval court of inquiry was nowhere mentioned.[21]

Semmes biographer Warren F. Spencer speculated that, notwithstanding the insufficient ballast, Semmes was exonerated quickly because the navy needed officers and it was then in the middle of a hot war.[22] The point here is not to question whether Semmes should have been held accountable by the navy, but only that the incident exposed his appetite for battle and was an early indication of his enduring disposition to gamble with the weather.

One aspect of this disaster has special significance for White's story: Semmes's typically self-serving assertions about his deep concern for those who could not swim and about the gallantry of men acting under his orders. In his 1851 memoir, he belabors this point and further elaborates, in a long footnote, on the exquisite care he and his crew took to save those men flailing in the water.[23] Much later in his career, after the sinking of the *Alabama*, Semmes would return to his explicit, if somewhat disingenuous, consideration for those who could not swim (discussed further in chapter 23).

The *Somers* was not the only vessel lost on blockade duty in the perilous gulf seas of December 1846. In an amazing quirk of fate, the same day the *Somers* court of inquiry was convening, John Ancrum Winslow, who eighteen years later would face Semmes in the fusillade of cannon fire off Cherbourg, lost another ship—the USS *Morris*, a renamed captured Mexican schooner known previously as the *Union*. Both the men and the circumstances could not have been more different.

Born in Virginia and educated in Massachusetts, Winslow in his family and career can be seen to represent another founding strand in the United States' ideological DNA. On his father's side, he was a descendant of *Mayflower* passenger Mary Chilton—reputed to be the first European woman to step ashore at Plymouth in 1620. Furthermore, Mary's brother-in-law, Edward Winslow, was an important Pilgrim father who signed the *Mayflower* Compact.

By the mid-nineteenth century, Puritan Calvinism had evolved into a number of different evangelical denominations and revivals. Among them, New England Puritanism developed into milder Congregationalism and radical abolitionism—especially as it pertained to believing Christians. John Brown himself was known to be strongly influenced by Puritanism, and Puritan religious ideology—such as that espoused by Wendell Phillips—significantly influenced Black activism and abolitionist rhetoric in Massachusetts.[24]

Puritan egalitarianism figures in a recent conservative critique of the *New York Times'* 1619 Project. That project sought to recenter North American history from the point of view of the enslaved and flagged the 1619 landing of the first enslaved people at Point Comfort, Virginia, as an important founding moment in American history.[25] In his book *1620: A Critical Response to the 1619 Project*, Peter W. Wood argues that a more appropriate American founding narrative derives from the egalitarian principles articulated in the *Mayflower* Compact.[26] Both approaches have strengths and weaknesses, since both employ powerful rhetorical devices to advance a point of view, and as founding narratives both deserve and invite interrogation.[27] Neither excludes the other. Semmes's defense of slavery and Winslow's Puritan abolitionism both can be seen as founding strands, among many, in America's ideological DNA.

On his mother's side, Winslow was descended from Col. William Rhett, a naval hero who in 1704 successfully defended Charleston harbor from French and Spanish attack, and who in 1718 captured the buccaneer Blackbeard.[28] At the risk of overextending the metaphor, these two genes in Winslow's own ideological DNA combined to form a somewhat heterozygote warrior: fearless in battle and en-amored of the navy but horrified by war and its consequences. Like Semmes, Winslow obtained his midshipman's appointment (in 1827) with the help of political connections, in this case, Daniel Webster, whose home, Marshfield, was located on the original Winslow es-tate.[29] He completed his lieutenant's exam in 1833, becoming a passed midshipman, and by 1839 had obtained his lieutenant's commission.

A political polar opposite of Semmes, Winslow hated this particu-lar war and eschewed glory. On the eve of the war in 1845, he was attached to the USS *Cumberland*, which was preparing for a cruise to the Mediterranean. With war on the horizon, the *Cumberland* was as-signed instead to Conner's Gulf Squadron fleet. Winslow also hated blockade duty, but expressed an exquisite sensitivity regarding the sufferings and political dilemmas of the Mexicans. In June 1846, he wrote home from Pensacola: "The vanity of courage and glory has no charm for me when I think of the misery and bleeding hearts that everywhere strew its tracks. I wonder how mad men become to be so tickled with emptiness."[30] Later that August, he again wrote home expressing his political take on the war: "Our Government is no doubt satisfied now that California is ours and our boundary se-cured to the Rio Grande, and desires peace. This has been an unjust war, coveting and seizing territory which did not belong to us; to the honorable lover of his country a source of pain that has been achieved at the loss of justice."[31]

Despite his misgivings, Winslow served with distinction espe-cially in the taking of Tampico, which he celebrated chiefly for the minimal loss of life. In a November 1846 letter home, he observed that "one has only to see the misery which war creates to become sick of its horrors . . . poor, miserable, unoffending persons [made into] marks for shots of an excited soldiery."[32]

In recognition of his heroism at Tampico, Winslow was given

command of the *Morris*. Not long after he took command, however, the ship grounded on a reef off Vera Cruz. In this case, Winslow had been instructed to position the *Morris* near the *John Adams*, stationed off Isla Pájaros, but for some reason the commodore was unable to supply Winslow with charts or instruments—even though the treacherous reefs around Isla Pájaros had been well charted since at least the eighteenth century. Winslow was supplied with a lead line and instructions to use the *John Adams*'s light as a guide, but the lead line broke in a norther, and the *John Adams* changed its position, providing a "false guide." The *Morris* was thrown on the reef, though eventually everyone was saved by boats from the *John Adams*. On December 19, 1846, Winslow wrote, "The Commodore could say nothing, knowing well that it was shameful in him to send me to sea without the least means of navigation in a sea so liable to heavy tempests.[33] Perhaps Winslow was being literal when he wrote that "the Commodore could say nothing," for there is no record of a court of inquiry into the loss of the *Morris*.[34] And as a prize vessel, perhaps it wasn't considered that much of a loss.

Although both ships were lost in the same waters and neither incident was widely reported in the American newspapers, the *Morris* debacle could not have been more different from that of the *Somers*. There is no known suspicion of Winslow's judgment, and his actions saved the lives of all of his crew. The *Somers* was arguably lost because Semmes, in pursuit of glory, exposed his crank vessel to a storm. The *Morris* sank because the commodore sent Winslow into a stormy sea unequipped.

Drying out on the flagship USS *Raritan* a few weeks later, Semmes and Winslow shared a stateroom and teased each other over cigars. No doubt Winslow heard the full story from Claiborne, Parker, and Clarke, all of whom were on board the *Raritan*. Perhaps with their experience in mind, Winslow wrote home on December 19, 1846:

On board our ship is the Captain of the *Somers*. He is one of our lieutenants and was temporarily in command of the *Somers* when she was wrecked. Think what an awful experience, a ship struck over in a squall and sinking under you and you obliged to trust to an oar or something such for life, however it is a joke now. All the officers and men saved are here in the ship. Semmes, the Captain that was, I am very intimate with, so I frequently say, "Captain Semmes, they are going to send you out to learn to take care of ships in blockade," to which he replies, "Captain Winslow, they are going to send you out to learn the bearing of reefs."[35]

Winslow drew one direct lesson from the *Morris* debacle: never to go to sea, let alone battle, without rigorous, if not relentless, preparation. In that sense, he had adopted an important lesson from another famous incident of early US naval history—the 1807 *Chesapeake-Leopard* affair, which sparked the War of 1812. Under the command of James Barron, the *Chesapeake* left its anchorage in Georgetown, stopping in Norfolk before heading out to sea in order to relieve the USS *Constitution* in the Mediterranean squadron. At the time, the British Royal Navy was suffering from an epidemic of desertion, and one of the safest ways for deserters to avoid arrest and punishment was to enlist in a foreign navy. More than a few deserting British sailors had made their way onto the *Chesapeake*'s crew with false identities.

In heading out to sea, Barron understood that the *Chesapeake* was not yet ready for battle—the deck was cluttered and the cannons unprimed—but he expected to complete preparations during the voyage. Given the perceived sense of urgency in relieving the *Constellation*, this may have seemed an acceptable risk, since no belligerent encounter was then anticipated so close to the American coast.

In the event, it soon encountered the HMS *Leopard*, whose commander, Salusbury Pryce Humphreys, had written orders authorizing the boarding and searching of the *Chesapeake* to recover any of the deserters.[36] When Barron demurred, Humphreys forced the issue with a cannon fire, and the *Chesapeake*, caught off-guard, was in no position to do battle. Barron was forced to strike his colors and allow the British to seize four crewmen, after which the *Chesapeake* limped back to Hampton Roads with three men dead and eighteen wounded. The defeat, stemming from insufficient preparation and a suspected lack of offensive spirit, was a national embarrassment, the shame from which Barron never recovered his reputation.[37] Winslow would not make those mistakes.

In retrospect, given what followed, Winslow may also have gleaned some useful insight into the character of his eventual opponent. He had observed Semmes to be a daredevil for whom glory in battle was a passionately held virtue. He may not have been specifically referencing Semmes when disparaging "the vanity of courage and glory" and "mad men tickled with emptiness," but he knew the type and he certainly knew Semmes. And as a pious Christian who, when in command, personally read from the Bible to his crew every Sunday morning, Winslow would have been informed by the observation in Jeremiah 13:23, that the leopard doesn't change his spots.

Chapter 7

~≈~

Secession

At the time of Lincoln's election in 1860, White was about fifteen years old and was already working at the Atlantic Hotel in Lewes. Over the following two years, he would witness increasing militarization in Sussex County—a local manifestation of a national phenomenon. At this juncture, several key historical events occurred that provide the national context for what White would see in Lewes and also help to illustrate Semmes's enthusiasm for the Confederacy: Lincoln's election in November 1860; the secession of South Carolina, Mississippi, Florida, Alabama, Georgia, Louisiana, and Texas, which together formed the Confederate States of America on February 8, 1861; Lincoln's inauguration on March 4, 1861; and the attack on Fort Sumter and the secession of Virginia on April 12 and 17, 1861. The months of April and May culminated in an excited patriotic fever—described by historian James McPherson as a *rage militaire*—sweeping both northern and southern cities.[1] A vivid account of this heady, if short-lived moment in the South was provided by James Morris Morgan in his 1917 memoir, *Recollections of a Rebel Reefer.*

The volunteers were composed of fresh, youthful-looking men, and almost every one of them was accompanied by a "body-ser-

vant" as negro valets were called in the South. They were also accompanied by a great number of baskets of champagne and boxes
of brandy . . . they had huge hampers containing roasted turkeys,
chickens, hams and all sorts of good things. . . . I saw some of these
same young men in the muddy trenches in front of Richmond in
1865, when they were clothed, partially, in rags and were gnaw-
ing on ears of hard corn, and would have gladly exchanged half a
dozen negroes or a couple of hundred acres of land for a square
meal or a decent bed to sleep on.[2]

For some, like Robert E. Lee, joining the Confederacy was a famously tortuous and difficult decision. After much agonizing, Lee
ultimately decided his first loyalty was to Virginia, and he resigned
his US commission only in April 1861, after his home state joined
the Confederacy.[3] Whether, rightly or not, Lee has conventionally
been remembered as an ambivalent warrior who ultimately felt com-
pelled to defend his own state, the same cannot be said for Semmes.
A strong advocate of secession, Semmes resigned his US commission
on February 15, just one week after the Confederacy's founding, two
months before Fort Sumter, and well before the *rage militaire* outbreak of April and May. Of the sixteen officers of commander rank
who resigned from the US Navy in 1861, Semmes was one of only
four who did so before April. In this case, Lee's stated logic—loyalty
to his state—doesn't even apply; Semmes hailed from Maryland, a
state not even in insurrection.

Lincoln declared the South in a state of rebellion on April 15, and
just a few days later, on April 19, Jefferson Davis replied by invit-
ing anybody who could equip a private vessel to apply for letters of
marque—that is, licenses to prey on enemy shipping in return for
keeping the captured vessels and cargoes. Lincoln responded by an-
nouncing a blockade of Southern ports.

With the establishment of the blockade, the new Confederate

Navy secretary, Stephen R. Mallory, immediately faced its lack of
ships and sailors. Officers were not so much a problem: indeed, the
South was so well represented in the antebellum US Navy that this
lode eventually provided a formidable officer core for the new Confederacy. Out of some 1,500 US Navy officers ranging from captains
and commanders to boatswains, gunners, and engineers, 373 resigned
or were dismissed—amounting to 24 percent of the US officer corps.[4]
Yet the South simply did not have a large enough merchant marine
from which to draw experienced crews. Out of a total freighter tonnage of 5,539,912, the South had only 500,000 tons, many owned by
Northern merchants.[5]

In targeting the US merchant fleet, the Confederacy was following
a long and storied strategy of American warfare. In fact, commerce
raiding on the high seas had been a central strategy of warfare glob-
ally, especially during the long-running European wars of the previous two centuries. During the Revolutionary War, the Continental
Congress had authorized some two thousand letters of marque. In
theory, it was the actual commission (the document) that made the
practice legal. In practice, use of the descriptor "privateer" or "pirate" generally depended on whether the predator or prey was doing
the talking, and whether the commissioning state was legally recognized by the other. The strategy's success was measured in rising
maritime insurance premiums paid by British mercantile interests.
In the subsequent War of 1812, American naval strategy was aimed
not so much at defeating English warships, but rather forcing England to the negotiating table by inflicting a severe economic penalty
on its influential merchant interests.[6]

It was thus logical for Secretary Mallory to target merchant shipping, but the difficulty was that by the 1860s, privateering had become
an antique form of warfare, said to be obsolete, like the Confederacy
itself. Confederacy naval historian Raimondo Luraghi explains that
privateering was a system that could work only in an age of "im-

mense seas and difficult communications."[7] Increases in the volume of trade, expanding international networks of wealth, and the advent of steam all made it impossible to privateer without hurting the interests of nonbelligerents. After the Crimean War in the 1850s, Great Britain, France, Russia, Austria, Prussia, Turkey, and Sardinia signed a treaty outlawing privateering altogether.

As Luraghi notes, the world "was under the illusion that the war on maritime trade was no longer possible or rewarding."[8] When the early Confederate privateers failed, Mallory and Semmes conceived a plan to build light, fast naval commerce raiders. These naval vessels would dispense with the private intermediaries and thereby destroy commerce under the direct command of the secretary of the navy. Mallory allowed Semmes to convert an unused vessel, the CSS *Sumter*, into a commerce raider. His reported instruction to Semmes is delicious for its unintended irony and brutal comment on the state of human affairs: "On reaching the high seas you are to do the enemy's commerce the greatest injury in the shortest time. Choose your own cruising grounds. Burn, sink, and destroy, and be guided always by the laws of nations and of humanity."[9]

The Confederacy had identified a vulnerable and ineffectually defended mark. A vibrant American merchant fleet carried a significant percentage of global trade in every sea, and these routes presented a fat target for the Confederate commerce raiders. Indeed, much of the US maritime trade of the 1860s can be seen in the routes and cargoes of the *Alabama*'s captures. An antebellum Golden Age of American shipping extended to the known reaches of the globe and included the North Atlantic lanes traversed by packet and cargo ships. These ships were taking grain, dried fish, rice, cheese, and other foodstuff from the mid-Atlantic and the North, and cotton from the South, and returning from Europe with manufactured goods—most importantly textiles but also luxury goods such as scented soaps, claret, and pâté de foie gras. American ships also traveled to the Baltic by way of

Havana with sugar and returned from Riga and Swedish ports with cargoes of iron and Russian hemp.[10]

In the Mediterranean, eastbound ships carried molasses, sugar, and rum and returned with figs, lemons, oranges, currants, nuts, raisins, olive oil, and fine wines. The China and East India traders sailed round the Cape of Good Hope with buffalo hides, jute, linseed, and shellac, and returned with tea, coffee, pepper, silks, ivory, and sandalwood. A South American trade exported lumber and returned with Argentine hides and Brazilian coffee. California clippers, circling Cape Horn, carried out prospectors and manufactured goods and, after 1849, returned with gold.

In the Caribbean, American ships carried flour, salmon, brandy, hams, peas, candles, soap, butter, herring, claret, glassware, juniper berries, cheese, indigo, and spruce and hickory hoops, returning with rum, coffee, sugar, pimientos, molasses, and bananas.[11] The maritime industry at this time included the massive cod and mackerel fisheries off the Grand Banks and, in the age when whale oil was used for lighting, whaling fleets in the Atlantic, Pacific, and Arctic Oceans. While underappreciated, there was also the thriving guano trade, which brought back much-needed fertilizer mined in remote islands along both the African and South American coasts. The trade thrived because by the 1860s, in an age before artificial fertilizer, some two centuries of farming had nearly exhausted much of the soil along the East Coast.[12]

Although its career as a warship lasted barely six months, the *Sumter* had taken eighteen prizes—of which it burned eight, bonded nine, and released one—before it was bottled up in Gibraltar by Union warships. Nevertheless, the damage done to Union commerce was substantial, and the diversion of Federal blockade ships to hunt down the *Sumter* was understood to be a success. Taken together, these factors led the Confederacy to have more purpose-built commerce raiders constructed in Birkenhead.

The resulting vessels, the *Florida* and *Alabama*, were the brainchild of James Dunwoody Bulloch, an experienced seaman from a Scotch-Irish and Huguenot family in Georgia. His father, James Stephens Bulloch, was one of the incorporators of the Savannah Steam Ship Company, which built the first steamship to cross the Atlantic in 1813. Bulloch Sr. was also a partner in a cotton mill and owned a large plantation with over thirty enslaved. James Dunwoody Bulloch had entered the US Navy on his sixteenth birthday. He saw extensive service in South American waters, the Mediterranean, the US Coastal Survey, and Panama. As Stephan Kinnaman relates: "By the late 1850s, he had obtained unexcelled experience with naval affairs and materiel, mercantile transactions and protocol, conduct of international diplomacy, steamships and their machinery, ship building, navigation and ship handling."[13] This experience made Bulloch uniquely qualified to take on the role of the Confederacy's secret agent in London and Liverpool.

Mallory's initial instructions to Bulloch were to identify usable British ships that might, like the *Sumter*, be bought and converted to raiders. However, Bulloch found no satisfactory vessel and concluded that it would be necessary to design and construct purpose-built vessels. He also found far more sympathy for the South in Liverpool, whose economy depended on the cotton trade, than in London, where there was more abolitionist sentiment and awareness of the political complexities of antagonizing the North.

Bulloch was ably assisted in Liverpool by John Low, a superb seaman whose later helmsmanship on the *Alabama* would save the vessel on at least one occasion. Born in Scotland in 1836, Low had much in common with Semmes: both were orphaned at a young age, and both were taken under the benevolent guardianship of uncles made wealthy by the slave economy. At the age of sixteen, Low joined the British Merchant Service, and in 1856, when he was twenty, he came to Savannah at the invitation of his uncle, Andrew Low, who had by then run up the cotton export market to become the wealthiest man in the city. By the outbreak of the war, John Low owned his own shipping supply business. Recognizing his seamanship, connections, and talent for business, Bulloch arranged for Low to join him in Liverpool to help secure and outfit the planned raiders.

Drawing on contemporaneous letters and diaries, Civil War historian James McPherson described the motivations which attracted combatants into the wartime militaries. McPherson noted that Southern officers were drawn mainly from the middle and upper classes, with nationalism, ideology, religion, and honor being among their primary incentives.[14] While all of these motivations in one form or another pertained to the *Alabama*'s designers and officers, in considering Bulloch and Low in particular, we should not omit the obvious incentive of self-interest. Both of these men also happened to be defending an industry—the transatlantic cotton trade—that at the time entirely depended on enslaved labor and formed the basis of personal family fortunes. Nor can self-interest be dismissed in the cases of Semmes, Galt, or Kell, all of whom came from slaveholding families.

Using cotton credits and the services of Messrs. Fraser, Trenholm & Company, a sympathetic merchant bank with deep commercial ties to the South, Bulloch contracted with Laird's Shipyards in Birkenhead to construct two raiders. One of these vessels was initially named the *Oreto* (later renamed the CSS *Florida*), which managed to slip down the River Mersey and escape to the open sea in March 1862. The other, variously called "Hull 290" and the *Enrica*, eventually became the *Alabama*.

An obstacle to building and equipping the new vessels was the British Foreign Enlistment Act of 1819, which governed the rules for what was permissible with regard to conflicts in which Britain was officially neutral. For one thing, it outlawed belligerents from recruiting British subjects as soldiers, sailors, or marines for any foreign state. Thus, while the raiders would be staffed by Confederate officers, the South would have to recruit ordinary sailors from wherever they could find them, and Liverpool was an obvious place to recruit. Another immediate problem was that section 7 of the act prohibited the "equipping, furnishing, fitting out, arming (or attempting or assisting to do so) any vessel with the intent that such vessel should be used to commit hostilities against any state" with which Britain was at peace.[15]

To the South's chagrin, in May 1861 the British foreign secretary, Lord John Russell, declared British neutrality and invoked the act. Not easily deterred, Bulloch developed an intricate and covert plan to construct the raiders under cover of various ruses and aliases, including a legalistic argument that building these vessels would not violate the law so long as the ships were not *armed* in Britain. The position was supported by a friendly Liverpool customs inspector who, despite American protests, repeatedly refused to sanction the vessels under construction. Another difficulty was a hyperalert US diplomatic corps that was not about to passively allow Confederate cruisers to take shape in Birkenhead yards.

Charles Francis Adams, the US ambassador and the son of former president John Quincy Adams, and his able deputy Benjamin Moran (who, in October 1862, would take an important deposition from Captain Julius of the *Tonawanda*) employed a sophisticated network of spies who not only shadowed Bulloch, but kept a close eye on the Birkenhead yards. Thus began an elaborate game of cat and mouse as the Confederates sought to evade British constraints. Semmes wrote to Secretary Mallory on June 15, 1862, "It will doubtless be a matter of some delicacy and management to get the Alabama safely out of British waters, as . . . Adams, the Northern envoy and his numerous satellites are especially vigilant in their espionage."[16] Although the

Americans were fully on their game, "Hull 290" was still able to escape down the Mersey thanks to Southern espionage and a British bureaucratic comedy of errors.

By the summer of 1862, Hull 290 was nearly complete. Matters came to a head when, early in July, Union detective Matthew Maguire managed to enter Laird's Shipyards at Birkenhead and transmit a full description of the vessel to Moran and Adams. The US consul in Liverpool, Thomas Haines Dudley, continued to press the American case that the vessel had been designed as a warship and should be seized. This demand was again rejected on July 21 by the Liverpool collector of customs. Dudley then sent an appeal to London, and in the interim, Adams hired a leading British barrister, Robert P. Collier, who examined the evidence and wrote on Wednesday, July 23, that "it appears difficult to make out a stronger case of infringement of the Foreign Enlistment Act, which if not enforced on this occasion, is little better than a dead letter."[17] By the end of the week, the American objections were forwarded to the Queen's Advocate, Sir John Harding, who had just fallen ill (from what has variously been described as a stroke, a nervous breakdown, and dementia), and his wife, anxious to conceal his condition and oblivious to urgent matters of state, allowed the package to lie undisturbed on his desk for three days.[18]

When law officers of the Crown finally read the documents, they immediately concluded that the construction of Hull 290 had indeed violated the Foreign Enlistment Act. The wheels of bureaucracy then turned but did not exactly spin; on July 29, an order to seize the vessel was hurriedly dispatched on Her Majesty's Service from London to Liverpool. It arrived too late. Confederate spies had realized that the British might imminently seize the vessel and it therefore would not be safe to leave the ship in Birkenhead.[19] On July 29, a matter of hours before the seizure instruction reached Birkenhead, and under the pretense of a sea trial and christening party, Hull 290 slipped away with a skeleton crew. Years later, an article in the *New York Times* described the scene:

> There were good friends at court who gave the Confederates information of what was to be done; and so, while a huge dispatch, "on Her Majesty's Service" was traveling from London to Liverpool, the "290" was heaving anchor ostensibly for a trial trip. To give color to this pretense, a number of fine English ladies, daughters, friends, and acquaintances of the Parliamentary builder, went with her. They flaunted their crinolines and scarfs over her deck and set their dainty lips to the champagne and salad provided for their delectation. When fairly clear of the port, and out of reach of arrest, a tug came alongside, the lovely guests went on board, and the "290" went on her way.[20]

On July 31, while Hull 290 was still off the coast, a telegram was sent to the Liverpool customs collector with the terse order: "Seize under Foreign Enlistment Act vessel 'two hundred and ninety' if she returns or can be met with."[21] The raider didn't return, and in the belligerent sense of the phrase, it wouldn't be met with for another two years.

Chapter 8

The *Alabama*

Now under the temporary command of James Dunwoody Bulloch, the unfinished vessel arrived on August 10 to a planned rendez-vous in the remote harbor of Porto Praya, on the Island of Terceira in the Azores. A tender, the *Agrippina*, also manufactured in Great Britain, was there carrying the necessary armaments, while Semmes arrived from Nassau on the *Bahama* to assume command.

After the vessel arrived in Porto Praya, there followed two weeks of furious activity to coal, store, arm, and staff the ship before Por-tugal—a relatively weak country at the time—could detect the vi-olation of its neutrality and assert authority.[1] Since the place was remote, and there was as yet no telegraph service, Semmes was able to hold off the local authorities for a while. However, he also had to finish the transshipment and commissioning of arms three miles out on a heavy sea.

The *Alabama* itself was a marvel. Since the vessel would become White's home—if not prison—for the following two years, it is worth relating key aspects of its design. Exceptionally well proportioned and graceful, the *Alabama* was admired by all who viewed it, includ-ing its enemies. It was 220 feet long, displaced 1,050 tons, and could fly across the water using wind or steam (figs. 8.1 and 8.2).

The vessel was designed to be more of a raider than a fighter—that is, it was built for speed, not stability, and was better armed than armored. It had "plenty of metal," including six thirty-two-pound cannons, and a large sixty-eight-pound, pivoting, rifled Blakely cannon, manufactured in Liverpool. While the world was transitioning to iron hulls, the *Alabama* was built with a wooden hull lined with copper; the rationale being that iron hulls tended to foul with barnacles, and could not be easily repaired in the remote ports the *Alabama* would be visiting. Although wood also fouled, the copper sheathing protected it, and was easier to repair on the fly.

On the upper deck, the ship's wheel had a motto cast in bronze: "*Aide toi et dieu t'aidera.*" Loosely translated it means "God helps those who help themselves"; an unofficial motto of the Confederacy, it was also engraved on Robert E. Lee's ceremonial sword.[2] Other notable features of the deck included the quarterdeck, a raised platform behind the main mast, a bridge (literally, a bridge) amidship just before the funnel, and in addition to the Blakely, another pivoting cannon (unrifled) aft of the funnel, and the relatively high bulwarks, apparent in photographs of the deck (Chapter 18), which had the advantage of concealing the cannons.

The *Alabama*'s design reflected the traditional practical arrangements necessary to keep officers and crew apart. The officer's cabins and berths were situated in the rear of the vessel, described as "a handsome suite of staterooms."[3] The crew slept and ate in the front, and were separated from the officers by the coal bunkers with "no communication."[4] Down the stairs by the mizzenmast, immediately aft was the captain's cabin with a small anteroom for Breedlove Smith, the captain's clerk. Forward of this was a state room used by the engineers and steerage officers, with cabins along both sides. Farther along was the stateroom (gun room) and cabins used by the petty officers and engineers, fitted up with charts and bookcases. Farther forward was the engine room and, amidships, the coal bunkers

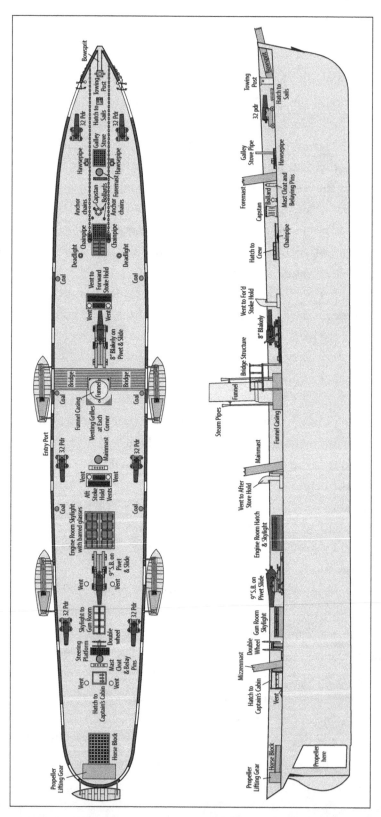

FIGURE 8.1. Upper deck of the *Alabama*, from above and in profile.
University of Alabama Press. Redrawn by Jade Myers.

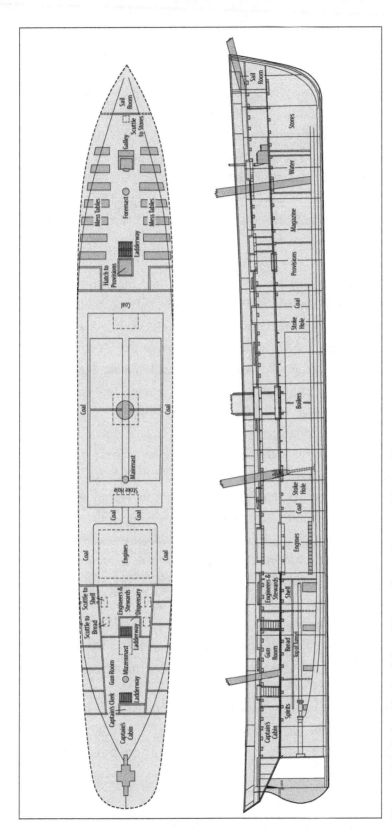

FIGURE 8.2. Below deck of the *Alabama*, from above and in profile.
University of Alabama Press. Redrawn by Jade Myers.

and boilers, with no passage to the crew's berths. A different hatch near the foremast led to the galley and to the crew's quarters, which were positioned just over the magazine and water stores. Here, the men slept in hammocks slung on hooks, with seats all around and space underneath for personal belongings.

In his deposition to Congress years later, Capt. Theodore Julius of the ship *Tonawanda*, from which White was captured, described the vessel:

> The *Alabama*, or *290*, is a splendid vessel, and the fastest under canvas I ever had my foot on board of, and I have no doubt she is under steam, as she has very powerful machinery. . . . She is calculated to remain at sea as long as they like, as they condense all the water they use; it takes one pound of coal to make a gallon of water. . . . I do not think there is a ship in our navy that can catch her.[5]

In retrospect, Julius identified two fateful design characteristics of the *Alabama*, one responsible for its success, the other for its demise. The first was speed. Its rigging indicates that its designers took full advantage of mid-nineteenth-century engineering, which efficiently captured the motive energy supplied by wind. As a "jackass" bark, it had three masts; the foremast was square-rigged; the main mast was partially square-rigged with topsails above and fore-and-aft-rigged sails below; and the mizzen or rear mast had fore-and-aft rigging. The square sails, set high up the masts, made it possible to capture relatively light wind, while the fore-and-aft sails enabled the vessel to point higher in the wind, thereby increasing maneuverability (fig. 8.3).

The application of the screw propeller to ocean travel—of which the designers of the *Alabama* took advantage—provided both speed and efficiency while allowing the engines and propulsion systems

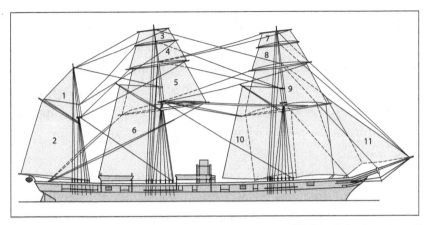

FIGURE 8.3. Principal rigging of the *Alabama*, a "jackass" bark: (1) gaff topsail; (2) spanker; (3) main royal sail; (4) main topgallant sail; (5) main topsail; (6) main trysail; (7) fore royal sail; (8) fore topgallant sail; (9) fore topsail; (10) fore trysail; (11) jib and staysails. *University of Alabama Press. Redrawn by Jade Myers.*

of warships to be positioned under the waterline in relative safety compared to vulnerable side-wheelers. The first US Navy ship outfitted with a propeller was the USS *Princeton*, designed by Swedish inventor John Ericsson. The *Princeton* departed Philadelphia in 1843 and proceeded to New York, where it raced and easily beat Isambard Kingdom Brunel's paddle-wheeler, the SS *Great Western*. In Great Britain, an iconic moment of the age was the staged tug-of-war competition in 1845 between the screw-driven HMS *Rattler* and the paddle steamer HMS *Alecto*; the former pulled the latter backward at 2.5 knots.

By 1861 engineers understood the problem that when not engaged by its motor, a screw created unwanted drag. The solution was a retractable propeller, which gave the *Alabama* all the advantages of both wind and steam propulsion. As *Alabama* officer John McIntosh Kell later recalled: "In fifteen minutes her propeller could be hoisted, and she could go through every evolution under sail without any impediment. In less time her propeller could be lowered; with sails furled and yards braced within two points of a headwind, she was a perfect steamer."[6] The ship's speed "independent" was 10 to 12 knots, but when combined under favorable circumstances, it could reach 15 knots. In an age when the average speed of most seagoing vessels was 5 to 8 knots, the *Alabama* could outrun all but the swiftest clippers.[7] On sighting a suspect vessel, it generally caught up to its prey with ease.

The second characteristic Julius identified was the water condenser, an untested new technology, which enabled the vessel to remain at sea for long periods of time without having to enter ports for freshwater, where it might be seen and reported. This apparatus, working off steam from the engines, vaporized and condensed seawater to provide potable water. It was a good idea but for a significant flaw: its water tanks were positioned adjacent to the ammunition stores, with the result that, over time, the ammunition became damp and dysfunctional.[8] Toward the end of the *Alabama*'s cruise, during target practice off Brazil, the problem became worrisome when one in three shells failed to explode and those that did were smoky and sounded off, as described further in chapter 20. This would prove fatal in the final battle with the *Kearsarge*.

Another problem contributing to the dampness was less one of design than of manufacture. In their haste to construct the vessel, Laird's used wood for the decks that was insufficiently cured; the white oak planks had been caulked in the damp English winter, but in the summer sun they shrank and pulled away from their joints.[9] Just a few months into the cruise, the *Alabama* began leaking and required constant caulking. As early as August 25, 1862, barely a month after its launch, Semmes wrote: "Everything is in confusion, and every body uncomfortable . . . the ship leaking considerably through her top works . . . Pump, pump. I thought I had gotten rid of the eternal clanking of the pump when I laid the *Sumter* up."[10]

Not the least of the logistical challenges was the recruitment of a satisfactory crew. The officers were the easy part. Bulloch and Semmes chose fellow southerners drawn mainly from those with whom they had sailed previously. Among them was Bulloch's younger brother Irvine, who served as midshipman, and John McIntosh Kell of Georgia, who became Semmes's loyal first lieutenant.

Like Bulloch, Kell also had much in common with Semmes; he came from a politically connected, enslaving Georgia family and had used his family's political connections to obtain a midshipman's warrant. Born in 1823, he was fourteen years younger than Semmes, and that much more vigorous. After extensive service in the South Atlantic and Pacific, Kell in 1847 entered the new US Naval Academy at Annapolis. Upon graduating in 1848, he became a member of the ambiguous class of officers known as passed midshipmen, which entitled him to wear a star over the anchor on his collar, to signify the new academy qualification. Despite the new ornament, the status of academy passed midshipmen remained undefined when compared to those who obtained the rank before the academy opened. The navy had created the credential but had not adjusted the command structure accordingly. It was described as a sort of purgatory.[11]

Until one could attain a regular rank of lieutenant, the opportunities for promotion remained bleak for midshipmen. It was estimated that those appointed in 1839 could under normal circumstances not expect to reach the rank of lieutenant before 1870. Consequently, many aspiring midshipmen resigned their commissions in despair.[12]

This ambiguity led to an incident that provides insight into both Kell's personality and his introduction to and affinity for Semmes. After graduating, Kell and three fellow messmates from the academy, all passed midshipmen now, were assigned to the ship *Albany*, under the command of Victor M. Randolph. The four soon learned that despite their new ratings, they were treated as ordinary midshipmen by the senior officers, and expected to carry out menial tasks to which they stridently objected. Seeing it as a matter of honor, Kell refused to follow the order to conduct the menial task normally done by sailors, of carrying and lighting a lamp for a succeeding watch.

A court martial was convened on the *Albany* off Pensacola. As it turned out, one of the accused was Midshipman Clarke, who had rescued Semmes from the sinking *Somers*. Calling in the favor, Clarke convinced Semmes, then stationed in Pensacola, to represent the accused midshipmen as their lawyer. The ensuing defense was based on the simple principle that a naval officer had an obligation to refuse an illegal order, and the instruction to conduct the menial task of lamp lighting was both illegal and dishonorable. In his deposition, Kell further exhorted the navy to abandon the constraints on career advancement.

Like Semmes, Kell advocated a noble principle that he applied selectively when it suited him. Here is a passage that can be read as either an anthem of self-empowerment or an oppressor's manifesto, and perhaps even as the basis of a shipboard curriculum in servitude: "Employments, like associations of men, have a powerful influence upon their characters. You do not find the high-toned gentleman as a rule under the leathern apron of the mechanic any more than you can draw an accomplished officer from before the mast. Men who are made menials of soon learn to feel and act as menials."[13]

In the end, Kell was convicted of insubordination and dismissed from the navy, yet there was plenty of sympathy for him, and Semmes was deeply impressed with Kell's forthright defense of his honor. Using family political connections once again, Kell was reinstated in the navy in 1850, and when Georgia seceded ten years later, he resigned and joined the Georgia navy, "within the hour."[14] He was assigned to the raider *Sumter*, where he and Semmes would consolidate their working relationship.

Two other senior officers were British and supplied critical seamanship skills. The first was John Low, the wealthy scion of a Savannah cotton-trading family who had assisted Bulloch in purchasing and outfitting the *Alabama* in Birkenhead. The other was George Townley Fullam, from Kingston upon Hull, who had been trained by his father, the owner of several navigation schools.[15] Fullam Jr. joined the Confederate Navy when he was twenty-one, having been recruited by James Bulloch. His biographer, Charles Summersell, describes "paradoxes" in his character—"he was very precise but by no means especially cautious."[16] He kept a detailed journal recording the many courts martial, insubordinate sailors, and desertions that afflicted the *Alabama*'s voyage. (Chapter 22 considers his actions in the immediate aftermath of the *Alabama*'s sinking.)

Another officer, Fifth Lieutenant Arthur Sinclair IV from Norfolk, Virginia, was the son and grandson of US Navy officers. After secession, Sinclair served on board the ironclad CSS *Virginia* during its battle on March 9, 1862, with the USS *Monitor*. In 1895, he published a memoir notable for its vivid, self-congratulating style of storytelling, stereotyping, contempt for the Liverpool "jacks," and descriptions of White (discussed further in chapter 22). While much of Sinclair's account may be dismissed as grandstanding, a recent analysis suggests that in some respects, his unguarded narrative is more revealing about actual events than those of the more politically astute officers aboard the *Alabama*.[17] Sinclair's is a key firsthand account to the effect that White did in fact drown.

Other noteworthy officers were the ship's surgeons, Francis L. Galt and David H. Llewellyn. According to Semmes, White became "the servant" of Galt, who was another trusted comrade, having previously served on the *Sumter*. The word "servant" is vague and opens the door to whether White acted as Galt's body servant, in the manner familiar to Confederate officers in both the army and navy or in the more specialized manner of a surgeon's assistant.[18] The few firsthand accounts offer no evidence that White ever acted as a medical assistant; his documented responsibilities seem to have been limited to the wardroom mess and attending to Galt's personal needs. Besides, Galt became paymaster and Llewellyn did most of the doctoring.

Born in Norfolk in 1833, Galt was also politically connected and hailed from an enslaving family. His father was related to President Zachary Taylor, and his mother, Anne White Land, was the daughter of a prominent plantation owner in Virginia Beach. As an "unreconstructed rebel," like many ex-Confederates who fled to South America after the war rather than live "under Yankee domination," he enlisted in the Peruvian navy.[19] Galt creditably served the Peruvian Hydrographic Commission, which surveyed the Amazon, and sympathetically described the benighted conditions of the local populace. His actions as the *Alabama* sank also deserve scrutiny and are addressed further in chapter 22.

Llewellyn was British and a late addition to the *Alabama*'s crew. He was the son of the Rev. David Llewellyn, Perpetual Curate of Easton. Educated at Marlborough College, he studied for the medical profession at Charing-Cross Hospital, where he achieved silver medals for surgery and chemistry. Llewellyn enlisted in Liverpool, perhaps out of sentimental attachment to the Confederacy or perhaps because he just needed employment. In any event, he turned out to be one of the best-liked figures aboard the *Alabama*, and is also notable for his actions at the battle of Cherbourg when compared to the survival of Galt.

In addition to serving Galt and the officer's mess, White would have worked closely under two petty officers: Richard Parkinson, the wardroom steward, and Henry Tucker, the wardroom cook, both of whom are little known. Yet these men were true believers, having signed on to the *Alabama* on August 24, 1862, in Terceira, and both were "honorably discharged" after the battle of Cherbourg.

Whereas assembling a staff was mostly a matter of using established networks, finding a crew was quite another matter. The initial crew was almost exclusively recruited surreptitiously in Liverpool from the Canning Street boardinghouses, as well as from two consort vessels, the *Bahama* and *Agrippina*, that rendezvoused with the *Alabama* in the Azores. Most of the crew were unmarried, with some being veterans of the Royal Naval Reserve who signed on to the *Alabama* using aliases. Others came from the merchant marine, which had considerably less regimentation than the military, and most did it simply for the money. They were mainly English but included Dutch, Welsh, Irish, French, Italian, Spanish, and Russian members. There is no substantiated evidence that any of the crew recruited were Black. Historian Warren F. Spencer mentions an Andrew Shilland listed as a "colored slave" who drowned in the battle of Cherbourg.[20] However, this individual is described neither as Black, enslaved, nor deceased in three identifiable lists (see chapter 17).

Life for an unemployed sailor was tough in Liverpool, so the gig was tempting. The Sailors' Home was available for those who took advantage of it, but "Seamen's Lodging Houses" abounded; many were notorious establishments from which a tar would be lucky to escape with his money. In *Redburn*, Melville describes the Canning Street houses:

> Besides, of all sea-ports in the world, Liverpool, perhaps, most abounds in all the variety of land-sharks, land-rats, and other vermin, which make the hapless mariner their prey. In the shape of landlords, bar-keepers, clothiers, crimps, and boarding-house loungers, the land-sharks devour him, limb by limb; while the land-rats and mice constantly nibble at his purse.
>
> Other perils he runs, also, far worse; from the denizens of notorious Corinthian haunts in the vicinity of the docks, which in depravity are not to be matched by anything this side of the pit that is bottomless.[21]

Apart from those recruited by Confederate agents from the boardinghouses, Semmes made a direct pitch to the British crew of the *Bahama*, offering them fortune, adventure, and the excitement of combat. It was illegal to recruit British sailors in Liverpool, but not out at sea, in this case just three miles offshore from the Azores. Perhaps wary or just seeking to drive a hard bargain, plenty of them held back. Nonetheless, eventually Semmes signed a crew, but he would have to increase his offer to double the usual wages, paid in gold, with prizes awarded on the value of the capture whether burned or sold. At the end of it, he revealingly grumbled, "The modern sailor has greatly changed in character, as he now stickles for pay like a sharper, and seems to have lost his former love of adventure and of recklessness."[22]

As the South lacked a substantive merchant marine from which to recruit experienced seamen, the Confederacy had no choice but to hire mercenary crews to man the commerce raiders, but the resulting cultural disparity exacerbated the normal social distance that existed between naval officers and crew. In *Citizen Sailors*, historian Nathan Perl-Rosenthal describes the "natural allegiance" that had existed in earlier centuries between sailors and officers who served the same king or country.[23] While there may have been some overlap, if not homogeneity of allegiance and culture, among sailors and officers in the Atlantic merchant fleets, this did not generally pertain to the Confederate commerce raiders, and specifically did not pertain to the *Alabama*.

Amid the activity at Porto Praya, Semmes described his new recruits somewhat hopefully:

The crew, comprising about sixty persons, who had been picked up, promiscuously, about the streets of Liverpool, were as unpromising in appearance, as things about the decks. What with faces begrimed with coal dust, red shirts, blue shirts, Scotch caps, and hats, brawny chests exposed, and stalwart arms naked to the elbows, they looked as little like the crew of a man-of-war, as one can well conceive. Still there was some physique among these fellows, and soap, and water, and clean shirts would make a wonderful difference in their appearance.

He got a crew, but it would take a lot more than soap and water to straighten them out. Stories of drunkenness, indolence, impertinence, and desertion permeate the memoirs of Semmes, Kell, Sinclair, and Fullam, and those are the charitable accounts. Enforcing discipline, when it was enforced at all, was a constant struggle. By December 1862, just a few months into the cruise, Semmes would bluntly refer to them as "a miserable lot from the Groggeries of Liverpool."[24] In return, making fun of his long, pointed mustachios, they simply referred to him as "Old Beeswax."

Chapter 9

≈

Prelude

By Sunday, August 24, 1862, the *Alabama* and its prospective crew were ready. Semmes's description of the moment is a typical example of his vivid, mellifluous prose:

> The ship having been properly prepared, we steamed out, on this bright and sunny morning, under a cloudless sky, with a gentle breeze from the southeast, scarcely ruffling the surface of the placid sea, and under the shadow of the smiling and picturesque island of Terceira, which nature seemed to have decked specially for the occasion, so charming did it appear, in its checkered dress of lighter and darker green, composed of cornfields and orange-groves.[1]

With the officers in full uniform standing by, and the prospective crew assembled on the quarterdeck of the *Bahama*, a gun was fired and the English flag on Hull 290 was hauled down and replaced with a Confederate ensign. A little band played "Dixie." Semmes then mounted a gun carriage and addressed the men with an appeal both to gold and adventure:

Now, my lads, there is the ship; she is as fine a vessel as ever floated. There is a chance which seldom offers itself to a British seaman— that is, to make a little money. I am not going to put you alongside of a frigate at first, but after I have got you drilled a little, I will give you a nice little fight. There are only six ships that I am afraid of in the U.S. Navy. We are going to burn, sink, and destroy the commerce of the United States. Your prize-money will be divided proportionately, according to each man's rank, something similar to the English navy.... Any of you that thinks he cannot stand to his gun, I don't want.[2]

Out on the high seas there were plenty of unfinished tasks, such as bolting down gun turrets and properly caulking the decks. There were also innumerable personnel matters, such as assigning berths, watches, and duties. More daunting than any specific task was developing a culture of order and discipline—forging a functional team from a motley crew of entitled Confederate officers and undisciplined mercenaries. At this, Semmes apparently had varying levels of success, depending on who was doing the writing.

Semmes himself kept his distance; by one firsthand account he "was an austere and formal man, and, with the exception of Dr. Galt, the surgeon, and Mr. Kell, his first Lieutenant, he rarely held any intercourse with his officers except officially. He waxed the ends of his mustache ... and he would pace his quarter-deck, alone, twisting and retwisting those long ends."[3]

An immediate problem presented itself when the chief engineer, Welshman Miles Freeman, who had served with Semmes and Kell on the *Sumter*, refused an order from Kell that he deemed inappropriate and used "improper language." Like the passed midshipmen of the Old Navy, engineers in the 1860s occupied an ambiguous position in naval hierarchy: they possessed special skills for which they expected privileges but their enhanced status threatened the distinctive pre-requisites of line officers. As a result, they were neither fish nor fowl.[4] A good engineer was hard to find; the job required considerable skill and it was not fun. Engine rooms of the period could run well over 100 degrees; the air was foul, and unless scrupulously cleaned, everything and everybody were saturated with oil, coal dust, and soot.

In this particular case, the tables were turned, because, in contrast to the *Albany* incident, Semmes and Kell were now in the position of enforcing, instead of objecting to, a "menial" status. Semmes could always manufacture a legal argument to support an assertion of power, and consistency was hardly a consideration. Freeman was suspended, but reinstated shortly thereafter.[5]

In the meantime, lookouts kept a keen watch for sails. Deception was key. The standard mode of attack would be to approach an unsuspecting merchantman while flying a British ensign. If the captain of the unfortunate vessel raised an American flag, the British ensign was lowered, a Confederate one raised, and a cannon revealed—sometimes with a shot across the bow. Semmes would send over a boarding party, then hold a prize court at sea. As a general rule, only property was destroyed and the captured crew was landed in the next friendly port. But the process was unruly, things often got out of hand, and several hair-raising accounts reveal what happened when the *Alabama*'s crew actually got their hands on a prize.

Deception was nothing new in naval warfare, but the line between honorable sleight of hand and dishonorable perfidy was blurry and depended on the perspective of the writer. As noted earlier, Decatur himself used deception when, in burning the *Philadelphia*, he used a Turkish ketch and Arabic hail to raid Tripoli harbor, albeit to recover an American vessel. Even the practice of using British ensigns as false hails was an old American tradition; Commodore David Porter, Admiral David Dixon Porter's father, used the strategy when attacking British whalers in the Pacific in 1812. Indeed, Semmes explicitly cited Commodore Porter's commerce raiding as inspiration for the Confederate raiders.[6] In wartime, deception was so regularly practiced that most large navies employed secret flag codes to confirm identification—but this was not the practice in the merchant marine. Semmes in effect took the traditional strategies of commerce raiding and deception and gave them the power of steam.[7]

After a few false starts, including brief, unremarkable encounters with a Portuguese and a French ship, the *Alabama* sighted the *Ocmulgee*, a Yankee whaler out of Edgartown, Martha's Vineyard, which was part of a larger fleet cruising around the Azores. The *Ocmulgee*'s crew had just killed a massive sperm whale. They had tied it up against the hull and were busy cutting blubber and bailing oil from a hole cut in the top of the whale's head. According to plan, Semmes raised the Union Jack and drew near. In return, the unsuspecting *Ocmulgee* captain, the twenty-nine-year-old Abraham Osborn Jr., from a prominent Edgartown whaling family, raised the American flag. Semmes then sent over a boat with twenty-one-year-old Master's Mate Fullam and nineteen-year-old Lt. Richard Armstrong, as well as several armed crew. At that moment, Semmes lowered the British ensign and raised a Confederate one. Weapons drawn, the officers demanded that Osborn fetch his papers and accompany them back to the *Alabama*.

When brought on board the *Alabama*, Osborn soon came to realize that Semmes was not only claiming to take the *Ocmulgee* as a prize but intending to burn it. Semmes instructed Osborn that he and his crew could pack their boats with provisions and anything else they thought they may need. He also demanded Osborn's chronometer—the first of sixty-four such prizes he would ultimately collect and proudly show off to visitors to his wardroom.

In seizing these instruments, Semmes was doing more than simply building a collection. Many of the chronometers were the personal property of the captured vessel's captains. For one thing, he was depriving them of an essential means of navigation and one of the most important tools of their trade. (Recall how careful the *Wyoming's* Captain Burton was to have his chronometer serviced in Liverpool.) But more importantly, Semmes was following a time-honored tradition of collecting trophies.[8] And as a classically educated, self-identified member of the "hordes of the Alani," Semmes might well have been aware of their most notorious belligerent practice of hanging scalps on their war-horses.[9]

Although relatively young, Osborn hailed from a long line of seasoned Yankee skippers and wasn't about to submit quietly. As reported in the *Vineyard Gazette*, "The moment was tense. . . . 'You have dined many times at my father's house and now you are burning his ship,' thundered Osborn, and he is credited with still angrier words of protest, until Semmes ordered his men to take the gallant young whaling skipper to the brig below."[10] Meanwhile, the *Alabama's* boarding crew was busy scouring the *Ocmulgee* for useful provisions, including salt pork, beef, and spare rigging. The *Ocmulgee's* thirty-six crewmen—no doubt bewildered and furious—were transferred to the *Alabama*, and though ultimately put safely ashore, it was a difficult and punishing passage because they were confined to the deck in irons, even as the weather deteriorated.

Opting not to attract attention by burning the *Ocmulgee* at night, the *Alabama's* crew began their preparations at first light. Two shots were heard, which turned out to be the dispatch of the *Ocmulgee's* two dogs.[11] Since this was all new to them, the *Alabama's* crew needed instructions on how to properly fire a ship. Lieutenant Sinclair obliged:

First, you cut up with your broadaxe the cabin and forecastle bunks, generally of white pine lumber. You will find, doubtless, the mattresses stuffed with straw, and in the cabin pantry part of at least a keg of butter and lard. Make a foundation of the splinters and straw, pour on top the lard and butter. One pile in the cabin, the other in the forecastle. Get your men in the boats, all but the incendiaries, and at the given word—"Fire!" shove off, and take it as truth, that before you have reached your own ship, the blaze is licking the topsails of the doomed ship.[12]

The *Ocmulgee* hardly needed such elaborate preparation; the cargo of whale oil, which was used in this prepetroleum era for lighting, was itself highly flammable. It was the 1862 equivalent of an oil tanker. The resulting conflagration on the morning of September 6, of both the *Ocmulgee* and the partially harvested whale, was the first of several that were so extraordinary that those who witnessed them never forgot the sight.

Through September and early October 1862, the *Alabama* found its stride and decimated the rest of the whaling fleet (table 9.1). The *Elisha Dunbar* was a large whaler, bulging with three years of gear and supplies. Almost a century later, popular historian Edward Boykin painted the scene: "Never was the crew of the *Alabama* treated to a more awesome spectacle than the burning of the *Elisha Dunbar*. Hanging to the rail with both hands, salt spray blown from the tops of the waves stinging their faces like small shot, the *Alabama*'s tars stood transfixed."[13] Vividly describing the thunder, black clouds, howling wind and tumultuous sea, Semmes wrote that the burning ship "was a beautiful spectacle, the scene being wild and picturesque beyond description."[14]

The *Dunkirk*, captured on October 7, yielded a consequential prize: George Forrest, who had deserted the *Sumter* and whom Semmes immediately conscripted onto the *Alabama*. Once taken on board, the captured crews had a rough time sleeping on the upper deck with the weather worsening. Some insight into what they endured may be gleaned from the reports of the various captains once they returned to US ports. A graphic example was reported in the *Philadelphia Inquirer* by the captain of the *Virginia*, Shadrach R. Tilton:

Table 9.1. Captures by the *Alabama*, September 5–October 7, 1862

Date	Ship	Home Port	From/To	Cargo	Disposition
September 5	Ocmulgee	Martha's Vineyard	Cruising	Whale oil	Burned
September 7	Starlight	Boston	Flores, via Fayal	Mail	Burned
September 7	Alert	New London	Cruising	Whale oil	Burned
September 8	Ocean Rover	Boston	Cruising	Whale oil	Burned
September 9	Weather Gauge	Provincetown	Cruising	Provisions	Burned
September 13	Altamaha	New Bedford	Cruising	None	Burned
September 14	Benjamin Tucker	New Bedford	Cruising	None	Burned
September 16	Courser	Provincetown	Cruising	Whale oil	Burned
September 17	Virginia	New Bedford	Cruising	Whale oil	Burned
September 18	Elisha Dunbar	New Bedford	Cruising	None	Burned
October 3	Brilliant	New York	London	Whale oil	Burned
October 3	Emily Farnham	Portsmouth, NH	Liverpool	Grain	Burned
October 7	Wave Crest	New York	Cardiff	Flour and grain	Released and made a cartel
October 7	Dunkirk	New York	Lisbon	Flour and grain	Burned
				Grain	Burned

Source: Official Records of the Union and Confederate Navies in the War of the Rebellion (hereafter O.R. Navy), Ser. I: Vol. 3, pp. 677–81.

I went on the quarter deck with my son, when they ordered me into the lee waist, with my crew, and all of us put in irons, with the exception of two boys, cook and steward. . . . The steamer was cruising to the west, and the next day they took the *Elisha Dunbar*, her crew receiving the same treatment as ourselves. The steamer's guns being kept run out the side ports could not be shut, and when the sea was a little rough, or the vessel rolled, the water was continually coming in on both sides and washing across the deck where we were, so that our feet and clothing were wet all the time, either from the water below or the rain above.

We were obliged to sleep in the place where we were, and often waked up in the night nearly under water. Our fare consisted of beef and pork, rice, beans, tea and coffee, and bread. Only one of our irons was allowed to be taken off one at a time, and we had to wash in salt water. We were kept on deck all the time, night and day, and a guard placed over us.[15]

To summarize the barely managed chaos that characterized the *Alabama* just days before White's capture on October 9, 1862: a state-of-the-art stealth warship, under the leadership of a daredevil sea lawyer, overflowing with angry, drenched prisoners and a toxic brew of empowered racist officers and seemingly feral mercenaries, all on a mission to burn, sink, and destroy.

Part II

VOYAGE

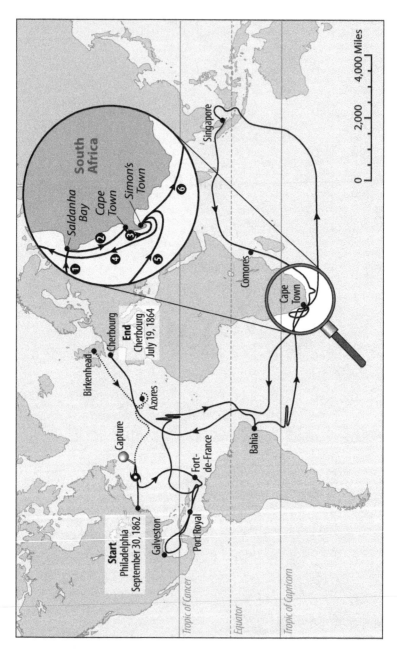

MAP 2. The voyage of David Henry White. The dotted line represents the *Alabama*'s track before White's capture from the *Tonawanda*. The inset includes numbered segments of the eastbound journey: (1) South Atlantic to Saldanha Bay; (2) Saldanha Bay to Cape Town; (3) Cape Town to Simon's Town; (4) Simon's Town to Lüderitz (Angra Pequeña); (5) Lüderitz back to Simon's Town; (6) Simon's Town into the Indian Ocean. (For clarity, the westbound return journey, stopping once again in Cape Town, is not shown in the inset.) *Cartography by Jade Myers.*

Chapter 10

⤳

Capture

On Tuesday, September 30, 1862, White was perhaps becoming familiar with the *Tonawanda*'s galley when, at 2:30 p.m., with the help of the steam tugboat *America*, the old packet departed the busy Front Street wharf and eased down the Delaware toward the Atlantic. Due to adverse winds, Captain Julius did not discharge the pilot and enter the open sea until October 3. Once again, there was a bit of drama getting started: this time, the *America* had a minor collision with a schooner and could not take the *Tonawanda* all the way out.[1] It was a slow beginning, but with all the news about the horrific battles in Virginia and Maryland, going to sea at this moment might have seemed a better option to White than unemployment in increasingly militarized Sussex County.

According to Captain Julius's log, on Thursday, October 9, the *Tonawanda* reached latitude 40°29' N and longitude 56°40' W, about a thousand miles east of Cape May, which meant that it had averaged about 165 miles per day, at an average 6 knots, since entering the Atlantic. The log notes "moderate breeze and rain showers, with variable winds from the North and Northeast."[2] In the meantime, the *Alabama* had been heading west from the Azores en route to New

York, where Semmes intended to attack ships in the harbor. At 1:30 p.m., he spied the *Tonawanda* and gave chase. By evening, just before sunset, the *Alabama* intercepted the *Tonawanda*, which turned out to be a prize wholly different from the whaling vessels so easily disposed of in the Azores.

Semmes sent over a boarding party under the command of twenty-six-year-old John Low, wearing two revolvers. Low instructed Captain Julius to accompany him back to the *Tonawanda*, where the crews of the *Wave Crest* and *Dunkirk*—both burned two days before—were restrained in irons on the deck. After a brief introduction and a desultory negotiation, Semmes rejected Julius's offer of "a reasonable sum" from his agents to let the ship off.[3] Meanwhile, the *Alabama* tore off after yet another sail, which turned out to be British. Semmes then resumed negotiations with Julius.

Julius understood that with all the other crews crammed on deck, Semmes had no room for the *Tonawanda*'s passengers and crew, so arson was not an option. After considerable haggling, they settled on a bond of $80,000, payable if the Confederacy won the war.[4]

White's exact experience during this critical moment is unclear from the record, but we may surmise that Low and his boarding officers mustered the *Tonawanda*'s crew and interrogated them. The two adult Black cooks, White's companions William Cannon and Luke White, were found to have Certificates of Protection—the documents provided by US port authorities to protect American seamen from foreign impressment. Like most junior sailors, White had no such certificate, and this fact would later be misrepresented as a quasi-legal rationale for his capture. In his deposition to Congress, Captain Julius recorded that after he signed the extorted bond aboard the *Alabama* and gave his word of honor not to try to escape, "all persons belonging to the *Alabama* returned to her, with one colored boy, our passenger-cook, he belonging to Delaware, a slave State, and being without protection or free papers."[5] Julius's son's log entry records: "They forced our passenger Cook a Negro boy to join them and took him on board his name was Henry White of Lewistown Delaware"[6] (fig. 10.1).

Now Low was made prize master and put in charge of the *Tonawanda*, which then followed in the *Alabama*'s wake. Next, the *Alabama* started to transship all of the prisoners from the whaling fleet to the *Tonawanda*. The plan was to burn the *Tonawanda* if the *Alabama* could find a ship less valuable on which to release the prisoners. The passengers' comfort was not a consideration. Later Semmes cuttingly related exactly what he thought of them. "Some of the passengers were foreigners, fleeing from the tyranny, and outrages of person and property, which had overtaken them, under the reign of the Puritan, in the 'land of the free, and the home of the brave,' and others were patriotic Puritans themselves running away from the 'City of Brotherly Love' to escape the draft."[7] Their experience was later described as "[filling] the air with piteous lamentations at what appeared to them to be a dreadful fate."[8]

As it turned out, on Saturday, October 11, Semmes spied the *Manchester* on its way from New York to Liverpool. It was a more valuable prize to burn because it was only one year old and had almost twice the *Tonawanda*'s cargo of wheat.

On that day the winds were easterly, and the weather moderate and fair, and by evening conditions remained moderate.[9] On Sunday, with Low at the helm of the *Tonawanda*, Julius's son didn't bother to record the course, writing only that it was "after the 290."[10] After

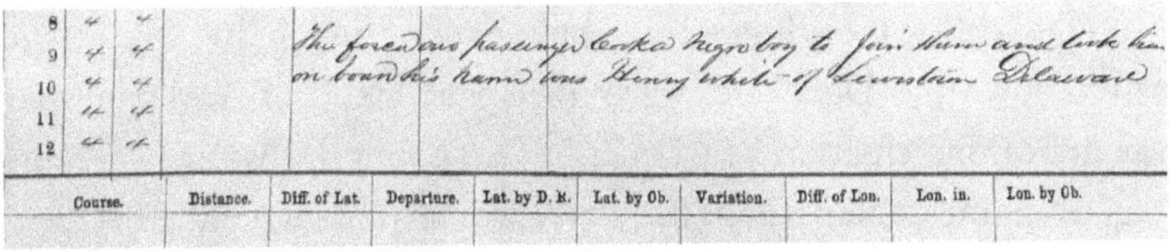

FIGURE 10.1. Excerpt from *Tonawanda* logbook, entry for October 9, 1862. *Avil Family Papers. Courtesy Avil Family.*

capturing the *Manchester*, the *Alabama* put its crew of twenty-two men on board the *Tonawanda* and set the *Manchester* on fire. Captain Julius remained on board the *Alabama* at end of day and overnight, sleeping in steerage.

The next day, Semmes informed Julius that he would load the *Tonawanda* with more prisoners and let him continue under bond to Liverpool. Another argument ensued about how much food and water would be required and about sleeping arrangements. Julius, angry and exhausted, appealed to Semmes's sense of honor and privilege. As the weather deteriorated, Julius made the case that they might lose the *Tonawanda* if he wasn't put back at the helm. Indeed the *Tonawanda*'s log recorded a freshening breeze during the night, and squalls around 3:00 p.m., making it necessary to haul up the mainsail and topsail. The weather notwithstanding, once again sighting a ship, Semmes cleared the *Alabama* for action and got steam up, but the new sighting turned out to be a Spanish vessel.

After four days of haggling, shuttling, sail chasing, and worsening weather, Semmes finally allowed Julius back on the *Tonawanda*. The old packet resumed its slow voyage to Liverpool, now loaded with more than two hundred men, women, and children—all crew and passengers of the *Wave Crest, Dunkirk, Manchester,* and *Tonawanda*—but without White, who had suddenly been conscripted into the Confederate Navy.

What made Semmes single out White for kidnapping? The *Alabama* was already reasonably well staffed—to the extent that there was room on the decks only for the captured crews. The *Tonawanda* brought with it the Philadelphia newspapers, which, by the time it sailed down the Delaware, were filled with news of Antietam and the draft Emancipation Proclamation. No doubt this would have enraged Semmes, and perhaps he just wanted to make a point. Historian William Marvel suggests that Semmes viewed White as legitimate "contraband of war," since Semmes later wrote in his memoir that

Delaware was "arrayed on the side of the enemy. I was obliged, therefore, to treat her as such."[11]

The contraband issue was certainly in the air. In May 1861, General Benjamin Butler had famously refused to return escaped slaves at Fort Monroe. While the army was at first reluctant to recruit Black men, the navy, now in need of crews to support the blockade, went all in. In August, the US Congress passed the Confiscation Act of 1861, which declared that any property used by the Confederate military, including enslaved people, could be confiscated by Union forces. On September 21, 1861, Navy secretary Gideon Welles authorized the recruitment of escaped enslaved willing to enlist. Further, Welles issued a directive to pay "persons of color, commonly known as contraband," in the employment of the Union Navy, $10 per month and a full day's ration.[12] Three weeks later, the Union Army followed suit, paying male "contrabands" at Fort Monroe $8 per month and $4 to women specific to that command.[13] In March 1862, it became a military crime for officers to return any contrabands to the enemy. By July of the same year, Congress had passed the Second Confiscation Act, which took a step toward emancipation by declaring that those enslaved taken "shall be deemed captives of war and shall forever be free."[14] Semmes was doubtless fully aware of and animated by the contraband issue, yet he never used the word "contraband" in connection with White. Perhaps he held back, conscious that his own usage of the word "slave" was duplicitous.

As to the particular role Semmes chose for White, his 1869 memoir provides yet another clue to kind of servant he sought. First, he described his former servant on the Sumter:

When I was fitting out the *Sumter* in New Orleans, a friend, and relative resident in that city, had kindly permitted me to take with me, as my steward, a valuable slave of his who had been brought up as a dining-room servant. Ned was as black as the ace of spades, and being a good-tempered lad, had become my right-hand man, taking the best of care of my cabin, and keeping my table supplied with all the delicacies of the different markets, to which we had had access.[15]

Ned turned out not to be so docile after all; he deserted the *Sumter* in Surinam. Semmes blamed the American consul in that country, remained bitter about the desertion, and smugly reported Ned's subsequent demise, telling his readers that Ned "died miserably."[16]

In discussing White, Semmes wrote, "We were in want of good servants and sent him to wait on the ward-room mess."[17] In his antebellum memoir, First Lieutenant Kell, when traveling to Bridgeport, Connecticut, was astonished "to find young white servant girls attending at the table."[18] Moreover, Kell's account of his early naval

FIGURE 10.2. "The Confederate Sloop-of-War '290,' or *Alabama*, Leaving the Merchant-Ship *Tonawanda*." *Published in* Illustrated London News *41, no. 1174 (November 15, 1862): 513. Author's collection.*

experience makes clear that this was a menial task they would have abhorred for themselves. As for being "in want" of servants, some seven weeks into their cruise, the officers had perhaps discovered that with the wardroom mess at the other end of the ship from the galley, and no passage between the two, if they wanted hot food they would need a "menial" to bring it.

Semmes's log entry of October 9 is notable for being the original documented lie regarding White: "Thursday, October 9. . . . The prize in company during the night. The master having reported that one of the black waiters on board his ship, was a slave, from Delaware, had him brought on board and entered as one of the crew, a waiter in the officers' messes."[19] Apart from downplaying the drama, antagonism, and discomfort of the four-day encounter with Captain Julius and his passengers, the entry is revealing for its dissembling on

FIGURE 10.3. "Capture of Packet Ship *Tonawanda* by Confederate Privateer *Alabama*, October 9th, 1862," by Franklin D. Briscoe, including depictions of Capt. Raphael Semmes, Capt. Theodore Julius, and First Mate Theodore Julius Jr. *Avil Family Papers. Courtesy of Avil family.*

the subject of White. All of the lies and distortions that were applied to White from Semmes's and his officers' accounts are summarized further in chapter 25. Here, it is enough to point out that the origin of the fiction that White was "a slave, from Delaware" begins in Semmes's daily log, on the day he was kidnapped (fig. 10.4).

With his sea-lawyerly skills, Semmes may have somehow convinced himself that White was enslaved, but it was disingenuous of him to enlist Captain Julius in this fiction—with the phrase that "the master" of the *Tonawanda* had told him so. Julius certainly informed Semmes that White was from Delaware, but it is difficult to imagine that he described White as enslaved. Julius had personally signed White on with William Cannon and Luke White. In the *Tonawanda* log, Julius's son reported that White had been "forced" on to the *Alabama*. Moreover, the moment Captain Julius stepped ashore in Liverpool, he reported White's kidnapping to the relevant authorities. This report is recorded in the diary of Benjamin Moran, who served as assistant secretary to the US ambassador to England, Charles Francis Adams, during the Civil War. Moran wrote in his diary on Friday, October 31, 1862: "We have a written statement from Capt. Julius of the *Tonawanda* thro' the consul at L'pool. The Capt. says the pirates number about 100, nearly all of whom are English man o'wars men. Semmes stole a free negro boy from the ship, & will no doubt carry him into slavery."[20]

Consider what White had just experienced. If he was like any

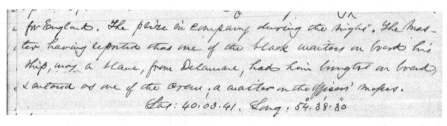

FIGURE 10.4. Semmes's *Alabama* log entry for October 9, 1862. *Semmes Family Papers, Alabama Department of Archives and History.*

other free Black teenager from Sussex County, Delaware, or for that matter any other Black sailor before the war, he had spent much of his life in fear of being kidnapped and sold into slavery. It is likely that he attempted to assert his free status; after all, he was trying to *avoid* servitude—not end it.

Scholars have well-documented the violence by which the newly enslaved were physically and psychologically subjugated through a practice known as "seasoning."[21] In his 1840 memoir of the voyage on the *Pilgrim, Two Years Before the Mast*, Richard Henry Dana provided a graphic example of such brutality at sea. Dana recorded how the *Pilgrim*'s captain treated a sailor only identified as "Sam":

"You see your condition! . . . Will you ever give me any more of your jaw?" No answer; and then came wrestling and heaving. . . . "You may as well keep still, for I have got you," said the captain. . . .

"I never gave you any, sir," said Sam; for it was his voice that we heard, though low and half choked.

"That's not what I ask you. Will you ever be impudent to me again?"

"I never have been, sir," said Sam.

"Answer my question, or I'll make a spread eagle of you! I'll flog you, by G—d."

"I'm no negro slave," said Sam.

"Then I'll make you one," said the captain; and he came to the hatchway, and sprang on deck, threw off his coat, and rolling up his sleeves, called out to the mate—"Seize that man up, Mr. A——! Seize him up! Make a spread eagle of him! I'll teach you all who is master aboard!"[22]

As for White, all we have of this moment is Semmes's account years later, which was presumably something of an understatement: "The boy" he wrote, "was a little alarmed at first."[23]

Chapter 11

༺❦༻

Storms

During the first few critical days aboard the *Alabama*, White would have had to weather an entirely new set of relationships and expectations, while the weather itself worsened. We may even surmise that White was emotionally traumatized, and perhaps attempted to resist.

At this early stage of his journey, White was probably learning, as the saying goes, that resistance was futile. A rare firsthand account of another such kidnapping, aboard the Confederate commerce raider *Shenandoah*, provides some insight into the mindset and capacity of Confederate raider officers, both generally and specifically. In this case, Midshipman Irvine Bulloch and the captain's clerk, W. Breedlove Smith, served both on the CSS *Alabama* under Semmes and later on the CSS *Shenandoah* under the command of Capt. James Iredell Waddell. Author Tom Chaffin recounts the experiences of John Williams, a Black steward taken from the bark *D. Godfrey*, southwest of the Cape Verde Islands in the central Atlantic.[1] In this case, the Confederates "triced-up"—that is, hung by the thumbs—several *D. Godfrey* crew members, including Williams. According to Williams, Waddell informed him that "I better join the ship as it would be better for me;

that as colored people were the cause of the war, if I did not go in it would go hard on me. . . . I offered to work but refused to join."[2]

Williams later stated that each time he refused to join, citing his loyalty to the Union, he received the same punishment: "I have been triced up by the thumbs seven times for upholding my country." Williams never wavered in his determined refusal.[3]

After releasing the *Tonawanda*, the *Alabama* continued west on October 14, with Semmes still nursing his plan to attack shipping in New York harbor. Unfortunately, he was on a collision course with the fifth tropical storm of 1862, known only as Hurricane Five, which was heading up the Atlantic Coast toward Georges Bank. Hurricane Five would today be termed a Category 1 storm, having a peak intensity of about 80 miles per hour. That same day, October 14, the schooner *Albert Treat*, on its way up the coast approximately 310 miles west of Bermuda, had been thrown onto its beam ends, suffering considerable damage with three men drowned. Two days later, the storm, methodically moving up the coast, finally caught up with the *Alabama* a few hundred miles east of Cape Cod.[4]

It was fortunate that on October 3 Semmes had offloaded onto the *Emily Farnham* most of the prisoners from his first ten captures (table 9.1): out on deck in this storm, they might have been doomed. The experience was terrifying for everybody, and the *Alabama* was one of the few ships then known to have sailed straight through the eye of a hurricane and emerged on the other side to describe it. Semmes, an experienced mariner who had been at sea on and off for at least twenty years, and who had lost the *Somers* in a gulf norther, recorded, "The bad weather . . . culminated, today, in one of the severest gales of wind I have ever experienced."[5]

It is not as though he had no warning. Atlantic mariners—especially southern ones—had long understood the meteorology of hurricanes; even Columbus himself learned how to predict the advance of these storms from the indigenous Taino people of the Bahamas. A strange portent of heavy weather ahead arrived, for example, when a flock of curlews landed on the ship's bulwark. At once, there was a conversation about whether they might be put to use in the officers' mess, but the superstitious sailors from Liverpool objected. What were curlews—a type of sandpiper shorebird—doing hundreds of miles off the coast? It turns out that since 1575, Spanish mariners understood that an early sign of an imminent hurricane was "odd behaviors among birds, which are exquisitely sensitive to shifts in barometric pressure. When they sense a pressure drop, they might try to outrun it. . . . The result is unusual species showing up in un-expected places, sometimes migrating from America to Europe to escape a hurricane."[6]

In any event, Semmes noted the worsening weather. On Monday, October 13, he recorded, "a real dirty Gulf day with the wind from the SE to the SW and the weather squally, thick, and rainy." The next day, he wrote, "Fresh wind from the S.W. with some sea on." Even so, Semmes took some time to chase a Danish ship running before the wind. He then noted, "Fresh winds from the SW with some sea on, weather variable, looking well and ill by turns. Bar. 29.5, fluctuat-ing a little."[7] For comparison, anything lower than the 29.8 inches of mercury is associated with warm air and rainstorms, while rapidly lowering pressure indicates a coming storm.[8]

According to Lieutenant Low, the weather intensified on the eve-ning of October 15, with "heavy squalls and heavy sea running, the barometer going gradually down all the time with the wind from the South West . . . it looking very black in the North West."[9] A barom-eter "gradually going down all the time" and starting from a low of 29.5 is a sign of trouble.[10]

In spite of these portents, Semmes continued to sail west. Al-though he did not have access to modern weather services, he knew enough about hurricanes that, when the *Alabama* encountered a lowering barometer and freshening wind in the North Atlantic in October, he might have taken the safe course and headed back east or hove to. In that way, he could have tried to avoid the cyclone's counterclockwise vortex. From his contemporaneous diagram (fig. 11.1), however, it is clear that, by the time Semmes hove to, he was about to enter into the upper-right quadrant of the vortex.[11] Because the wind from the east pushes a vessel into its path, the upper-right quadrant of a hurricane is the most dangerous.

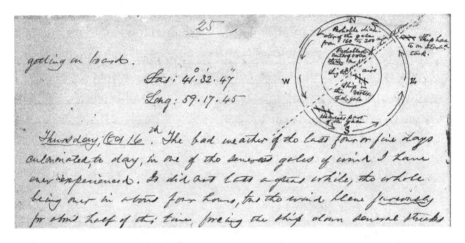

FIGURE 11.1. Semmes's *Alabama* log entry for October 16, 1862, showing his diagram of the hurricane the ship traversed. *Semmes Family Papers, Alabama Department of Archives and History.*

A possible explanation is that by the time it became clear the *Alabama* was heading into a hurricane, it may have been impossible to head east, against the wind. Another is inflexible attachment to an *idée fixe.* Author Rachel Slade provides the example of Capt. Michael Davidson of the container ship *Faro,* lost in October 2015 during Hurricane Joaquin. Glued to a plan, Davidson persistently ignored warnings from his crew that the ship's course would put them in peril of colliding with the storm.[12] In Semmes's case, he may simply have been willing to place his fate in the hands of the Almighty. It perhaps was no accident that he inscribed his logbook with a quote from "The Shipwreck," a sentimental and descriptive poem by William Falconer (1732–69).

Perhaps this storm is sent, with healing breath.
From neighboring shores to scourge disease and death!
'Tis ours on thine unerring laws to trust:
With thee, great Lord! "whatever is, is just."[13]

Semmes's description of a ship suddenly blown onto its side in a growing storm, of which there was warning, resonates with the *Somers* disaster in the Gulf of Mexico. At the moment of extreme peril, the main topsail parted, and the fore-topmast staysail threatened to pull

The Alabama in a cyclone, in the Gulf Stream, on the 16th October, 1862.

FIGURE 11.2. "The *Alabama* in a Cyclone in the Gulf Stream on the 16th October, 1862." *Illustration from Raphael Semmes,* Memoirs of Service Afloat During the War Between the States *(Baltimore: Kelly, Piet and Co., 1869). Author's collection.*

the ship into the trough of the sea. Smith valiantly clambered up and cut it away, leaving only the little storm staysail to carry the ship. Boarding Officer Fullam noted Smith's heroism:

> 9:30 (AM) Blowing a perfect hurricane, the sea rising to a fearful height, and the ship laboring heavily. Shortly after, a squall of extraordinary violence struck us, and we being under close reefed main topsail, reefed main trysail and foretopmast staysail. The heavy strain on the main braces, caused the weather bumkin (short boom) to snap in two, the yard flew forward bending upwards until it was almost double, when with a sudden crash it broke in two splitting the topsail with a noise equal to the loudest thunder. A sea striking immediately after smashed in the whale boat; it was soon cut away. No sooner had the main topsail gone, then the foretopmast staysail was cut away by the Capt. of the forecastle, thereby preventing the ship falling off into the trough of the sea.[14]

Another seaman who acted heroically and without credit was Lieutenant Low. According to both Sinclair and Low's biographer Hoole, after the ship survived the north-northeast side of the storm, passed through the vortex, and entered the equally violent south-southwest side, it was Low who saved the ship.[15]

Where was White during this tempest? He may have been down below or with the other Boys, lashed to the weather bulwark, as indicated by Marvel: "The officer of the deck, Lieutenant Low, ordered all the unoccupied hands and the boys of the watch to gather on the quarterdeck, where he had them lashed against the weather bulwark to avoid losing them over the side to leeward when the ship rolled."[16]

It remains unclear why these crew members were lashed to the quarterdeck bulwarks. It was a high spot, which might have provided some shelter from the crashing seas, but the quarterdeck was probably no safer than the decks below, and certainly a lot wetter. Had the ship rolled over, either place would have been deadly. In any case, it would have been harrowing for anybody. The *Alabama* was built for speed, not stability. Years later, Semmes provided a thrilling, if incomplete, account: "She was soon enveloped in its [the storm's] folds; and the winds, running around the circle, in that mad career represented by the arrows, howled, and whistled, and screeched around her like a thousand demons. She was thrown over, several streaks, and the waves began to assault her with sledge-hammer blows, and occasionally to leap on board of her, flooding her decks, and compelling us to stand knee-deep in water."[17]

Sinclair's description is similarly wrenching: "To convey an idea of the force of the wind would beggar language. . . . The officers and men were cowering under the weather bulwarks, or lashed at important stations. The wheel doubly manned, and in spite of this precaution it at one time, during the violent laboring of the vessel, got away from control, and with a whirl, threw a man completely over it to leeward."[18]

According to Hoole:

That night, Lieutenant Low, the man who had saved the ship, wrote these few modest, unassuming words in his logbook: "a little before daylight we wore ship around on the starboard tack. From 8 to meridian blowing a very heavy gale, carried away the main yard, main topsail, blew away fore-staysail, stove in and cut away whale boat, stove in hammock nettings forward, carried away lower studding sail boom, set main storm topsail; at 11:30 gale moderated."[19]

Finally, after nearly five hours of pure terror, the wind subsided. Semmes then wrote, "I must capture another ship now directly . . . to enable me to repair damages and replace my boats."[20] White would have had no way of knowing—nor do we—whether Semmes had risked his vessel and their lives by doggedly sailing west or, for that matter, whether Semmes's seamanship had saved both the ship and his life.

Chapter 12

❧

Reports

A few weeks later, news of the *Tonawanda*'s capture reached the
United States. The *Philadelphia Public Ledger* reported the news
first on November 14, and then it was picked up by both the *New York
Times* and the *New York Herald*. The *New York Times* article headlined
the account "The Depredations of the *Alabama*: Interesting Letter
from Capt. Julius, of the *Tonawanda*" (fig. 12.1). The article quoted
Captain Julius's statement that "all persons belonging to the *Alabama*
left for their ship, taking with them a colored boy, named DAVID
HENRY, our passenger cook, belonging to Delaware, and being
without protection of free papers [*sic*]."[1]

A more detailed account was published in the *New York Herald* on
Thursday, December 11, 1862, describing a "highly interesting letter
from one of the passengers of the *Tonawanda*" (fig. 12.2):

THE PIRATE *ALABAMA*

The Capture of the Packet Ship *Tonawanda*

Journal of the Voyage and Incidentals of the Capture

FIVE DAYS IN THE MESHES OF THE PIRATE

The Pirate Steals a Colored Boy from the *Tonawanda*

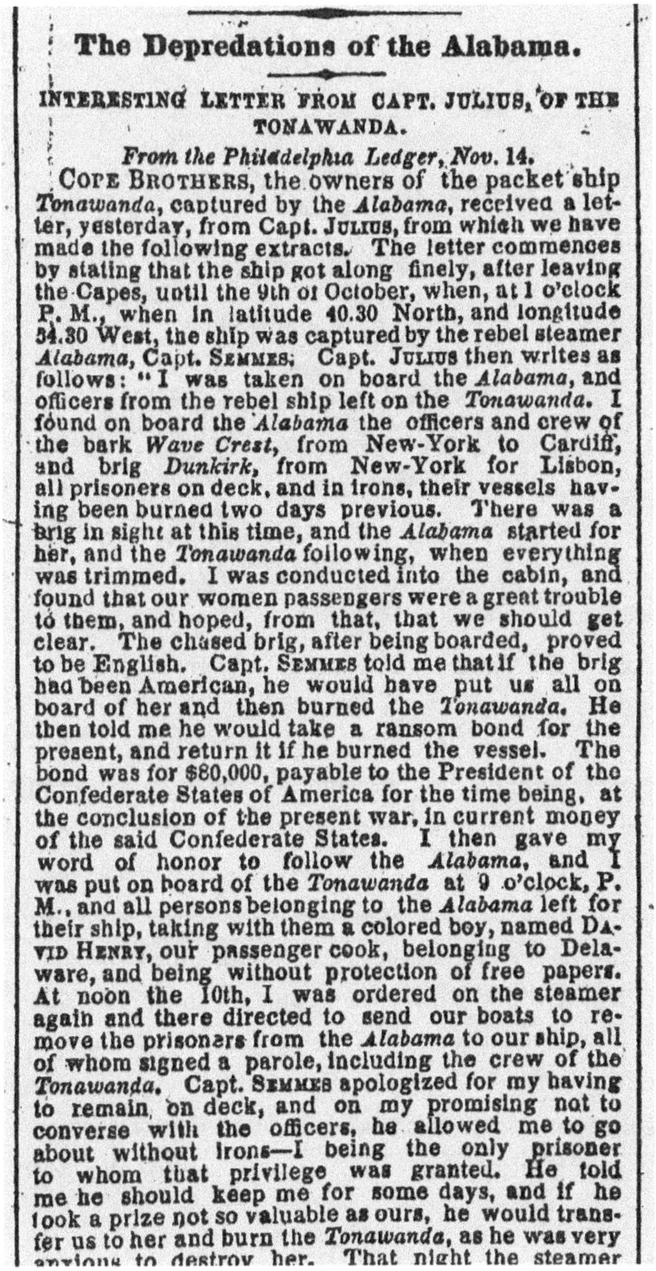

The Depredations of the Alabama.

INTERESTING LETTER FROM CAPT. JULIUS, OF THE TONAWANDA.

From the Philadelphia Ledger, Nov. 14.

COPE BROTHERS, the owners of the packet ship *Tonawanda*, captured by the *Alabama*, received a letter, yesterday, from Capt. JULIUS, from which we have made the following extracts. The letter commences by stating that the ship got along finely, after leaving the Capes, until the 9th of October, when, at 1 o'clock P. M., when in latitude 40.30 North, and longitude 54.30 West, the ship was captured by the rebel steamer *Alabama*, Capt. SEMMES; Capt. JULIUS then writes as follows: "I was taken on board the *Alabama*, and officers from the rebel ship left on the *Tonawanda*. I found on board the *Alabama* the officers and crew of the bark *Wave Crest*, from New-York to Cardiff, and brig *Dunkirk*, from New-York for Lisbon, all prisoners on deck, and in irons, their vessels having been burned two days previous. There was a brig in sight at this time, and the *Alabama* started for her, and the *Tonawanda* following, when everything was trimmed. I was conducted into the cabin, and found that our women passengers were a great trouble to them, and hoped, from that, that we should get clear. The chased brig, after being boarded, proved to be English. Capt. SEMMES told me that if the brig had been American, he would have put us all on board of her and then burned the *Tonawanda*. He then told me he would take a ransom bond for the present, and return it if he burned the vessel. The bond was for $80,000, payable to the President of the Confederate States of America for the time being, at the conclusion of the present war, in current money of the said Confederate States. I then gave my word of honor to follow the *Alabama*, and I was put on board of the *Tonawanda* at 9 o'clock, P. M., and all persons belonging to the *Alabama* left for their ship, taking with them a colored boy, named DAVID HENRY, our passenger cook, belonging to Delaware, and being without protection of free papers. At noon the 10th, I was ordered on the steamer again and there directed to send our boats to remove the prisoners from the *Alabama* to our ship, all of whom signed a parole, including the crew of the *Tonawanda*. Capt. SEMMES apologized for my having to remain on deck, and on my promising not to converse with the officers, he allowed me to go about without irons—I being the only prisoner to whom that privilege was granted. He told me he should keep me for some days, and if he took a prize not so valuable as ours, he would transfer us to her and burn the *Tonawanda*, as he was very anxious to destroy her. That night the steamer

FIGURE 12.1. "Depredations of the *Alabama*," *New York Times*, November 16, 1862. *Public domain image in the NYPL collection; photo by Andrew Sillen.*

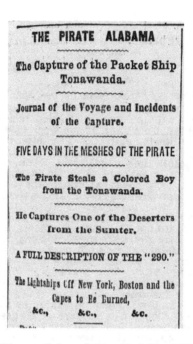

FIGURE 12.2. "The Pirate *Alabama*," *New York Herald*, November 13, 1862. *Public domain image in the NYPL collection; photo by Andrew Sillen.*

The article contained the following passage, notable not just for the account of the kidnapping but also for the casual dismissal of its importance:

> The only levy made on the *Tonawanda* by the privateer was to take a little colored boy from us—an assistant in the galley—because he was unprotected by free papers. He was an apprentice under the laws of the state of Delaware and would be free when of age (twenty-one). This has been truly a day of congratulation and one of a series which all of us at present on the *Tonawanda* will never forget.

The article also contained the following passage, quoting Captain Julius:

[Captain Semmes] . . . told me he would take ransom bond for the present, and return it if he burned the vessel. The bond was for $80,000, payable to the President of the Confederate States of America for the time being, at the conclusion of the present war, in current money of the said Confederate States. I then gave my word of honor . . . and all persons belonging to the *Alabama* left for their ship, taking with them a colored boy, named DAVID HENRY, our passenger cook, belonging to Delaware, and being without protection of free papers [*sic*].[2]

Captain Julius also provided a deposition of his ship's capture to the US consul in Liverpool, which was eventually entered into the *Congressional Record.* Julius wrote, "All persons belong to the Alabama [were] returned to her, with one colored boy, our passenger-cook, he belonging to Delaware, a slave state, and being without protection or free papers [*sic*]."[3]

Possibly, the substitution of the word "of" for the word "or" is a distinction without a difference ("without protection *of* free papers" for "without protection *or* free papers") but there is arguably a subtle explanation for the error.

The linguist Geoffrey Pullum coined the term "eggcorn" to denote a word or phrase that enters the language because it has a plausible meaning, even though it is based on a mishearing of the originally intended word or phrase.[4] The classic example of an eggcorn is the phrase "for all intensive purposes," which is of course an incorrect adaptation of "for all intents and purposes." It enters the language not because it is correct but because it makes sense to those unfamiliar with the original.

"Without protection of free papers" is such an eggcorn. The erroneous phrase made sense to those who were unfamiliar with the original and who might have assumed that servitude was a default status to which White was subject without a document to the contrary. Had

White been manumitted, his transmission to freedom might have been recorded in a deed-book registered in a county courthouse, but as an individual born free, he had no such official registration other than the census. Had he been indigent, his "binding to service" would have been similarly recorded—but it was not. As for "without protection," as recorded in the Philadelphia Port archives, the phrase simply meant that, like most junior members of merchantman crews, he had not yet obtained an identity document provided by ports to protect US seamen from foreign (historically British) impressment.

The application of the term "without protection" to White's predicament subtly suggests that he was impressed, rather than kidnapped. That is, the word "impressment" implies the imprimatur of a legitimate governing power, acting under the umbrella of law, for which some official document—a certificate of protection—would provide immunity. Even were it to be applied to White's capture, impressment remains among the most un-American of naval practices. In fact, objection to impressment was one of the original twenty-seven colonial grievances enumerated in the Declaration of Independence. The War of 1812 was itself precipitated by the *Chesapeake* affair, but in that particular case, one of the four sailors taken had previously served on British ships and had deserted. In any event, the practice was widely understood to be egregious and inefficient—some 25 percent of impressed sailors in the British navy at one time or another deserted.[5] After the defeat of Napoleon, England by 1815 contracted its navy, reformed its means of recruitment, and thus ended impressment. In 1853, England could fight a war with Russia without resorting to impressment.

Therefore, White was kidnapped—not impressed—because, by 1862, impressment as a legitimate form of naval recruitment had long been obsolete. Further, Semmes had no legal authority to remove him from the *Tonawanda*, much less to enslave him. White was not "contraband" because he had never been a slave—and Semmes knew it. As Domby made clear with his use of the word "lie," in this instance use of the word "impressment" rather than "kidnapping" might render the act innocuous.

In any event, the excitement was short-lived; the news of the kidnapping did not appear to have much impact. There were none of the speeches, family interviews, marches, or journalists that might have taken up White's cause, as would be the case in this century. With the exception of two muster rolls, he disappears from the primary documentary record. After the war, when the time came to settle with Great Britain in the first-of-its-kind international arbitration, $15.5 million in reparations—an astounding sum in its day—was accorded through the *Alabama* claims international arbitration by Great Britain to the United States for the damage to US commerce.[6] White is mentioned in Julius's deposition to the Court of Arbitration, but there was never any consideration of reparation to his family. When the time came to settle up with Great Britain, White's life was never a consideration.

Chapter 13

❧

Mutiny

Semmes then turned southwest to pursue commercial shipping that traveled the sea lane between New York and Liverpool. Over the following few weeks, the *Alabama* chased and released nine neutral vessels, ransomed one, and burned six (table 13.1).

By now the American papers had caught on to the flamethrower. The captain of the *Brilliant*, which burned on October 3, arrived in New York two weeks later, and all hell broke loose. According to Boykin, "The hurricane that struck the *Alabama* on October 16 was, relatively, no fiercer than the furor swirling about Secretary of the Navy Welles at Washington that same day."[1] Welles sent new orders to the US steam sloop *Mohican*, to search for the *Alabama* at latitude 50° North. However, by October 31, the *Alabama* had already turned south toward Martinique, out of the lane.

In his *Naval History of the Civil War*, Admiral Porter expressed chagrin at the Navy Department for not protecting Union commerce and anticipating Semmes's moves:

Why the United States Government should have left this great highway unprotected no one to this day can conjecture. The vessels that were sent to look for the "Alabama" always went to the

Table 13.1. Captures by the *Alabama*, October 9–November 8, 1862

Date	Ship	Home Port	From/To	Cargo	Disposition
October 9	Tonawanda	Philadelphia	Liverpool	Grain	Converted into a cartel and released on ransom bond
October 11	Manchester	New York	Liverpool	Grain, cotton	Burned
October 15	Lamplighter	New York	Gibraltar	Tobacco	Burned
October 23	Lafayette	New Haven	Belfast	Wheat and corn	Burned
October 26	Crenshaw	New York	Glasgow	Flour and grain	Burned
October 28	Lauretta	Boston	Gibraltar	Herring, flour, pipe staves, nails	Burned
October 29	Baron de Castine	Bangor, ME	Cuba	Lumber	Released on bond and made a cartel
November 2	Levi Starbuck	New Bedford, MA	Cruising	Whalebone and provisions	Burned
November 8	Thomas B. Wales	Boston	Calcutta	Linseed oil, saltpeter, jute	Burned

Source: O.R. Navy, Ser. I: Vol. 3, pp. 677–81.

wrong places, when it must have been known that she would seek
the highways of trade as naturally as a bluefish would seek the
feeding grounds of the menhaden. Whatever success the federal
government may have had in blockading the enemy's ports, its
attempts to protect the merchant marine were nearly always fail-
ures; and it shows how necessary it is for a nation to keep on hand
in time of peace vessels that will prove useful in time of war.[2]

Historian Warren Spencer has provided one answer to Porter's
question: the US secretary of the navy "obviously considered the
blockade more important than the merchant ships."[3] In a dispatch
to Welles that October, the New York Chamber of Commerce was
blunt: "The American flag, pride of the nation, and once the emblem
of its power to protect cargo and passenger on every sea, is dishonored and in disrepute, or is withdrawn from the seas."[4]

In fairness to Welles, Semmes aided himself in the evasion of
Union warships with a rigorous practice of scrutinizing the latest newspapers captured from his prey. Years later, he revealed his
method:

> The *Manchester* brought us a batch of late New York papers, and
> I was much obliged to the editors of the New York "Herald," for
> valuable information. I learned from them where all the enemy's
> gunboats were, and what they were doing; which, of course, en-
> abled me to take better care of the *Alabama*, than I should oth-
> erwise have been enabled to do. The Americans effected many
> reforms in the art of war during our late struggle. Perhaps this
> was the only war in which the newspapers ever explained, before-
> hand, all the movements of armies, and fleets, to the enemy.[5]

The *Alabama* captured the *Thomas B. Wales* on November 8, scav-
enged its main yard, and burned it. It went down with its valuable

cargo of jute, linseed oil, and most importantly, saltpeter, used for making gunpowder. Among the displaced passengers were George H. Fairchild, a former US consul in Mauritius, his wife, and their three daughters. Perhaps Winslow Homer had them in mind—or the *Tonawanda*'s passengers—when he drew *The Approach of the British Pirate Alabama*, which appeared in the April 25, 1863, edition of *Harper's Weekly* (fig. 13.1).[6]

FIGURE 13.1. "The Approach of the British Pirate 'Alabama,'" by Winslow Homer. Harper's Weekly, *April 25, 1863, 268. Author's collection.*

Having stayed as long as he dared in the northern sea-lane, Semmes then spent the first two weeks of November sailing south to Fort-de-France, Martinique, where he hoped the *Agrippina* would be waiting with coal in a prearranged rendezvous. By now both officers and crew were living on "salt horse" (actually beef, not horse, preserved in salt) and hardtack (a dense biscuit made from flour, water, and salt), so Semmes also needed to provision the ship with fresh food and antiscorbutic.

By this point, White would have become accustomed to his new duties, much of which can be described from firsthand accounts of officers such as Sinclair; the experience of other sailors on similar vessels, such as the *Georgia* and *Shenandoah*, and even from the maritime archaeology of the *Alabama* itself.

Historian Barbara Brooks Tomblin describes the daily routine and responsibilities for sailors on Confederate vessels. A typical day began at dawn or before with a trill from the boatswain's pipe, with the boatswain's mate shaking hammocks and shouting orders to "Rise and shine! Lash up and Stow!" On Confederate ships, sailors had about ten minutes to wrap their hammocks and bedding into a bundle and stow them behind heavy rope nets along the sides. Then came about an hour of heavy work, including holystoning the decks and attending to rigging, before inspection and breakfast.[7] White was probably exempt from this heavy work, but nevertheless would have been fully engaged, both as Galt's manservant and as a steward to the officers' mess. One notable firsthand account lists among the steward's responsibilities helping officers shave and dress, and giving the cook a hand in the galley once the officers sat down to breakfast.[8]

The day's work began in earnest with the carpenter's team maintaining the hull and masts, the boatswain's mate training landsmen and new crew members, the engineer's team maintaining the tricky machinery, the firemen shoveling coal, and the sailmaker's team sewing and repairing the massive bolts of canvas. In the wardroom,

White would likely have been tasked with washing and polishing the officers' tableware and perhaps helping the cook in the galley to prepare the afternoon meal. A cabinet in the wardroom mess contained the tableware, some of which has been recovered in excavations: it consisted of three sets (blue, green, and brown) of Davenport transfer-printed dishes produced in 1862 in Staffordshire, England.

The Naval History Command describes the dish sets:

The blue set features a blue fouled anchor surrounded by a garter in the center of the dish and a twisted rope around the edge. The green set consists of two crossed anchors surrounded by a garter in the center and a twisted rope border around the vessel's edge. The brown set consists of only one anchor in the center with a twisted rope border around the vessel's edge. The three sets include dinner plates, side plates, bowls, and soup tureens.[9]

The different colors were not intended for variety: they were a material manifestation of the hierarchical world in which the officers lived: gold for the captain, blue for the wardroom officers, green for the steerage officers, and brown for the crew.[10]

Around 4 p.m. a light supper was served in the officers' mess. Semmes generally dined alone and remained aloof from the junior officers and crew.[11] The officers themselves were divided into categories: the most senior were the ten wardroom officers; they were followed by steerage officers, masters mates, assistant engineers, four warrant officers (the boatswain, carpenter, sailmaker, and gunner), each the head of his respective department, and finally some thirty petty officers, including the cook, Henry Tucker, and the wardroom steward, Richard Parkinson, under whom White worked.

In this situation, White may have had access to a better diet than the common sailor, who rarely had it as good as the cabin passengers of the Cope Line packets. Before the invention of refrigeration, it was necessary for vessels to regularly obtain fresh provisions before resorting to the monotonous and unhealthful diet of salt-horse and hardtack. The officers generally had it better, and Sinclair related that, whenever they had the opportunity on land, officers hunted for pheasant, hare, quail, snipe, plover, curlew, and turkey. The captured prize ships regularly provided the officers and crew with fresh food, including pigs, fowl, potatoes, and onions.[12] Among the luxurious items taken from larders and cargoes were champagne, oysters, wines, brandies, sardines, cheese, fruitcake, olives, and pâté de foie gras.[13] There was also plenty of line fish, from which the cook, Tucker, made a favorite chowder.

Following dinner, the sailors who were not on watch had free time until taps sounded. In his account of the *Georgia*'s voyage, Morgan writes that this was one hour in which discipline on that ship was suspended. After the day's work, men gathered on the upper deck, sang songs, told stories, and smoked. During this period, crewmen could speak freely with the officers.[14]

According to Sinclair, the crew frequently played checkers. The officers played chess and backgammon in the wardroom, but cards were strictly prohibited. Most smoked tobacco, either in meerschaum pipes or as cigars if they could get them. In the dark and smokey lower deck, White is likely to have found some companionship, if not comradery among the Boys and crew. The *Alabama*'s crew hailed mainly from the seagoing community of Liverpool; White knew the place, and by this time, Black men had long been a ubiquitous and normal presence on board the British ships from which they were recruited.[15]

Or perhaps not. In *Black Jacks*, Bolster points out that Black stewards of the time inhabited an ambiguous social sphere, belonging neither to the officers nor to the men, and as cabin servants, they were often regarded as the captain's "flunkies."[16] White was likely among the very few on this vessel who regularly worked in the rear for the officers but slept in the front with the crew. Like it or not, the teenage White would have had to navigate these shoals and now would experience the full expression of early- to mid-nineteenth-century naval culture—often described and perceived as a kind of situational slavery—but also enriched with a vivid and captivating tradition of yarns (stories), songs (including chanties), superstitions, high jinks, and inebriation.

While Semmes thought of himself as a strict but fair disciplinarian, and while there may be some truth to this self-image, order could unravel the moment he was out of sight. Down in the lower deck, White would have had to use all his wits to survive the rough-and-tumble regime lived by the mercenaries. Now White would see what happened to those sailors—white no less—who ran afoul of this captain. It would be a vivid lesson.

Once in Fort-de-France, Martinique, Semmes and his senior officers left the ship to have dinner on a French corvette. One of the sailors got into a fight with some of the corvette's petty officers, and as a result liberty was canceled. The *Alabama*'s sailors were not ones to be denied the pleasures of shore leave, and George Forrest, the sailor who had deserted the *Sumter* and had been impressed back into service from the *Dunkirk* on the day of the *Tonawanda*'s capture, took advantage of the situation. That night, he slipped down the cable, made his way to shore, and returned with five gallons of what Fullam called "spirits" and Sinclair dubbed "Oh be Joyful."[17]

At this time, a grog ration in the form of rum was regularly issued to the crew, as had long been the practice in the US and Royal navies. Congress had voted to end the practice in September 1862, but the Confederacy kept it, as did the Royal Navy (until 1970). Given much of the crew's demand for and expectation of alcohol, the daily ration was no doubt a necessary expedient, but the difficulty was that alcohol itself encouraged mischief.

For Capt. Thomas Truxton, one of the first commodores appointed by President George Washington, and commander of the USS *Constellation*, the problem presented its own solution; since most of the disciplinary problems onboard were the result of drunkenness, stopping a man's grog, he noted, "answers the purpose intended much better than public flogging, and is more humane, and not so degrading to man."[18] Perhaps that was Semmes's plan A in denying his crew shore leave, but he hadn't counted on Forrest. No matter—Semmes had a plan B.

Based on the various accounts, all of which in this case more or less agree, here is what transpired. Forrest, considering himself a prisoner and not bound by the rules, distributed the liquor—without imbibing any himself—and incited mutiny. When the first officer of the watch appeared, the drunken sailors hurled various objects at him, and the boatswain was knocked down by a blow from a belaying pin. Kell then arrived on deck and ordered those men who appeared sober to seize their drunken comrades, but not a hand was raised; instead Kell also had to duck a flying belaying pin. Then the officers, with the sober portion of the crew, charged the drunken lot, and a furious melee ensued during which at least one man was severely stabbed in the arm.

Semmes had been enjoying fresh fruit in his cabin as he pondered the confusion of noise and trampling of feet on the deck above him.[19] He arrived on deck to find a surly crowd of drunken sailors gathered near the foremast. He then ordered the men to quarters to the beat of a drum, which had some effect, and eventually they fell into a line. As he walked by them, one by one, he picked out the sots—twenty in all—and had them placed in irons.

Semmes professed to understand the difference between drunken rampage and true mutiny. Most of the rowdies were put in irons, placed on a gangway, gagged, and repeatedly drenched with buckets of ice-cold seawater. At first they laughed and swore: "Come on with your water; we're not afraid of water!"[20] As bucket after bucket was emptied over them, however, they began to gasp and choke and were soon begging for mercy. That was the kind treatment.

Forrest, the ringleader, did not fare as well. He was spread-eagled on the rigging—by one account for two hours at a time, with two hours on and two hours off, and by another account for four hours at a time—for at least twenty times.[21] More trouble than he was worth, Forrest was eventually bound and left on the desolate island of La Blanquilla, located more than 150 miles from the mainland of Venezuela and populated mainly by donkeys and goats.

Imagine these events through White's eyes: having just been kidnapped, he then experienced the unimaginable terror of the hurricane and now saw the potential violence of the ship's crew, which was mitigated only by an undependable sobriety and exercise of raw power.

Chapter 14

＝

South to Galveston

For the last six weeks of 1862 and through the long hard year of 1863, the *Alabama*'s voyage would settle into a pattern of deception, attack, and burn, punctuated by visits to friendly ports to rest, take on coal, obtain provisions, and offload prisoners. The end of 1862 saw yet another two ships ransomed and one burned (table 14.1).

Two other crew members—Robert Egan and Antonio Bartelli— were closer in age to White, and he may well have spent much of his time with them. Egan was an incorrigible scamp. Along with three other orphans or runaways from Liverpool, he had found his way on to the *Bahama* and subsequently signed on to the *Alabama* in Terceira. The British, US, and Confederate navies limited minors, but teenagers up to the age of eighteen could commonly serve in the junior rank of Boy.[1] For £2 per month, they served the officers, assisted the cooks, and carried messages. As Marvel relates, "In their abundant leisure [they] played pranks and acted like the children they really were."[2]

Sinclair relates one incident in which Egan really landed in trouble. Some of the sailors had brought along a pet cat from Terceira, of which they were immensely fond. When the cat went missing,

Table 14.1. Captures by the *Alabama*, November 21–December 7, 1862

Date	Ship	Home Port	From/to	Cargo	Disposition
November 30	Parker Cook	Boston	Santo Domingo	Provisions	Burned
December 5	Union	Baltimore	Jamacia	General	Released on ransom bond
December 7	Ariel	New York	Aspinwall (Colón)	Assorted cargo	Released on ransom bond

Source: O.R. Navy, Ser. I: Vol. 3, pp. 677–81.

Egan was suspected of mischief, spread-eagled on a mast, and interrogated. At first, he denied any knowledge of the cat, but, just then,
a sail was sighted and one of the guns readied for action. When the
cover was taken from the muzzle, the frightened animal jumped out
of the barrel. Unable to withstand the punishment any longer, Egan
confessed, and when asked why he had done it, replied, "Oh to see
what effect the firing would have on the cat!"[3] Although he was incorrect about White's legal status, Marvel makes an insightful comment
about the Boys as a group: "Six of them served the ship, including
the erstwhile slave David White, who, considering his background,
probably behaved himself."[4]

Bartelli was Semmes's personal steward; he had been another captain's steward on the *Bahama*, but had had a rough time of it. According to Semmes, he had been treated too harshly. Bartelli was possibly
an alcoholic, but Semmes saw potential and was drawn to his forlorn
manner. They made a deal that, if Bartelli stayed sober on board the
Alabama, he could "have a little frolic on shore" so long as he always
returned sober. As usual, Semmes described Bartelli in stereotypical
terms: "He was an Italian, evidently of gentle blood, and as, with the
Italians, drinking to intoxication is not an ineradicable vice, I felt
confident that he could be reformed under proper treatment."[5]

Semmes's description of his *Sumter* steward Ned, described in
chapter 10, suggests that he liked his servants docile, and Bartelli fit
the bill perfectly. Semmes described Bartelli as a

> pale, . . . delicate, and soft-mannered young man . . . an obedi-
> ent, respectful, and attentive major-domo. . . . He took care of my
> linen like a woman, washing it himself when we were at sea, and
> sending it to some careful laundress when in port. I shall, per-
> haps, astonish a great many husbands and heads of families, when
> I tell them, that every shirt-button was always in its place, and
> that I never had to call for needle and thread under difficulties!

My mess affairs never gave me the least trouble. My table was always well supplied, and when guests were expected, I could safely leave the arrangements to Bartelli; and then it was a pleasure to observe the air, and grace of manner and speech, with which he would receive my visitors and conduct them into the cabin.[6]

Although the captain doesn't mention it, Bartelli's duties also included waxing and curling Semmes's mustaches into long narrow points. A faithful servant to the end, he drowned along with White in the battle off Cherbourg.

One notable clash early in the new year—a battle with the Union gunboat *Hatteras* just off Galveston—may have added yet another lesson to White's curriculum in servitude. From captured newspapers, Semmes was aware that a naval expedition under Nathanial Banks was to gather near Galveston by January 10, in order to invade Texas. Semmes's plan—in Admiral Porter's words, "bearding the lion in his den"—was to attack the fleet under cover of darkness, sink and scatter what he could, and retreat.[7] However, when he arrived off Galveston, all that he found were five second-rate blockade enforcers, among them the USS *Hatteras*, a slow, commercial side-wheeler the navy had refitted in 1861. Seeing an unfamiliar ship in the distance, the *Hatteras*, under the command of Lt. Homer C. Blake, was sent out to investigate.

As usual, deception would be key, but here Semmes may have stepped over a line. Approaching the *Alabama* as the sun set, Blake's officers called out "What ship is that?" whereupon Kell replied that it was the HMS *Petrel*. Suspicious, Blake indicated that he was sending over a boat. As the boat arrived, Semmes continued the ruse by expressing his willingness to receive the American officers. When the two ships were close enough that he was sure his guns would be decisive, he gave the order for the *Alabama* to let loose its entire starboard battery.[8]

The Combat between the Alabama and the Hatteras, off Galveston, on the 11ᵗʰ of January, 1863.

FIGURE 14.1. "The Combat between the *Alabama* and the *Hatteras*, off Galveston, on the 11th of January, 1863." *Illustration from Semmes,* Memoirs of Service Afloat. *Author's collection.*

Blake and the *Hatteras*'s crew put up a fierce fight.[9] But even without the element of surprise, the *Hatteras*—lesser armed and designed primarily as a side-wheel riverboat—was no match for the *Alabama.* After the surprise broadside, it sank in about twenty minutes with two dead and about five injured.[10] Some twenty years after this battle, Porter described Semmes's actions as "perfidy."[11]

Porter was in a position to know, but he too had his own agenda. As previously mentioned, he was born into one of the most storied and distinguished families in the US Navy; his father, David Porter Sr., was a midshipman on the *Constellation* during the capture in 1798 of the French frigate *L'Insurgente.* During the First Barbary War (1801–7), Porter Sr. was first lieutenant on the *Philadelphia* and was taken prisoner when it ran aground in Tripoli harbor. The father went on to command the USS *Essex* in the Pacific and, later, the frigate *John Adams*. David Dixon Porter inherited from his father a deep understanding of the navy and of maritime warfare, as well as an aggressive fighting spirit. He also played a pivotal role in the Civil War, commanding the flotilla that took New Orleans in April 1862, and then working closely with Gen. Ulysses S. Grant to open up the Mississippi at Vicksburg. After the war, he remained a close confidant of Grant and an important commandant of the Naval Academy.

Porter was hardly in a position to complain about deception in mercantile warfare: after all, Semmes was emulating Porter Sr.'s tactic, while commanding the *Essex* during the War of 1812, of raising British colors to allay enemy suspicions. With the *Hatteras* incident, however, Porter draws a line—albeit a blurry one. It is acceptable, he seems to have said, to board a merchantman under false colors, but another thing entirely to receive an enemy's military emissary under false colors and then fire a broadside.

Lieutenant Low's biographer, Hoole, makes an interesting, if unsubstantiated, comment about this battle: "With six shell holes in her upper hull and 118 prisoners of war crowding her deck, the *Alabama* worked her tedious way back out of the Gulf of Mexico, southeastward toward Jamaica, every rebel aboard from Raphael Semmes to David White swelling with pride: in fair combat with an enemy warship of her own age, tonnage, and armament she proved herself as sweet a fighting ship as ever sailed the sea."[12]

In reality the attack on the *Hatteras* could hardly be described as "fair combat," not only because the ship was a vulnerable sidewheeler taken by deception, if not deceit. It was also outgunned. The *Hatteras* had four 32-pounder cannons, two Parrot 30-pounder rifles, one 20-pounder rifled cannon, and one 12-pounder howitzer, for a total of 220 pounds. The *Alabama* carried six 32-pounders, an 8-inch pivot shell gun, and a rifled 100-pound Blakely pivot cannon—360 pounds in all.

Nor is there any known primary account of White's reaction to the battle—Hoole's inference conveniently reinforces the conventional racist trope. Given White's limited experience, however, he might conceivably have drawn the wrong conclusion—that under the command of this captain, battle with a Union warship would be among the least of his perils.

Chapter 15

~≈~

Port Royal, the *Olive Jane*, and the *John A. Parks*

Back in the Northeast, as if the devastation of a whaling fleet was not humiliating enough, news of the sinking of an American navy warship was explosive. It took ten days for word of the *Hatteras* battle to travel north from Galveston. The *New York Tribune* reported the incident in a front-page column on January 27, 1863. As more detailed reports arrived, the *Tribune, Times,* and *Herald* provided continuous coverage over the last few days of January and well into February. And that was just New York—the sensational news traveled around the world. It didn't matter that the *Hatteras* was an obsolete side-wheeler—outgunned and overpowered by deception—the bottom line was that Semmes had vanquished the US Navy.

The battle had two important consequences. First, it turned Semmes into a genuine international celebrity: going forward, he would not just be greeted, but positively fêted by citizens in neutral ports sympathetic to the Confederacy. Second, outraged US authorities put intense diplomatic pressure on nominally nonaligned countries—especially British colonies—to enforce rules of neutrality. From now on, whenever the *Alabama* entered a port—Port Royal, Bahia, Cape Town, Singapore, and ultimately Cherbourg—there would always be a delicate interplay, if not clash, between these somewhat oppositional forces. Against this background was Semmes's constant struggle to keep the crew from deserting, or just falling off the wagon.

By the time news reached New York that the *Alabama* had sunk the *Hatteras*, Semmes had made for Port Royal, Jamaica, where the ship docked from January 20 to 26. To exit the Gulf, he had to sail through the narrow Yucatán channel between Mexico and Cuba. The nine-day voyage was exhausting and difficult since the *Alabama* was sailing against the wind and the currents, and because of the constant vigilance necessary to avoid US Navy vessels. In addition, he had more than one hundred enemy prisoners from the *Hatteras* on board. Here Semmes may have learned from the experience of John Roberts, the naval officer who became a national hero in 1799 by navigating the captured *L'Insurgente* to friendly St. Kitts with a small, well-armed crew, all the while vastly outnumbered by the captured French sailors.

The first evening in Port Royal, Semmes would add a musical lesson to White's curriculum: a vivid demonstration of British naval and port officials' sympathy for the Confederacy. The *Alabama* was docked alongside the British warship *Greyhound*, while Homer Blake, the captured captain of the *Hatteras*, was yet to be released. As a gesture of goodwill, the deck officer of the *Greyhound* instructed his ship's bandmaster to play "Dixie," which the band did—in Semmes's words—with "slowness, sweetness, and pathos."[1] Blake objected, and in response, the band played "Yankee Doodle" but with such a willful, cacophonous imitation of musicality that the Confederate officers were in stitches. As later described by Porter, "The military bands played that lovely air Dixie with all the pathos they could throw into the music . . . while . . . they performed Yankee Doodle with all their drums, cymbals and squawking clarionets in the harshest manner, as if in mockery of the American nation."[2]

The formal correspondence, which followed a few days later, literally papered over the incident so as to preserve both Blake's honor and British neutrality.[3] The official correspondence omits the part about the mangled "Yankee Doodle" and "squawking clarionets," but Semmes just couldn't help chortling in his memoirs that "the effect was electric; the officers had to hold their sides to preserve their dignity."[4]

White would have known nothing of the official correspondence and formal declarations of neutrality. There is little doubt, however, that he would have witnessed the evening's entertainment, and no doubt at all of the vivid musical lesson it conveyed: that this vessel was only stopping in Confederacy-friendly ports. That lesson was reinforced by the thralled excitement with which the population of the city greeted the ship.

Then transpired the kind of bifurcated shore experience—Semmes's versus the crew's—that would become the pattern. Semmes gave a speech to the Kingston Chamber of Commerce in which he expounded on the benefits of slavery to an audience that "cheered lustily."[5] Mentioning that he needed some rest and recreation to restore his "wasted energies," Semmes was hosted by his "excellent friend" Mr. Fyfe (*sic*) at Flamstead, one of the most storied plantation homes in Jamaica, located 3,300 feet above sea level in the Blue Mountains.[6] Years later, Semmes waxed lyrical about his love for nature, interior décor, hospitality, books, servants, and horses:

I was awakened the next morning by the merry songs of a hundred birds, that came appropriately blended with the perfume of the flowers that clustered around my windows; and I have seldom looked upon a more beautiful picture, than when I threw back the blinds, and caught a view of the landscape, rejoicing in the morning's sun, with all its wealth of tropical fruits and flowers, and the sea—the glorious sea—glittering like a mirror in the distance. . . . With a library, servants, and horses at your command, you are literally left to take care of yourself—meeting the family in the parlors and sitting-rooms, as much, or as little as you please.[7]

While Semmes was enjoying his repose, back in Port Royal the crewmen on leave were pursuing diversions of another kind. US consul John W. Camps kept a record of the crew's drunken misbehavior.[8] Lieutenant Sinclair had a devil of a time rounding up sailors from the local brothels, and many were brought back in irons. Meanwhile, the paymaster, Clarence B. Younge, helped himself to some gold from the ship's safe and defected. Kell then went ashore with an armed patrol, found Younge in a brothel, and without any interference from the local authorities, had him dragged back to the ship, where he was summarily court-martialed. At that point, Galt took over as paymaster and let Llewellyn do the doctoring.

White would have known about all of this, but perhaps another incident carried with it an even more formidable message. Two sailors, Tom Bowse and Bill Bower, having been forcibly brought back to the ship, attempted to return to shore by commandeering a dugout canoe that had come alongside the *Alabama* paddled by two Black men. Observing this attempted escape, Semmes ordered a cutter to pursue the canoe. In an effort to outrun the cutter, Bowse and Bower lightened the canoe by simply tossing the Black men into the shark-infested waters of Port Royal Bay. After the sailors were captured and forcibly brought back to the *Alabama*, Semmes interrogated them before the mast:

Semmes: "You're a pretty pair of fellows. You not only tried to desert your ship and flag, but you endeavored to commit murder, in your attempt to escape!"

"Murder!" Blurted Bowse with a start of horror. "We never thought of such a thing, sir. Them Jamaica n——s, they take to water as natural as South Sea Islanders. There's no such thing as drowning them, sir."

"That was it, your honor," put in Bower; ". . . it was only a bit of a joke, you see, sir, played on the officer in the cutter. We knew he'd stop to pick 'em up, and so give us the weather gauge of him."[9]

"That may do very well for the murder," rejoined Semmes. "What about the desertion?"

"No idea of deserting your honor, . . ." insisted Bowse. "We only meant to have another bit of a frolic, and come back in good time, before the ship sailed."[10]

White may have understood that even white men were not allowed to leave this vessel and would be dragged back if they tried. But more significantly, he might have noticed the casual disregard for the life of Black men, shared both by Semmes and at least some of the *Alabama*'s crew. The assertion that Black men can't drown was sufficient defense against a charge of attempted murder.

Semmes knew that he couldn't stay in the port long enough to allow word to reach the US Navy. So, on the night of January 25, the *Alabama* slipped out of Port Royal and headed toward Santo Domingo. After a brief sojourn in the capital, in which Semmes visited the Cathedral of Santa María la Menor, the *Alabama* headed east into the Atlantic, then south to Bahia. Along the way, four vessels were ransomed and a further sixteen met their fiery demise (table 15.1).

One capture, the *Olive Jane*, had an exceptional cargo that required exceptional measures. On its way to Boston and New York from Bordeaux, it was loaded with luxury French goods including Bordeaux wine, brandy, goose liver pâté, and other delicacies. Semmes and his officers realized there would be hell to pay if his crew got anywhere

Table 15.1. Captures by the *Alabama*, January 26–March 2, 1863

Date	Ship	Home Port	From/to	Cargo	Disposition
January 26	Golden Rule	New York	Aspinwall (Colón)	Food, medicine	Burned
January 27	Chastelaine	Boston	Guadeloupe	In ballast	Burned
February 3	Palmetto	New York	Puerto Rico	Lumber	Burned
February 21	Golden Eagle	New Bedford, MA	Cork	Guano	Burned
February 21	Olive Jane	New York	Bordeaux	Wine, brandy, luxury goods	Burned
February 27	Washington	New York	Cork	Guano	Released on ransom bond
March 1	Bethiah Thayer	Rockland, ME	Cork	Guano	Ransomed
March 2	John A. Parks	Hallowell, ME	Montevideo	Lumber	Burned

Source: O.R. Navy, Ser. I: Vol. 3, pp.677–81.

near that cargo, and he actively feared another spirit-driven mutiny. The solution, which worked, was to set out a table on the *Olive Jane* and allow the boarding crew to feast and drink under the watchful eye of the officers, in a controlled repast. Then he wasted no time in burning the *Olive Jane*, before anyone could smuggle the coveted liquor on board. Semmes remarked on the extraordinary spectacle:

> What a splendid libation was here to old Neptune! I did not permit so much as a bottle of brandy, or a basket of champagne to be brought on board, . . . though, I doubt not, the throats of some of my vagabonds, who had so recently cooled off, from the big frolic they had had in Jamaica, were as dry as powder-horns. There were the richest of olives, and pâtés de fois gras, going to tickle the palates of the New York shoddyites, and other nouveau-riche plebeians, destroyed in that terrible conflagration. I should have permitted Bartelli, and the other stewards to have a short run among these delicacies, but for the wine and the brandy. A Fouché could not have prevented the boats' crews from smuggling some of it on board, and then I might have had another Martinique grog-watering on my hands.[11]

It is interesting, and understandable, that Semmes prevented Bartelli, a recovering alcoholic, from getting anywhere near the *Olive Jane*'s luxurious spirits. Yet for all the incessant boozing in port, the smuggling of alcohol from captures, and the constant battles to keep the *Alabama*'s crew sober, as meticulously documented by all of the ship's officers, there is no association of White with alcohol at all. This makes sense, since he appears to have been associated with Powell's temperance-advocating sailors' network.

There were other moments of excitement up on the deck. Sinclair tells the story of Johnny Raw, a bird that reached the quarter boat one day, exhausted and starved. The sailors had adopted him as a pet.

He was described as black as a raven, about the size of a field lark, with a noble carriage. The bird had a remarkable gait, hopping both legs together rapidly with giant leaps. One day, Johnny Raw happened under the lee of the mainsail and was dashed into the sea. At the crew's request, the main topsail was hove to the mast, and a boat lowered to retrieve the cold, wet, shivering, forlorn-looking bird. He soon recovered, returning to his "piratical expeditions to the mess-cloths."[12]

At this early stage, a modicum of good feeling still existed between the officers and crew, which may have been most vividly expressed with music in the evenings. According to Semmes, the *Alabama* had signed on a valuable asset in the form of an Irish fiddler named Michael Mahoney, who would desert in Cape Town to Semmes's great consternation.[13] Semmes describes an evening scene:

> After duties of the day were over, [the crew] would generally assemble on the forecastle, and with violin, and tambourine—they would extemporize a ball-room, by moving the shot-racks, coils of rope, and other impediments, out of the way, and, with handkerchiefs tied around the waists of some of them, to indicate who were to be the ladies of the party, they would get up a dance with all due form and ceremony; the ladies, in particular, endeavoring to imitate all the airs and graces of the sex—the only drawback being a little hoarseness of the voice, and now and then the use of an expletive.[14]

According to Semmes, at the end, all joined in the inspiring refrain "We'll live and die in Dixie!" At 8 p.m., the night watches were set with the strike of the ship's bell, and festivities ended.[15]

On March 2, in the middle of the Atlantic, the capture of the *John A. Parks* (carrying lumber from Maine to Montevideo)[16] gave Semmes access to the latest batch of newspapers, which carried the news of the formal adoption of the Emancipation Proclamation. Semmes doesn't say much about it, but the report must have festered, and three weeks later, he couldn't resist a dig at the "'sainted' Abraham."[17]

Thus, news that the Emancipation Proclamation had been formalized in January 1863 took more than two months to reach the *Alabama*, then about 1,500 miles east of Bermuda in the North Atlantic. Sooner or later, White would have heard; but Emancipation didn't pertain to him, since he was already free, and anyway the proclamation itself didn't apply to Delaware's enslaved, as it was not a state in insurrection. The proclamation nevertheless had a profound effect in Delaware itself, where the legislature responded out of concern that the state would become overrun with runaways from the Deep South.

The April newspapers in Delaware announced the passage of a new "Act in Relation to Free Negroes and Mulattoes."[18] Section 1 of the act included an important change to the exemption under which White had traveled to Philadelphia. It stated that "no free negro or free mulatto can gain a legal residence, and any resident free negro or free mulatto who shall voluntarily leave the State for five days shall be deemed a non-resident, unless such person be a mariner or waterman engaged in that occupation and on board of some vessel *belonging to a citizen of this State*" (emphasis added).[19]

With this act, the Delaware legislature made it harder for free Blacks to enter the state, reduced the time it allowed Delaware's free Blacks to be out of state from sixty to five days, and eliminated the 1807 exemption under which White had been allowed to sign onto a Philadelphia packet. From then on, free Black men could no longer sign onto a Cope Line vessel, enjoy all the benefits of wages earned outside the state, and expect to return without penalty. We will never know if White was aware of this change in the law, but it is possible that Semmes, a sea lawyer with an avid and insatiable interest in captured American newspapers, would eventually have found out.

In any event, the impact was the same: with no specific grandfather clause, the new law applied to White, who from this point, had no legal option to return to Delaware.[20]

Chapter 16

~≋~

Brazil and the South Atlantic

E arly in March, Semmes turned the *Alabama* south and headed
for Brazil, crossing the equator at 5 p.m. on March 29, 1863.
Semmes logged the wind and the current but made no mention
of the traditional maritime initiation normal for landsmen. Kell,
however, recorded what transpired on the *Sumter*, describing it as a
"christening [of] all young sailors who are for the first time passing
from one hemisphere to the other, after which initiation they are ever
thereafter entitled to roam old ocean [*sic*] as one of Neptune's own."[1]
Plausibly, White was subjected to this initiation. "If permission was
granted by the captain," Stephanie Koenig observes,

> the entire crew would partake in a performance, in which Nep-
> tune was portrayed by one of the oldest sailors, a veritable "Jack
> Tar of the olden time," with a great curling wig, an immense
> beard rope yarn, bearing in his hand a trident, and drawn aft upon
> the deck in his car of state, fitted out of a gun-carriage. . . . After
> saluting the officer of the deck, asked "permission to examine the
> crew that he might learn if there were any on board that ship to
> be christened. . . ." The attendant who acted as Neptune's bar-
> ber then lathered the face and beard most thoroughly with tar,

and with a huge wooden razor scraped the face vigorously. He was then plunged in a boat filled with salt water, and rising from this [he] presented a most forlorn and deplorable picture, and all hands saluted him as an old tar, the son of the Great Neptune, to the merry enjoyment of his brother sailors.[2]

Along the way, Semmes ransomed another two ships and burned ten more, adding another twelve chronometers to his collection (table 16.1). Fox has noted the distance between Semmes's anodyne descriptions of these captures and the testimony of the captured. Among these accounts, Frederick Adams, first officer of the *Nora*, captured on March 25, said that he and sixty other prisoners were forced to huddle on the open deck of the *Alabama* in a space 20 square feet. They were fed "wormy biscuit and half-rotten pork" taken from a captured whaler that had been at sea for four years.[3] The crew was undisciplined and inept. As for the ship, "she was dirty, never in what a sailor calls a shipshape condition, and there was about as much wasted by the men as they consumed. . . . While the prisoners were starved, the pirate crew had an abundance, and waste was the rule. The armament of the ship and the small arms of the men were alike in a slovenly condition, and neither were in proper condition for use."[4]

According to a newspaper report:

The sailors appeared like a lot of thieves, taking everything they could stow about their persons, and not appearing to take any notice of their officer, the officer himself not seeming to know much about the ship [under capture], except as regards the burning of her. . . . So little discipline was there that the Alabama's men were smoking segars [*sic*] in the boat that took the Captain on board the Alabama's decks. The men were lying about aft, as well as forward, smoking pipes and segars. . . . The ship was very dirty, and everything looking in disorder.[5]

Table 16.1. Captures by the *Alabama*, March 15–May 3, 1863

Date	Vessel	Home Port	From/to	Cargo	Disposition
March 15	Punjaub	Boston	Calcutta	Guano	Released on ransom bond
March 23	Morning Star	Boston	Calcutta	General	Released on ransom bond
March 23	Kingfisher	New Bedford, MA	Cruising	Whale oil	Burned
March 25	Nora	Boston	Calcutta	Salt	Burned
March 25	Charles Hill	Boston	Montevideo	Salt	Burned
April 4	Louisa Hatch	Rockland, ME	Cardiff	Coal	Burned
April 15	Lafayette	New Bedford, MA	Cruising	Whale oil	Burned
April 15	Kate Cory	Westport, CT	Cruising	Whale oil	Burned
April 24	Nye	New Bedford, MA	Cruising	Whale oil	Burned
April 26	Dorcas Prince	New York	Shanghai	Coal	Burned
May 3	Union Jack	New York	Shanghai	General	Burned
May 3	Sea Lark	Boston	San Francisco	General	Burned

Source: *O.R. Navy*, Ser. I: Vol. 3, pp. 677–81.

At the beginning of April, the *Alabama* reached the remote Brazilian island of Fernando de Noronha, a tiny, seldom-visited penal colony described by Boykin as "a prodigious marker standing on one of the principal commercial thoroughfares of the world; it was a milepost from which passing mariners took new departure and sailed on. It was sighted by more ships, yet visited by fewer, perhaps, than any other spot on the civilized globe."[6] It was also governed by a petty military official, Maj. Sebastião José Basilio Pyrrho, who cravenly hosted Semmes at his home and allowed him to land prisoners, obtain provisions, sell coal from the captured *Louisa Hatch*, and wait around for a hopeful rendezvous with the tender, the *Agrippina*. Basilio also looked the other way when the *Alabama* made a foray from the neutral coast, then captured and burned two more American whalers, the *Lafayette* and the *Kate Cory* (table 16.1).

By this time, Union fury at the *Alabama*'s swath of destruction was seriously threatening already poor British and American relations. The same April 2, 1863, edition of *Harper's Weekly* that carried Winslow Homer's illustration also fired a rhetorical broadside, arguing that "there has never been a time when hatred of the English was so deep or so wide-spread as it is at present. There has never been a period at which war with England could have been more generally welcomed than at present—if we were free to engage in a foreign war."[7]

Two weeks later, having torched the *Union Jack* and the clipper *Sea Lark* on May 3, the *Alabama* reached Bahia. The day before was a disastrous one back home: one of the Confederacy's key generals, Stonewall Jackson, was fatally shot by friendly fire. It was said that "the wail of the stricken South resounded through the land."[8]

The going was tough. It was no simple matter to transport the sixty or so prisoners taken off the *Union Jack* and the magnificent clipper *Sea Lark*. One incident, in particular, stands out, both for what actually happened and for what Semmes omitted from his log and memoir.

The captain of the *Union Jack*, Charles P. Weaver, was traveling to China with his family as well as an American minister, the Rev. Franklin Wright (on his way to take up his appointment as US counsel to Fuzhou), Wright's wife, and an Irish stewardess. Sinclair tells us what Semmes left out:

An Irish stewardess was brought on board from one of the prizes, and sad to relate, a little "how came you so" [that is, drunk]. This charmer was given a free ride over the side, it being necessary to rig a "whip" from the yard-arm for her accommodation. She was particularly severe upon our gallant though modest commander, applying to him epithets of so emphatic a character that we omit them mostly, but "pirate, rebel, freebooter," etc. were the mild ones.[9]

Here, once again, Semmes omits the odd details that might compromise his self-serving narrative, but also notable is the snarky mirth with which the officers regularly described the anger expressed and anguish experienced by their prisoners.[10] Sinclair gleefully applied this tone to the rage and terror of an Irishwoman having no connection to their conflict. He makes sure to tell his readers she was "how came you so" (inebriated) in order to diminish her social standing and reason, and therefore the legitimacy of her opposition. Together with the incessant stereotyping, caricaturing, and insulting of Yankees, Mexicans, jacks (the Liverpool sailors), Italians, Portuguese, and Brazilians (and these were just the white folks), this practice suggests that the approach of Semmes and his officers to racial and cultural identity reflected, among other things, a reflexive contempt for those who looked and spoke differently from themselves.

The *Alabama* arrived in Bahia on May 11, and there began once again the familiar round of diplomatic negotiations, grandiose welcoming galas for the officers, and drunken imbroglios by the crew.

The US consul, Thomas Y. Wilson, wrote nothing in his official correspondence about the *Alabama*'s crew. His chief concerns centered on the cargo of the captured vessels and preventing the *Alabama* from being coaled.[11] Here the authorities were more emphatic, invoking a neutrality rule and asking Semmes to leave within twenty-four hours. Taking advantage of the weakness of the Brazilian authorities, he simply rejected the request and threatened the vengeance by the future Southern Confederacy—which was all it took for the Brazilian authorities to back down. A British merchant then invited Semmes and his officers to a lavish reception. "Mr. Ogilvie's tasteful residence overlooked the bay . . . his grounds, redolent of the perfumes of tropical flowers, were brilliantly illuminated, and a fine band of music charmed not only the revelers, but the numerous ships in the Bay."[12] As for the crew, Semmes merely reports that "Jack had his frolic."[13]

On May 22, the *Alabama* finally left Brazil and headed east into the South Atlantic. Before reaching the remote, bleak port of Saldanha—some 60 miles north of Cape Town—Semmes added another eight chronometers to his collection (table 16.2).

By now the crew and captain of the *Alabama* were showing signs of disorder and fatigue; the ship itself was deteriorating under the strain of the long and arduous voyage. Capt. John McCallum, whose ship *Gildersleeve* was burned on May 25, reported that discipline on the *Alabama* was "of the worst description, as bad as none at all. The men are a hard-looking lot—of all nationalities."[14] Capt. W. Loveland of the *Amazonian*, burned on June 2, reported that he was treated with great scorn: "Told . . . he could not expect any favor, being from Boston, . . . the captain was sent to sleep on deck and to mess with the motley crew of that and another vessel. There seemed to be no want on board the *Alabama*. Many articles lay around in sad waste and confusion, such as curiosities of every kind, parrots, albums, ornaments, musical instruments. The passenger was left with a general impression of squalor, greed, and disorder."[15]

Table 16.2. Captures by the *Alabama*, May 25–August 5, 1863

Date	Ship	Home Port	From/to	Cargo	Disposition
May 25	Gildersleeve	New York	Calcutta	Coal	Burned
May 25	Justina	Baltimore	Rio de Janeiro	In ballast	Ransomed
May 29	Jabez Snow	Buckport, ME	Montevideo	Coal	Burned
June 2	Amazonian	Boston	Montevideo	Candles, soap	Burned
June 5	Talisman	New York	Shanghai	Coal	Burned
June 20	Conrad	Philadelphia	Buenos Aires	Wool	Fitted up as tender Tuscaloosa
July 2	Anna F. Schmidt	Boston	San Francisco	General	Burned
July 6	Express	Portsmouth, NH	Valparaiso	Guano	Burned
August 5	Sea Bride	Boston	Cape Town	Cloth, notions	Sold

Source: O.R. Navy, Ser. I: Vol. 3, pp. 677–81.

Even Sinclair noted that the ship was "storm-beaten and rusty."[16] On June 15, Semmes wrote in his log: "An ugly morning, with the weather squally; wind blowing half a gale, and quite a sea on. Our ship has certainly got to be very dull under canvas, for with a press of sail, and the wind a point free, she has made to-day but 8 knots. The consequence is that a stern chase has become a forlorn hope with us."[17]

Two weeks later, Semmes commented on his own senescence: "Monday, June 29: Ugly stormy-looking weather, with a rough sea and half a gale from the east. . . . Ship rolling and tumbling about, to my great discomfort. The fact is, I am getting too old to relish the rough usage of the sea. Youth sometimes loves to be rocked by a gale, but when we have passed the middle stage of life we love quiet and repose."[18] Here perhaps he was channeling James Biddle, another luminary from the early navy who served on board the *Philadelphia* together with David Dixon Porter's father, when it was grounded in 1803 in Tripoli. Biddle was sixty-three years old in 1846 when he wrote, "I have become heartily tired of the sea and all its anxieties and all its discomforts. I am aware that life at sea is just what it was forty-six years ago, when I first knew and liked it, and that the change is not in it, but in me."[19]

Meanwhile, the war back in the States had arrived at another key milestone: passage of the Enrollment Act in the North, which resulted in four days of dreadful riots in New York City (July 13–16), with much of the anger directed at the city's Black population. Among those caught up in the "bloody destructive episode," which included dozens of lynchings, was William Powell, who by this time was living with his family at the Colored Seamen's Home on Pearl Street.[20] He and his family narrowly escaped the mob when it came to ransack and burn the Seamen's Home. As he described their experience:

My family, including my invalid daughter, took refuge on the roof of the next house. I remained till the mob broke in and then narrowly escaped the same way. This was about 8 ½ p.m. We remained on the roof for an hour. It began to rain, as if the very heavens were shedding tears over the dreadful calamity.

How to escape from the roof of a five-story building with four females—and one a cripple—without a ladder was beyond my *not* excited imagination. But God came to my relief in the person of a little deformed, despised Israelite who, Samaritan-like, took my poor helpless daughter under his protection in his house. He also supplied me with a long rope. Though pitchy dark I took soundings with the rope to see if it would touch the next roof, after which I took a clove-hitch around the clothesline which led from one roof to the other over a space of about one hundred feet. I managed to lower my family down to the neighbor's yard. We were secreted in our friend's cellar till 11 p.m. when we were taken by the police and locked up in the station house for our safety.[21]

All this took place against the backdrop of the Battle of Gettysburg (July 1–3, 1863) and the success of the Vicksburg campaign (May 18– July 4, 1863)—a period often described as an inflexion point of the war. It may also be thought of as an inflexion point for the *Alabama* and specifically for Semmes, as reflected in the decreasing efficiency of the whole enterprise. In one way the sojourn in Brazil in May 1863 represented the apex of the voyage: in terms of captures, it was downhill from there. In the first nine months of its voyage, sailing from the Azores to Galveston, then to Jamaica and on to Brazil, the *Alabama* had traveled more than 11,000 nautical miles and captured 48 vessels: on average about 1 capture per 230 nautical miles. From Brazil to the coast of Africa, the ship had traveled some 3,500 miles and captured 10 vessels, or 1 per 350 nautical miles. From here on—Cape Town to Singapore, back to Cape Town, and finally to Cherbourg—it would travel 19,000 nautical miles and capture only 10 vessels: just 1 capture per 1,900 miles.

The diminishing returns notwithstanding, this record is a testament to Semmes's able, if not gifted, seamanship. Even while flaunting his lifelong affinity for danger and battle, he roamed the seas for three years with minimal external support, significantly impairing Union commerce, evading capture, and managing not to kill anyone during the captures—save the two crewmen of the *Hatteras*—all the while leading an unruly and undisciplined crew. Whether the ends justified the means is another matter entirely.

Approaching the coast of Africa in late June, the familiar sound of the wind and rigging was suddenly pierced by the scream of a circling petrel (described as a Cape pigeon), a bird that in Semmes's words "delights in the commotion of the elements." Boykin described it as a "harbinger of tempest."[22]

Chapter 17

☙

Cape of Good Hope

In the Southern Hemisphere winter of 1863, a year into the voyage and with no other choice, White had settled into whatever servile role the Confederates had set for him, including both waiting tables in the officers' mess and acting as a servant to Dr. Galt. Although his role may have been set early on and remained unchanged to the end, this isn't to say that White himself did not change. The period of his capture was critical because it spanned his growth from ages seventeen to eighteen. For most male teenagers, whether in bondage or not, this is a time of biological transition, from child to man.

Still, in two separate manifests, White's position on the *Alabama* is recorded as that of Boy: once in Semmes's muster roll of July 7, 1863 (fig. 17.1), and in an undated muster roll reported after the Battle of Cherbourg. Although the original is lost, an undated typescript copy can be found in the miscellaneous papers of the former Museum of the Confederacy, now in the collections of the Virginia Museum of History and Culture (fig. 17.2). The change in White's status from passenger cook on the *Tonawanda* to that of Boy on the *Alabama* was accompanied by a commensurate reduction in salary. In 1862, Semmes authorized the salaries of all seamen and recorded the salary of Boys as £2 per month (or $9.68/month, as he calculated). In his muster roll of July 1863, he recorded each seaman by name, station, and salary. On October 10, 1862, White was listed as Boy, still at a salary of £2/month.[1] Semmes added the designation "(cld)," perhaps acknowledging that by this time White was no longer a minor, and the status "colored" was more a matter of consistency with the default applied to adult Black men, as was the practice in the Union Navy until December 1862.

Now off the coast of Africa, Semmes sought a safe harbor where he could rest, make some repairs, and reconnoiter before approaching the cosmopolitan city of Cape Town—in those days still a British colony. The west coast of Africa had few suitable harbors south of Sierra Leone, so he chose Saldanha Bay, a magnificent natural harbor some sixty miles north of Cape Town.

Unlike Cape Town, Saldanha provided shelter from the furious winds from the northwest that bedevil ships anchored in Table Bay in winter. Semmes actually wondered in his memoirs why the Dutch built the city at Table Bay instead of Saldanha. The answer is simple: they founded Cape Town for the main purpose of provisioning ships coming and going from Batavia (the Dutch East Indies). They

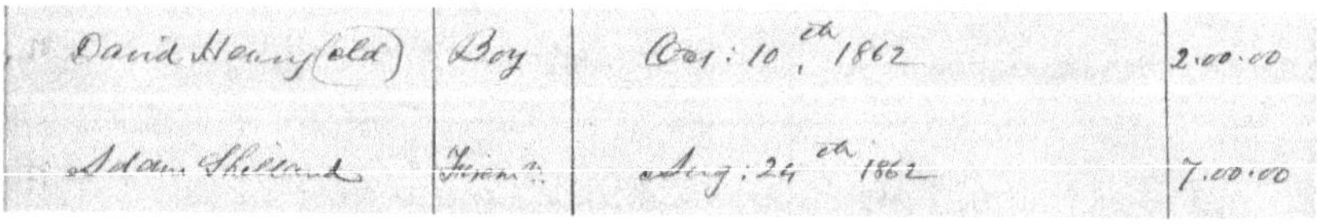

David Henry (cld)	Boy	Oct: 10th 1862	2.00.00
Adam Shilland	Firem.	Aug: 24th 1862	7.00.00

FIGURE 17.1. *Alabama* muster roll, July 7, 1863. *Semmes Family Papers, Alabama Department of Archives and History.*

David H. White*	Slave from Delaware	9 Oct. '62	(Wardroom Boy) Drwoned June 19/64.

FIGURE 17.2. Extract from *A General Muster-Roll of the Officers, Petty Officers, and Firemen of the* C. S. Steamer Alabama, *from the Day She Was Commissioned August 24th, 1862, to the Day She Was Sunk, June 19th, 1864. Virginia Museum of History and Culture.*

needed to grow fresh fruit and vegetables, but unlike the Cape of Good Hope, Saldanha had very little freshwater or wood. Saldanha was surrounded by a relatively barren coastal plain suitable mainly for game and hardscrabble grazing.

The ship was greeted warmly by the poor Afrikaner farmers who had settled on the bleak coast. They came from miles around and brought all sorts of exotic gifts that might have delighted the teenager: a wild peacock, a brace of pheasants, ostrich-eggs and feathers, springbok horns, and so on. There is no indication, however, that he ever left the vessel on this coast. In any event it all would have been alien; from a strictly geographic point of view, White was no more African than Semmes was French.

In this safe spot, over the following five days, Kell put the men to work making urgent engine repairs, applying long-overdue caulk, painting, and generally getting ready for the inevitable attention they expected when they entered Table Bay. For amusement, there was a great deal of excitement among the officers and crew about the prospect of hunting. Semmes too was thrilled by the abundance of game, including "quail, pheasant, deer in several varieties, and even the ostrich, lion, and the tiger."[2] Of course, there are no tigers in Africa, but it was a common misconception.[3]

Even in this remote outpost, where there wasn't a pub for sixty miles, the crew got into trouble—with one drawing a revolver on a master's mate. "The fact is," wrote Semmes of this moment, "I have a precious set of rascals on board—faithless in the matter of abiding by their contracts, liars, thieves and drunkards."[4]

All of this was prologue. The most significant thing about the Saldanha sojourn was that word of the *Alabama*'s arrival spread down the coast to Cape Town, which now eagerly anticipated the manifest. By August 4, US consul Walter Graham knew the *Alabama* was at Saldanha, and presumably the whole city knew as well.[5] The stage was now set for the familiar port opera seen previously in Jamacia and

Brazil, but this time even grander. All the elements that had contributed to the excitement were amplified: the *Alabama* was even more famous, the American consul was even more upset, and the city of Cape Town even more sympathetic to the Confederacy. But now, on August 5, as the *Alabama* approached the city that was eagerly awaiting its arrival, it encountered a sail that turned out to be an American bark, the *Sea Bride*, which Semmes captured in full view of the city. With this feat, the *Alabama* became something more than just an exciting curiosity, and veritably sailed into folklore (fig. 17.3).[6]

At this moment in its history, Cape Town had a heterogeneous population of some 22,000, about half of whom were white and half Cape Colored. In its heyday, before the Suez Canal opened in 1870, Cape Town was known as the "Tavern of the Seas." Unlike Fernando de Noronha, which Boykin described as a place that every ship saw and skipped, Cape Town was a place every passing ship saw and stopped.

No matter that the harbor itself was notoriously poor and exposed to the furious wind from the northwest that whipped the Cape in winter. Capetonians have an affectionate term, the "Cape Doctor," for the persistent, dry southeasterly wind that blows from spring to late summer (September to March in the Southern Hemisphere), but it is the winter northwesters that do the damage. The Dutch found this out the hard way in May 1697, when a number of Dutch East India Company (VOC) ships were blown from their anchors and two important vessels, the *Waddinxveen* and *Oosterland*, were lost. Driven east by a furious northwester, they foundered near Paarden Eiland beach and Milnerton lagoon on the eastern shore of Table Bay. In fact, a subsequent review by Dutch officials in Batavia suggested using Simon's Town, located on the other side of the Cape, as an alternative anchorage for the Dutch fleets. It took another forty-five years and some fifteen more disasters before VOC vessels were actively prohibited from anchoring in Table Bay between mid-May

Figure 17.3. "*Daar kom die Alibama*," as sung in Afrikaans (*traditional*). See note 6 for a translation.

and mid-August.[7] By entering Table Bay in early August, Semmes was once again tempting fate by daring the wind.

The billowing white clouds—known as the tablecloth—tumbling off Table Mountain high above Cape Town were startlingly beautiful, and for over two hundred years, despite the wind, the port had been the central pivot and victualing station on the main highway between the Atlantic and Indian Oceans.[8] Diversions abounded for visiting sailors. Among the most famous was Black Sophie's bordello—the eponymous Sophie, a notorious crimp and madam, who lured sailors who patronized her establishment into the guano mines on Dassen Island.[9]

Once again, White would likely have been unaware of the diplomatic imbroglio that resulted from the capture of the *Sea Bride*, the purported violations of neutrality, and the interactions with a consort vessel, the *Tuscaloosa*.[10] Sinclair refers to "a long and tedious correspondence . . . a cross-fire of formidable documents."[11] The contentious correspondence between Consul Walter Graham, commander in chief of British naval forces Sir Baldwin Walker, governor of Cape Town Sir Philip Wodehouse, and Lord Russell is indeed voluminous, much of it eagerly followed by readers of the *New York Times*.[12]

Graham's dispatches to Washington focused primarily on the *Sea Bride*'s capture, disposing of prize cargoes, and sorting out living and transport arrangements for prize crews, including those of the *Sea Bride* and *Rockingham*. Different US consular officials had slightly different foci in their reports, but all appear to have been chiefly concerned with prize crews and cargoes. Graham never mentions White, which is odd given how well White's kidnapping had been covered in the Philadelphia and New York newspapers. It would have been out of character for Graham, as consul, to omit encountering White if it had ever occurred.

None of this would have been known to White, who certainly experienced the frenzied reception in Cape Town, of which there are several astonished descriptions, including this one, from Sinclair:

> The scene on the hill-tops commanding the sea, the morning of the capture, as viewed from the deck of the *Alabama*, beggars description . . . every vehicle that could be commanded was pressed into service, for the ride to the point of vantage, and price was no

object to the sight-seers. . . . It is safe to say Cape Town was almost depopulated, and the excitement emphasized by the general
turnout to visit the ship at her anchors. Every imaginable form
and model of boat were represented in the throng around the ship
. . . anything that could float was brought into requisition.[13]

According to the *Cape Argus* of August 8:

The inhabitants, rich and poor, halt, maimed, lame and blind—not
only men and maidens, young men and children, but old women
"dragons and all deep" went off to see the Alabama, her captain
and her officers . . . they rushed up the ladder, up the sides of the
ship, swung up by the rattlings [*sic*], crawled through port holes,
over the rails, wherever there was space to crawl, or anything to
get hold of, there were human beings swarming like bees about
a hive. They hung in bunches, scrambled over each other, buzz-
ing, bawling and waspy old gentlemen, lazy old drones, queen
bees, honey bees and bees of every description hung together and
squeezed each other with dreadfully desperate determination. . . .
When the decks were full the persevering ones mounted the sides
of the ship, climbed the rigging, sat about on the gun carriages,
went from aft to for'd from fa'd to below in the cabin, engine
room, and forecastle—everywhere.[14]

Bartelli exulted in his role as majordomo, standing outside
Semmes's cabin, and White was probably also involved as the wardroom Boys were summoned to help out.[15] Semmes later described
the scene in his memoir:

Bartelli, my faithful steward, was in his element during the con-
tinuance of this great levée on board the *Alabama*. He had dressed
himself with scrupulous care, and posting himself at my cabin-

door, with the air of a chamberlain to a king, he refused admission to all comers, until they had first presented him with a card, and been duly announced. Pressing some of the ward-room Boys into his service, he served refreshments to his numerous guests, in a style that did my menage infinite credit. Fair women brought off bouquets with them, which they presented with a charming grace, and my cabin was soon garlanded with flowers. Some of these were immortelles peculiar to the Cape of Good Hope, and for months afterward, they retained their places around the large mirror that adorned the after-part of my cabin, with their colors almost as bright as ever. During my entire stay, my table was loaded with flowers, and the most luscious grapes, and other fruits, sent off to me every morning, by the ladies of the Cape, sometimes with, and sometimes without, a name.[16]

A correspondent in the *Cape Town Advertiser and Mail* wrote, "There is hardly a man now living and moving in the realm of Christendom who has a better prospect of hereafter passing into a hero and becoming the principal character of an epic poem or drama than Captain Semmes of the *Alabama*."[17] Some twenty years later, Admiral Porter indeed compared Semmes to a principal character of an epic poem—albeit not the heroic kind intended by the newspaper's correspondent.

Chapter 18

꩜

Simon's Town

So it went for several days, until Friday, August 7, when the wind intervened. On that evening, a Bremen brig was wrecked off Paarden Eiland, not far from where the *Oosterland* had foundered in 1697. The second edition of Semmes's postwar memoir, published in 1887, includes a graphic illustration of the turbulent harbor from the perspective of Paarden Eiland and Milnerton, a northwester pushing the *Alabama* dangerously toward the eastern shore (fig. 18.1).[1]

Discretion being the better part of valor, in this instance, as soon as the gale subsided the next morning, the *Alabama* left Cape Town for Simon's Town in False Bay. As the Dutch had learned, Simon's Town offered much better shelter from the wind. Besides, it was now a British naval installation, where Semmes was warmly welcomed by the friendly British admiral Baldwin Wake Walker, and where he could secure further repairs. It wasn't far from Cape Town—some 30 miles by stagecoach—and by 1863, there was reliable telegraph service between the two closely related ports. In Simon's Town, Semmes was able to replace copper sheathing, repair the engine, and continue with caulking.

In mid-August—taking a hint from Admiral Walker that an American warship, the *Vanderbilt,* was in the neighborhood, Semmes

The Alabama in a Gale at Cape Town

FIGURE 18.1. The *Alabama* in a gale off Cape Town. *Illustration from Semmes,* Memoirs of Service Afloat. *Author's collection.*

left Simon's Town, returning a month later for a week. Leaving again, on Sunday, August 23, he remarked in his log, "Had the usual jail delivery upon coming out of port; read the proceedings of the court-martial and a general order. Intemperance and rascality seem to have taken a deep hold of my villains, and it is troublesome to manage them, whenever it [is] possible for them to get drunk and make beasts of themselves."[2]

During this interlude, he sailed up the coast to Angra Pequena, now called Lüderitz Bay, a remote harbor in what is now Namibia, where he rendezvoused with his tender, the *Tuscaloosa*, and also with the captured *Sea Bride*, which Semmes had arranged to sell to a local merchant for one-third of its assessed value in gold. Here, the accounts of what exactly transpired diverge, but Sinclair implies that Semmes purposefully allowed the crew to observe the gold transaction, as a way to assure their good behavior. However, the problem was that, a year into the voyage, nobody had seen any of the promised prize money in gold—nor were they going to. As Fox points out, "The crew's misbehaviors though surely inevitable and traditional for seafaring men, yet implied more than just the random unleashing of confined animal spirits. They were also a kind of labor protest, however inchoate and inarticulate, acted out instead of spoken."[3]

In *White Jacket*, Herman Melville begins by emphasizing the importance of the phrase "homeward bound": "Quick take the wings of the morning, or the sails of a ship, and fly to the uttermost parts of the earth. There, tarry a year or two; and then let the gruffest of boatswains, his lungs all goose-skin, shout forth those magical words, and you'll swear 'the harp of Orpheus were not more enchanting.'"[4] But, for the crew of the *Alabama*, there was never any homeward bound; this voyage seemed to have no end.

Back at the Cape, the crew had indeed become virtually unmanageable. Twenty-one men and Boys deserted, including the valued fiddler and the incorrigible Egan, of cat-in-cannon fame. A number of drunkards on liberty were brought back to the ship in irons with the help of the Simon's Town police.[5] Cape Town's authorities declined to intervene, however, resulting in a slew of "desertions," a usage recorded in the *Alabama*'s general muster role, though one that is open to interrogation. The US consul in Cape Town, Walter Graham, wrote to Seward on September 3, mentioning only prize prisoners. Further, on October 26, he reported to his superiors: "Fourteen seamen taken prisoners from American ships ... and who subsequently joined her crew to get out of irons, made their escape from her while here ... and are now under my protection."[6]

Indeed, the *Alabama*'s muster role reveals that more than a few of the "desertions" at the Cape were of sailors who had mysteriously "enlisted" in the middle of the Atlantic, either on the same day or within days of a capture.[7]

Among the visitors who thronged the *Alabama*'s decks was Cape Town–based photographer Arthur Green, whose significant pictures taken of the vessel in Simon's Town are now held in the South African National Archives and at the Maritime Archives at the National Museums Liverpool. These pictures give us a wonderful view of what White experienced on the deck of the *Alabama*, and perhaps even of White himself.

One photograph is probably the best-known of Green's series (fig. 18.2). In it, Semmes is weirdly standing on a coil of rope, leaning on the carriage of the aft pivot gun situated along the vessel's midline. In back of him, Kell, keeping a respectful distance, is leaning on a framework for the hoist over the gunroom skylight, just in front of the ship's famous inscribed wheel. In the background, an awful lot of clutter on the deck bears graphical witness to the numerous reports of untidy disorder.

FIGURE 18.2. The deck of the *Alabama*, photographed by Arthur Green in the port of Simon's Town. Capt. Raphael Semmes stands closest to the camera, with 1st Lt. John McIntosh Kell behind him. *US Navy, Naval History and Heritage Command NH Series NH 57000, NH 57256-KN.*

In another of Green's photos (fig. 18.3), Kell stands before the vent, facing forward. He is next to the hatch to the crew accommodation and galley. In front of the hatch is the grating that covered access to the stores in the lower deck. Kell's stance is one of authority, the crew hanging back and seemingly shrinking in their pose. In the background, an unidentified individual is watching from the bridge at the point of the ladderway. It has been suggested that this may be the boatswain, Benjamin Mecaskey.[8]

FIGURE 18.3. John McIntosh Kell (*center*) with crew members on the *Alabama* in Simon's Town. *Photo by Arthur Green. South African National Archives, Morrison Collection.*

In yet another in Green's nautical series (fig. 18.4), Kell is on the side of the aft pivot cannon with his hand on the breech rope. The engine room skylight, with bars over the glass, is clearly visible at the bottom left. Just behind the aft pivot cannon is the wheel. Laundry hangs from the rigging. In this picture, the untidy clutter is again apparent, both near the wheel and at the rear.

In another photo, Green captured Lieutenants Arthur Sinclair (left) and Richard F. Armstrong, leaning on one of the *Alabama*'s

FIGURE 18.4. John McIntosh Kell on the *Alabama* in Simon's Town. *Photo by Arthur Green. South African National Archives, Morrison Collection.*

32-pounders (fig. 18.5). An unidentified Black man—possibly the elusive Adam Shilland (chapter 8)—is standing in the background. A striking sight is the high bulwarks amidships—a design feature perhaps intended to disguise both the 32-pounders and the large pivot cannons.

A sixth photo from Green's shoot on board the *Alabama* (fig. 18.6) is interesting both for its content and for having been largely overlooked. The reason is clear—the subjects were simply not considered to be important at the time. In this picture, taken from a similar perspective but from a point a few feet back compared to the previous one (fig. 18.5), Green captured two young men, about the age and dress of Bartelli and White, looking almost suspiciously at the camera, under the watchful eye of an officer. In the background the stack can be clearly seen, along with the mainmast, with main trysail lashed along its length. The bridge is clearly visible, along with one of its ladders. The two young crewmen lean against the gunroom skylight, with the hatch to the officers' quarters in the foreground.

Skin tones are difficult to determine from such old black-and-white photographs, so there is no way to know if the figure on the right is White. However, the photo provides an excellent idea of how Bartelli and White might have looked from a distance, and what they would have seen while on deck.

FIGURE 18.5. Lieutenants Arthur Sinclair and Richard F. Armstrong on the *Alabama* in Simon's Town. *Photo by Arthur Green. South African National Archives, Morrison Collection.*

FIGURE 18.6. Unknown crew members aboard the *Alabama* in Simon's Town. *Photo by Arthur Green. South African National Archives, Morrison Collection.*

A picture from the Liverpool Museum Archives captures another individual who is a more likely candidate for White (fig. 18.7). This photo is most revealingly viewed in successive frames of depth. In the foreground (fig. 18.7A) Semmes's clerk, W. Breedlove Smith, is standing next to the high bulwark. Breedlove Smith, a Louisianan, had served as Captain Semmes's secretary on the CSS *Sumter*, then subsequently during the entire *Alabama* cruise, after which he joined the *Shenandoah* until the war's end.

Farther aft, Sailing Master Irvine Bulloch is leaning against the gunroom hoist, just in front of the wheel (fig. 18.7B). His stance connotes casual confidence, power, and control.

At the stern, among the clutter, a group of Boys, sailors, and officers are gathered by the flag locker and propeller-hoisting gear (fig. 18.7C). A sailor at the back right is wearing a "scotch cap." A tall individual, possibly B. K. Howell, lieutenant of the marines, is watchfully surveying the scene, a pair of binoculars dangling from his right hand. One individual, toward the left, among the Boys, appears to be young and Black. He could very well be White.

FIGURE 18.7A. Deck of the *Alabama* in Simon's Town. *Photo by Arthur Green. National Museums Liverpool.*

FIGURE 18.7B.

FIGURE 18.7C.

Chapter 19

～

The Indian Ocean

O ut in the Indian Ocean, despite some spectacular captures, the pickings were slim. The ship continued to deteriorate, and the crew became ever more disorderly and dangerous.[1] All this was punctuated by short visits to the friendly ports of Condore (Con Son Island, then part of French Indochina), off Vietnam; Singapore; and the Comoros before returning to Cape Town.

October 1863 began with persistent foul weather and leaks, and the constant damp took a toll. When the sun finally appeared, Semmes wrote, "we are airing clothes, bedding, etc., trying to get things a little dry once more, for the ship . . . has taken in water enough through the seams of the bends to wet all the bedding in the wardroom and to leak down a little into my bookcases, etc."[2] That month would be a long, boring stretch at sea with no captures or land in sight.

Back in Liverpool, however, there was more than enough excitement. On October 16, the American abolitionist Henry Ward Beecher, brother of Harriet Beecher Stowe and pastor at Brooklyn's famous Plymouth Church, delivered a hotly contested speech on the subject of slavery. A widely regarded, gifted orator, he was described as "the Most Famous Man in America."[3] During 1863 he had been on a world tour organized to help him recover from depression resulting from the death of a close friend, Lucy Bowen. Beecher observed hostility to the Union on the Continent and therefore avoided the subject of slavery—especially as the first six months of 1863 were not auspicious for the Union. But the situation changed during July when Lee's invasion of the North was turned back at Gettysburg and Grant seized control of the Mississippi at Vicksburg, thereby completing the North's grand strategy of cutting the Confederacy in two. Suddenly, all the Confederate sympathizers in Europe went silent. Beecher understood how important it was to keep European states from recognizing the Confederacy. Not unlike modern-day economic warfare, the North's strategy of attrition could only work if the rest of the world did not recognize the Confederacy.

With the improving military picture back home, Beecher decided to speak. If ever a moment could be characterized as entering the lion's den, this was it. As noted earlier, Liverpool's economy depended largely on the cotton trade, and it had created great wealth and many jobs. There was also the issue of the "cotton famine" among Manchester's textile laborers who were thrown out of work due to the Union's blockade of Southern cotton exports. In his speech, Beecher offered essentially an economic argument—that slavery was bad for business. The transcript states that Beecher's entrance was met by "a vast shout of mingled welcome and disapprobation . . . his audience became repeatedly little more than a shouting mob, tempered by periodical exhaustion, so strong were its sympathies with the Southern cause." The transcript shows that, no less than fifty times over the hour-and-a-half-long speech, Beecher was interrupted by "cheers," "applause," "hisses," "laughter," "immense applause and hisses," "hisses and continued uproar," "interruption and uproar," and so on.[4]

While courageously abolitionist, unlike Wendell Phillips or William Powell, Beecher's vision of social justice stopped well short of integration and actual equality. He had already been cuttingly mocked in the Black-run *Anglo-African,* reprinted on the front page of the *Brooklyn Daily Eagle*—then the largest circulation newspaper in America. "We are pained at such exhibitions of 'spinal weakness.' . . . We have heard of some men who did not know enough to go in doors when it rained; and what they have been called, surely Mr. Beecher must be classed with such, if in the pouring down of heavenly light and love which is showering this nation . . . he has not sense enough to keep that bi-lingual tongue of his from outdoor exposure."[5] The *Eagle*'s editors "mildly protested at this colored onslaught" of Beecher, but also chortled that, in opposing both slavery and equality, Beecher had only managed to alienate everybody.

Meanwhile, during the remainder of 1863 and until June 1864, the *Alabama* destroyed another nine vessels (table 19.1). In November, the raider captured two of the most magnificent clipper ships of the era, the *Winged Racer* and the *Contest*. The captain of the *Contest*, Frederick Lucas, thought he could outrun the *Alabama*, and nearly did. In an exciting two-hour chase, with a 14-knot wind blowing, the *Contest*, built for speed, appeared to be getting away. Semmes sought more speed from his tired engines, though he was told that "the tea-kettle will stand no more; if we attempt it we shall scatter the pieces for the chase to pick up."[6] Nevertheless, Semmes's luck held. Just after noon, the wind died to a 6-knot breeze, and that was the end for the *Contest*; by that evening the ship was in flames.

Sinclair, at least, understood the loss. "We never captured so beautiful a vessel," he later wrote. "She was a revelation of symmetry, a very race-horse. A sacrilege, almost a desecration to destroy so perfect a specimen of man's handiwork."[7] Semmes too remarked on the *Contest*'s beauty as it plowed its way through the sea "with the grace of the swan. . . . I was sorry . . . to burn this beautiful ship, and regretted much that I had not an armament for her, that I might commission her as a cruiser."[8] But that didn't stop him.

Possibly there were still moments of respite and entertainment. Narrative storytelling and music were highly valued among the crew.

Table 19.1. Captures by the *Alabama*, November 6, 1863–April 27, 1864

Date	Ship	Home Port	From/to	Cargo	Disposition
November 6, 1863	Amanda	Bangor, ME	Manila	Sugar, hemp	Burned
November 10	Winged Racer	New York	Manila	Sugar, hemp	Burned
November 11	Contest	New York	Yokohama	Japanese curios, tea	Burned
December 24	Texan Star	Galveston	Singapore	Rice	Burned
December 26	Sonora	Newburyport, MA	Singapore	In ballast	Burned
December 26	Highlander	Boston	Singapore	In ballast	Burned
January 14, 1864	Emma Jane	Bath, ME	Burma	In ballast	Burned
April 23	Rockingham	Portsmouth, NH	Cork	Guano	Burned
April 27	Tycoon	New York	San Francisco	Assorted cargo	Burned

Source: O.R. Navy, Ser. I: Vol. 3, pp. 677–81.

In the crews quarters, as on the *Wyoming* and the *Tonawanda*, during the long interludes, White would have heard stories, like the sailor whose head was recovered from the belly of a shark after he fell from a transfer boat, when one captain was visiting another for dinner. Or he might have heard tales of famous earlier voyages, such as the many Arctic voyages undertaken to search for the lost 1845 Franklin expedition.

Sir John Franklin's instructions were to search for the long-sought Northwest Passage to "penetrate the icy fastness of the north, and to circumnavigate America."[9] Using the latest technology, including steam engines, steam heat, propellers, and canned rations, he was to sail first to Greenland, then on to Baffin Bay and Lancaster Sound, through to the Bering Strait—completing for the first time a Northwest Passage. The expedition's two ships, HMS *Erebus* and HMS *Terror* sailed from the Thames on May 19, 1845. In early August, they passed two whaling ships in Baffin Bay and were never heard from again. Subsequently, their fate was pieced together from stories told by the Inuit, from artifacts found by numerous search expeditions, and by the recovery of frozen bodies of crew members. The evidence points to incredible privation, starvation, and ultimately, cannibalism.

The Liverpudlians would have known "Lady Franklin's Lament," a popular ballad, first published in 1850, reflecting on the arrogance of the age. The melody survived as Bob Dylan's "Bob Dylan's Dream," from his 1963 album, *The Freewheelin' Bob Dylan*:

> *Through cruel hardships they vainly strove*
> *'til their ships on mountainous ice was drove*
> *Where the Eskimo [Inuit], in his skin canoe*
> *Was the only one of them, to ever get through.*

There were probably chanties, of course, and whatever a little band played with a violin, tambourine, and concertina. According to Semmes, "The favorite dancing tunes were those of Wapping and Wide Water Street."[10] These tunes might have included "Maggie May," the traditional folksong about a prostitute who robbed a "homeward bounder" (later recorded by the Beatles). A more plaintive chantey on the same theme is "Off to Sea Once More" (ultimately recorded by Jerry Garcia and David Grisman). The officers formed a glee club and endlessly sang "Bonny Blue Flag" and "Dixie."

Nevertheless, from Marvel's and Fox's research to depositions and reports of the official records of the Union and Confederate navies, a number of important accounts testify to the deteriorating conditions on board over this period. Among them, Isaiah Larrabee, the captain of the *Amanda*, captured on November 6, 1863, reported that "the crew of the *Alabama* seemed to be dissatisfied with their long cruise and uncertainty of obtaining their prize money, but order was preserved on board."[11] On the other hand, George Cumming, captain of the *Winged Racer*, captured a few days later on November 10, described a "most disorderly set of fellows, apparently under no discipline whatever, and the officers comparatively ragged."[12]

The capture of the *Contest* a day later, on November 11, was described by its first officer, James D. Babcock:

Crew much dissatisfied, no prize money, no liberty, and see no prospect of getting any. Discipline very slack, steamer dirty, rigging slovenly. Semmes sometimes punishes, but is afraid to push too hard. Men excited, officers do not report to captain, crew do things for which would be shot on board American man-of-war; for instance, saw one of the crew strike a master's mate; crew insolent to petty officers; was told by at least two-thirds of them that [they] will desert on first opportunity. . . . Except at muster, no uniforms worn. Crew rugged. . . . Officers on duty have cutlass and revolver; never saw Semmes in uniform; puts on sword at muster. Have given up small-arm drill afraid to trust crew with arms.[13]

A passenger on the *Contest* also wrote, "The leader of the boarding party was a most rascally and seedy looking individual with a sword at one side and a pistol at the other." This observer further described Captain Semmes as "villainous in appearance" and the crew as "composed chiefly of the offscourings of the English service, and is in quite an insubordinate condition."[14]

About that time—November 13—Semmes attempted a gesture of reconciliation with his crew by distributing cigars taken from the *Winged Racer*. In a signal of contempt that came to be known as the cigar-box mutiny, a number of the sailors simply tossed their cigars overboard. Infuriated, Semmes responded with a court-martial.[15] One of the ringleaders was demoted to ordinary seaman, forfeited his three month's pay, and was confined to double irons and restricted to bread and water for thirty days.[16] Another seaman was given a more painful punishment: "Court Martial sentenced Michael Mars (sea.) to lose one month's pay, to do police duty [cleaning the ship] 3 months, and to be triced up three hours daily for one week."[17]

In late December, Lawrence Brown, captain of the clipper *Sonora*, captured on December 26, refused to accompany Lieutenant Armstrong back to the *Alabama*, and so witnessed the boarding party ransack his ship. He reported:

> They entered the cabin and searched around, feasting on what they could find to eat and drink; taking everything they could hide upon their persons. They soon stripped the cabin of the valuable things it contained, and one of them told me they were not allowed to do so but their officers would not say anything as they had the first pick . . . they emptied several bottles of wines that they found, and seemed to have turned their morning call into a first-class picnic. The whole affair was of rather a ridiculous, undignified nature. On the cruiser there seemed to be little order on board, more like everybody for himself.[18]

The *Times of India* published the following report, based on an account by Francis C. Jordan, captain of the *Emma Jane*, captured January 14, 1864, who was accompanied by his wife:

> While [the ship] was burning, the officers of the *Alabama* were shouting and crowing, and doing all they could by word and gesture to distress Captain Jordan and his wife. They amused themselves in tearing up Mrs. Jordan's silk dresses to make pocket-handkerchiefs for themselves. Captain Semmes is described as a small man, of unpleasant visage, coarse manners, and foul tongue, the very type of a Southern slave driver. His officers seem to maintain their position by terror, being constantly armed cap-a-pie, with swords, daggers, and revolvers. The petty officers told Captain Jordan that they were determined to seize the ship, and were watching for an opportunity . . . that none of them ever gets wages or anything else, and would desert if they could get a chance. While in dread of their lives from the officers, there is no discipline among them. They curse and swear at each other boisterously all day and frequently fight like fiends; while their night orgies are described as frightful. Indeed, the vessel is described as a floating hell.[19]

The stops in the Indian Ocean ports such as Singapore followed the familiar pattern of sumptuous entertainment for the officers in British colonies, but in this part of the world, there was a somewhat less fawning welcome from the local populace. Reports of the American vice-consul at Singapore, Francis D. Stobb, focus on disbursements to sailors made destitute by the captures of the *Amanda* and *Winged Racer*, complaining about the "confinement" of American shipping and requesting special instructions.

US consul Stobb, like his counterpart in Cape Town, was concerned with imprisoned prize crews. His message to Secretary

Seward—that the crew was confined and that he could get nowhere near them—is of exceptional interest, given Semmes's later claims that consuls had interacted with White. Stobb reported on December 22, 1863: "I endeavored to communicate with the crew of the 'ala' last night but was prevented by no boats being permitted to approach her sides. The wharf at which she coals is capable of being shut in and hence preventing any desertion of the crew." In a subsequent message Stobbs wrote that "the report of her crew being discontented and insubordinate I can confirm, the confinement in irons and strict watch prevented much desertion."[20] Here the *Alabama* became locally known as the *kappal hantu*, or the Ghost Ship.[21]

Semmes avoided Bombay (Mumbai) entirely for the simple reason that while under British control, Bombay nevertheless had its own independent cotton industry and so the Confederacy was, if anything, a competitor. When it appeared possible that the *Alabama* would stop in Bombay (Mumbai), the *Times of India* let loose: "Shall we receive them as they were received at Cape Town, as heroes of a righteous war? . . . Semmes scoured the seas . . . in search of weak, defenseless vessels; boards them, removes their crews, possesses himself of what valuables are easily removed, and then burns the goodly ships with their freight?"[22] The *Bombay Gazette* correctly predicted that the *Alabama* would skip Bombay.[23]

In contrast, the local French authorities on Condore Island, off Vietnam, were friendlier. In December 1863, Semmes noted that the French commandant, Mr. Bizot, visited and "expressed sympathy for the cause. Brought me a chart of the islands. Brought a present of a pig and some fruit; later present of coconuts."[24]

The following February, the *Alabama* also received a warm greeting in the Comoros, where Semmes, for one last time, indulged in a bit of repose at some high-end real estate, noting "the prince's garden, a beautiful wilderness of cocoa and betel nut, sweet orange, and mango, with heterogenous patches of rice, sweet potatoes, and beans, with here and there a cotton plant.... The people met us everywhere with kindly greetings. . . . The price of a slave here fresh from the coast is $5.00."[25]

The locals embraced slavery, but eschewed alcohol. As none was available in the Comoros, the crew was less troublesome. Nevertheless, on Sunday, February 14, four men went missing. As usual, the local authorities cooperated in bringing the men back in irons. "We afterwards learned," Semmes wrote, "they had taken to the hills, of course with the intention to abscond. I offered a reward for them, and after night they were brought on board to me."[26]

The *Alabama* now headed back to the South Atlantic, stopping briefly again in Cape Town for coal and provisions. It was March 1864, and the news from home was disturbing. The war was not going well for the South, and conscription was extended to all white males from seventeen to fifty years of age. Grant's formidable successes had earned him a promotion to lieutenant general—a rank previously only given by promotion in wartime to George Washington. The international community—mainly Great Britain and France—was beginning to hedge its bets. Nor could Semmes tarry at the Cape for he was in danger of losing his entire crew. Therefore, he stayed for only three days, and would have left sooner but for the wind.

Once underway, the *Alabama* had few sightings, but toward the end of April, 1864, it captured the Portsmouth ship *Rockingham*, with a cargo of guano. Very late in the game, about 400 miles east of Brazil, Semmes finally drilled the crew on firing the cannons. After offloading the *Rockingham*'s crew, instead of simply burning it, he had the crew use it for target practice.

Indications were not good; given the constant dampness, the powder had become unreliable: one in three shells failed to explode, and those that did were "sluggish," giving off no sharp, quick, vigorous reports. Nevertheless, Semmes was confident that the crew had aimed the cannons with good effect. The captain of the *Rockingham* later testified that twenty-four shots were fired at 500 yards, and that only four hits were made in the *Rockingham*'s hull and three in the spars and rigging. Why was even this precision of 29 percent not repeated in the final battle at Cherbourg? Marvel provides one answer: at 500 yards, the shots at the *Rockingham* did not simulate the more distant range that would count in battle.[27] Admiral Porter provides another: unlike the *Rockingham*, the *Kearsarge* fired back.[28]

Semmes and his ship were now boxed in by the urgent need for repairs. The *Alabama*'s copper sheathing was stripping, and it had become "a very tub" in sailing. Its engines were worn, and there was a constant thumping and fizzing in the engine room. Counting on the hospitality of the French, who had received him so royally at Martinique and the Comoros, the sympathy of Napoleon III to the Confederate cause, and possibly the diplomacy of Confederate agent Slidell in Paris, Semmes fatefully—and fatally—set a course for the French naval port of Cherbourg. Of this period, he later wrote of the ship's deterioration, his own exhaustion, and the change in political fortunes:

The poor old *Alabama* was not now what she had been. . . . She was like the wearied fox-hound, limping back after a long chase, foot-sore, and longing for quiet and repose. Her commander, like herself, was well-nigh worn down. Vigils by night and by day, the storm and the drenching rain, the frequent and rapid change of climate, now freezing, now melting or broiling, and the constant excitement of the chase and capture, had laid, in the three years of war he had been afloat, a load of a dozen years on his shoulders. The shadows of a sorrowful future, too, began to rest upon his spirit. The last batch of newspapers captured were full of disasters. Might it not be, that, after all our trials and sacrifices, the cause for which we were struggling would be lost? Might not our federal system of government be destroyed, and State independence become a phrase of the past; the glorious fabric of our American liberty sinking, as so many others had done before it, under a new invasion of Brennuses and Attilas? The thought was hard to bear.[29]

In his 1886 overview, Porter had little patience for this "melancholy moralizing" and wondered whether Semmes anticipated a fate like the one that befell Conrad in Byron's *Corsair*:

> *'Tis idle all—moons roll on moons away,*
> *And Conrad comes not—came not since that day—*
> *Nor trace, nor tidings of his doom declare*
> *Where lives his grief, or perish'd his despair!*[30]

In this epic poem, Byron tells the story of the pirate (corsair) Conrad, who sails away from his home and wife to attack the Pasha on another island. The attack at first goes well, but then goes awry while Conrad saves Gulnare, a slave in the harem. As a matter of honor, he refuses to kill the Pasha in cold blood and demands a fair fight. Eventually, he returns home, only to find that his wife, Medora, has died from grief and despair.

Given what would transpire in Cherbourg, the following couplet, from the same epic poem, might be added as an epitaph:

> *He left a Corsair's name to other times,*
> *Linked with one virtue and a thousand crimes.*

Chapter 20

⠀⠀⠀⠀⠀⠀⠀⠀⠀⠀⠀⠀⠀⠀⠀⠀⠀⠀⠀⠀⠀⠀⠀⠀⠀

The Looming Battle

The circumstances of White's birth and short life having been described, this chapter considers other relevant developments—notably Capt. John Ancrum Winslow's preparations over the course of 1863 and 1864—that contributed to the circumstances of White's demise. Given all that White had experienced on the *Alabama* and his own navigation of the manifold perils he had encountered, we may wonder at his survival skills. But, whether or not he was aware of it, the danger to him was all the while increasing as the US Navy finally closed in.

As with all research pertaining to the *Alabama*, the descriptions of the final battle between it and the *Kearsarge* are tiger territory for the unwary. What actually happened—as opposed to constructed histories—is obscured by conflicting accounts and images, some appearing within days, many constructed years after the events, and many tailored to suit a political narrative. Nineteenth-century audiences were thrilled by the battle, leading to many fictionalized accounts and images, including, alas, Manet's famous painting.[1] Perhaps the most unreliable account of all was Semmes's own, colored by his Southern and naval codes of honor, in which defeat was itself an unacceptable infraction.[2] In defense of that honor, he employed two of his favorite rhetorical weapons: recrimination and mendacity.

To fully understand the battle's trajectory and outcome for White, it would be helpful at this point to further consider both Captain Winslow and his vessel, the *Kearsarge*. One irony of White's story is that the proximal cause of his demise was the clinical military competency of this passionate abolitionist. After briefly summarizing Winslow's preparations and his ship's arrival off Cherbourg, this chapter describes some of the relevant events that took place in the tense five-day period between the *Kearsarge*'s arrival at Cherbourg on Tuesday, June 14, 1864, and the final battle on Sunday, June 19.

Winslow detested the war, but passionately believed in the abolitionist cause. It is also ironic that Semmes, a zealous defender of slavery, and W. E. B. Du Bois—a cofounder of the National Association for the Advancement of Colored People (NAACP)—had in common the view that in Du Bois's words, "the North did not conquer the South to abolish slavery."[3] If they were right, individuals like Winslow, with his pious Puritan background, were important exceptions.

On July 21, 1862, two months before the draft Emancipation Proclamation was issued, and seeing the suffering and devastation in Memphis, Winslow wrote home: "The officers are all sick at Cairo—this river uses every one up. I do not see any end to the war. If the President does not emancipate the slaves and use energetic measures of confiscation, we might as well make peace at once for our armies support instead of harass the South."[4] On hearing the news of Pope's loss to Lee at the Second Battle of Bull Run, he was accused of disloyalty for remarking, "I was glad of it. I wish they would bag old Abe."[5] According to historian Jim Dan Hill, "To him Lincoln, with all his blather about the Union, was just another third-rate politician. The primary objective in Winslow's mind was not to save the Union but to free the slaves, concerning which, to that date, the administration had taken no action."[6]

In defending himself to Welles, Winslow wrote that, far from being unfaithful to his trust, he was "[more] nearly an abolitionist and a person who believed that Wendell Phillips was fifty years in advance of the age."[7] Continuing this theme in a letter dated September 4, 1862, Winslow directly connected his appetite for battle to his religious abolitionism: "Until the slaves are manumitted we shall do nothing, then we shall go onward to fight God's battles and relieve thousands of His praying Christians."[8]

At the end of 1862, while Semmes was hitting his stride on the *Alabama*, Winslow was back home in Roxbury, Massachusetts, weak as a kitten. He had been badly injured on the Mississippi squadron, was periodically incapacitated from malaria, and also suffered from a mysterious and painful malady that was slowly destroying his right eye.

The draft Emancipation Proclamation, published in late September, gave Winslow a reason to fight, and despite his infirmities, he welcomed a new command. This is not to say that, like most whites of the period, Winslow did not in his letters express language that would survive a presentist analysis. While Winslow's allusion to Phillips indicate that he was progressive for his time, he was mainly notable for defending Christians and for arguing that the war be fought against slavery, or not at all.[9]

Finally, his orders came in December 1862 to travel to the Azores to take command of the *Kearsarge* and hunt the Confederate raiders, including the *Alabama*, which was by then four months into its cruise of fire. Winslow reached the Azores only after an arduous journey punctuated by his own fever and "neuralgia." Even getting down to New York for passage to the Azores was a trial, as the train carrying him from Roxbury was wrecked in a blizzard. Arriving in Fayal in January 1863, he was shocked to find the *Kearsarge* was nowhere in sight, the ship having been delayed by a suspiciously slow refit in Cádiz.

When the *Kearsarge* finally arrived, Winslow assumed his command, and over the course of a year, he made three important decisions. First, in May 1863, he took the advice of his first officer, James S. Thornton, who served with Farragut on the Mississippi squadron, and had surplus chains draped over the *Kearsarge*'s hull amidships as a kind of armor-plating to protect the boilers and engine in battle, and then hid them behind painted wooden cladding.[10]

The hidden armor created something of a controversy when, years later, casting about for excuses for losing, Semmes accused Winslow of deception, writing that Winslow "did not show me a fair fight" and that the hidden armor was "a cheat."[11] This argument was preposterous, since, as later noted by both Admirals Porter and Farragut, everybody in both navies knew that the practice had been used on federal Mississippi gunboats since at least 1862.[12] Moreover, according to his own officers, the Cherbourg authorities had specifically informed Semmes about the *Kearsarge*'s chain armor.[13] More than ironic, it was just a bit rich coming from Semmes, who, in a storied American naval tradition going back decades, had used deception as his central strategy of warfare, most notably when fighting the USS *Hatteras*.

Second, Winslow had realized by August that it was a poor strategy to cruise what his biographer called "the trackless ocean," searching for raiders, particularly the *Alabama*, which by then had become popularly known worldwide as the Ghost Ship.[14] He proposed instead to anchor in centrally located European ports that had a telegraph line and access to coal, and lie in wait for a sighting. At first he chose Brest, but after wearing out his welcome with the French, he ended up in Vlissingen (Flushing), Holland.

Third, during the long and frustrating year of 1863, Winslow used his time to methodically prepare his ship and crew. In Cádiz, he put into drydock, had the bottom scraped clean, and installed new crank-shaft bearings. During June, he drilled his crew on the *Kearsarge*'s two big 11-inch Dahlgren pivot guns, 32-pounder guns, and small arms. In Brest he had the bilges cleaned, the engines painted, the valves cleaned, leaky boiler tubes replaced, the masts tarred and new sails installed. He recruited a full complement of crew and contin-ued to drill relentlessly both on aiming the cannons and in hand-to-hand combat. Among them, Charles A. Poole, a housepainter from Bowdoinham, Maine, remarked that the ship was "one of the world's greatest workshops, where superiors seemed willing to take anything apart and reassemble it, merely to keep you at work."[15] Later, Poole remarked with frustration that they must have had the sharpest-looking engine room in the US Navy.[16] Perhaps it felt like overkill, but all that preparation would matter.

Sunday, June 12, 1864 found the *Kearsarge* at anchor in the River Scheldt, off Vlissingen. According to *Kearsarge* seaman William Wain-wright, who kept a diary, the morning was rainy, so there was no Sun-day inspection, but by the afternoon those who had not gone ashore were enjoying the music of four local musicians—two accordion and two violin players. Winslow had gone ashore, where he received a telegram from William Dayton, the American minister in Paris, say-ing that the *Alabama* had been sighted in Cherbourg. Returning to the *Kearsarge*, he immediately called for steam and fired a cannon, a prearranged signal recalling everybody to the ship. By eight o'clock that evening, the *Kearsarge* was underway.[17]

Winslow made a brief detour to Dover to pick up a new trysail and topsail he had previously ordered and might need should the engagement turn into a chase, but also to send messages.[18] Since Cherbourg harbor had two entrances, from Dover Roads he asked for another steamer, the *St. Louis* (then at Gibraltar), to join him at Cherbourg and sailed directly to Cherbourg, the officers and crew engaged in "considerable betting" on whether the *Alabama* would still be there. Land was sighted about 7 on the morning of the 14th, and Cherbourg was "in plain sight" about half past 9. The Ghost Ship had arrived just three days previously (fig. 20.1).

On his arrival at Cherbourg, Semmes had asked the local authorities if he could offload prisoners and make use of a drydock. The first request was immediately met, but not so for the second. The difficulty was that Cherbourg was a naval harbor, so there were no commercial docks where Semmes could contract for a refit. Had he entered Le Havre, it might have been a different matter, but the use of a naval dock in Cherbourg required the permission of the emperor. No doubt Semmes was counting on the personal sympathy of Napoleon III for the Confederacy, but he may not have realized that over the past few months, the political environment had changed, as it looked increasingly likely that the North would prevail in the war. In any event, at that moment Napoleon III was unavailable, en-

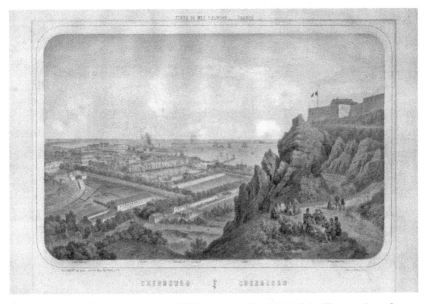

FIGURE 20.1. "General view of Cherbourg," 1866. This illustration shows the harbor's breakwater with its western channel. *Lithograph by Isidore Laurent Deroy (1797–1886), printed in Paris by L. Turgis. Author's collection.*

joying a holiday at Biarritz. While the French authorities, including Vice-Admiral Adolphe-Augustin Dupouy, head of the Cherbourg naval district, and the minister of marine and the colonies, Prosper de Chasseloup-Laubat, considered their response and waited for the emperor, the *Kearsarge* arrived.

That afternoon, the *Kearsarge* steamed in slowly past the Cherbourg breakwater by the eastern channel and stopped near the *Alabama* without anchoring. Winslow was doing more than just getting a good look at his elusive quarry. Given the long tradition of naval duels in which each of these two men were steeped, and given his Mexican-American War experience with Semmes, the move was a dare, and a highly strategic one. Winslow simply put Semmes in the position of choosing between bravery and cowardice.

Winslow was also keenly aware of neutrality rules, adopted first by Great Britain in 1862 and then by France in February 1864, according to which belligerent vessels could not fight in territorial waters, and those anchored in neutral ports could not leave within twenty-four hours of each other. He sent a boat ashore to briefly communicate with the Union agent and with French authorities, asking to pick up the prisoners who had been allowed to leave the *Alabama*—a request that was denied. However, given the twenty-four-hour rule, he was careful not to anchor and soon left by the western channel, then steamed slowly back and forth within site of the port but never in territorial waters, a large American flag flying gamely from the top of the highest mast.

Now Semmes had to make a choice. On one hand, he and his crew were exhausted, and the ship was worn out. Kell reminded him of all this and especially emphasized the problem of the damp ammunition and the failure of shells to explode on the *Rockingham*. On the other hand, Semmes well understood that if he did not come out and fight, other Union ships would arrive and the *Alabama*, like the *Sumter* in Gibraltar, would be bottled up in Cherbourg forever.

Semmes's response to Kell was classic: referring to the US ensign proudly flying high atop the *Kearsarge*'s mast, he said, "Mr. Kell—*I am tired of running from that flaunting rag!*"[19] The same day, Semmes wrote the following message to the Confederate agent in Cherbourg:

C.S.S. *Alabama*

Cherbourg June 14, 1864

SIR: I hear that you were informed by the U.S. consul that the *Kearsarge* was to come to this port solely for the prisoners landed by me, and that he was to depart in twenty-four hours. I desire to say to the U.S. consul that my intention is to fight the *Kearsarge* as soon as I can make the necessary arrangements. I hope these will not detain me more than until to-morrow evening, or after the morrow morning at furthest. I beg she will not depart before I am ready to go out.

I have the honor to be, very respectfully,

your obedient servant,

R. SEMMES,

Captain.[20]

Two days later, the *Alabama* still had not moved. Wainwright wrote on the 16th: "Well there is no signs of the *Alabama* showing herself to day so all our preparation amounted to nothing but then it is well enough to be ready in case of she should try to play any game on us. . . . Well let him come our Captain knows him and knows what he will try to do. He was with him in the Mexican war and he gives him the credit of being a brave man."[21] Wainwright added, "There is one thing certain if he comes out and doesn't run either the *Alabama* or the *Kearsarge* will be passed repairing [*sic*] when the fight is over."[22]

Chapter 21

～

The Battle of Cherbourg

As it happened, Semmes waited until Sunday, June 19, before steaming out of the harbor, and this delay later became a source of suspicion. During this period, an important series of events transpired that became the subject of intense, endless, and still unresolved controversy.

Among the vessels anchoring in Cherbourg that week was the British yacht *Deerhound*, the vessel depicted in the upper-right-hand corner of the Manet painting, and the vessel on which Semmes would ultimately escape. The somewhat unresolved controversy is whether the *Deerhound*'s owner, John Lancaster, a British coal magnate and Confederacy sympathizer, or its captain, Evan P. Jones, and crew deliberately conspired in advance with the *Alabama* to rescue Semmes and his officers, should the *Alabama* founder in battle. The charge was explicitly made, among others, by seaman James Magee of the *Kearsarge*, who related that captured American officers and crew from the *Rockingham* (who had been released in Cherbourg) reported that the *Deerhound* had brought out experienced gunners and that some twelve men had joined the *Alabama* in port.[1] Otherwise, there is no hard evidence of such a conspiracy, and Lancaster forcibly denied the allegations, both in a letter to the British foreign minister and in an indignant 1,700-word letter to the *London Daily News*.[2]

Yet two thorough reviews, one by Frederick Milnes Edge in 1864 and the other by Fox in 2007, make a convincing, if circumstantial, case that there was, indeed, coordination. Among their observations were that, first, the vessels had a shared history. Both were designed by the same naval architect, Henry Laird, were built at the same shipyard in Birkenhead, and for a while were lodged there together. Second, according to testimony of three members of the *Alabama*'s crew, the *Deerhound*'s officers did in fact come on board the *Alabama* at various times on Saturday, June 18, in the period *after* Semmes had indicated he would leave Cherbourg. Brent Johnson, a quartermaster on the *Alabama*, later recalled that visiting sailors had the name *Deerhound* in gilt letters on their caps. Third and most significant, the roster of those saved was heavily weighted toward the officers.

To be specific, Semmes, Kell, twelve other wardroom officers, and eight petty officers were saved, along with five firemen and fourteen sailors. "How," Fox asks, "in a supposedly random, unplanned purely humanitarian act of kindness, had Lancaster and Jones managed to save such a high proportion of the Confederate officers, especially the commander and the first lieutenant?"[3] A plan was evidently hatched, if the *Alabama* went down, for men from the *Deerhound* to find the key Confederates in the water.

Perhaps more than anyone else aboard the vessel, save Kell, Semmes fully understood the danger of going into battle with his tired ship and vagabond crew. He had valuables and 38 kilograms of gold coins removed from the *Alabama*, along with his precious collection of sixty-four chronometers—one taken from each of his captures over the preceding twenty-two months.

The night before the battle, Semmes hosted a dinner with his officers, where White, we are told, dutifully served fresh strawber-

ries and cream. Sinclair remarked on his cheery and fearless countenance:

> There is many a joke passing around the mess-table, all having
> direct reference to the present state of the nerves, and banter is
> the order of the meal hours. Poor little Dave, . . . our colored
> wardroom boy, . . . is jokingly catechized as to the state of his cour-
> age. The little fellow seems perfectly contented, evidently having
> every confidence in the ability of those he is serving to bring him
> through all right, and shows his ivories at each banter. Faithful
> Dave! Your goal is about reached. "Well done, good and faithful
> servant." Like Llewellyn, Steward Bartelli, and some other, poor
> little Dave could have saved his life by the mere mention that he
> was unable to swim.[4]

So much is disturbing about this passage that it is difficult to know
where to begin. We can start with the lighthearted tone, inasmuch
as Sinclair is referring to a matter of life and death. There is the familiar racist referral to Blacks in the realm of wild animals—using a
term for White's teeth otherwise generally applied to the dentin of
elephants. There is the deeply awkward confession that these officers
were actually making fun of White for his expression of confidence
in *them*.

The last sentence—regarding swimming—is perhaps the most
egregious. There are only two possibilities: either it was true or
false that Sinclair, or for that matter Semmes or Kell, never knew
that White could not swim. By this time, all the officers had spent
eighteen months at sea in close quarters with White while he daily
served their meals. During the Mexican-American War and again
following the Cherbourg battle, Semmes expressed an exquisite sensitivity to the special care given to those who could not swim. But,
for argument's sake, let us give Semmes, Sinclair, Kell, and Galt the

benefit of the doubt: they didn't know. We are left with the conclusion that White drowned not for the random reason that he couldn't swim, but for the not-so-random reason that nobody cared to find out.

That weekend, Cherbourg's hotels were filled with vacationers who had arrived on the new excursion train from Paris.[5] By that Saturday, it was no secret that a battle was imminent; the only question was when. Although not exactly prearranged, nothing quite like this had ever happened in full view of the city before, and for well over a thousand gathered spectators the excitement was palpable. Early on Sunday morning, as the *Alabama*'s stack began to spew smoke, crowds gathered on rooftops and bluffs overlooking the city. The little village of Querqueville, four miles to the west, provided a commanding view of Cherbourg harbor and the English Channel for the hundreds of tourists who gathered there, as well as nuns and parishioners who had just left Mass at the tenth-century chapel of St. Germain.

Once the boilers had generated enough steam, at ten o'clock, "just as the bells of St. Trinity's basilica tolled the hour along the Cherbourg waterfront," the *Alabama* undocked and headed out into the Channel; not far behind it was the *Deerhound*.[6] Now Semmes had the crew—presumably White was included—gathered while he climbed atop a gun carriage for a speech. Of course, it wasn't recorded, but again let's take his word that his 1869 memoir reflects the spirit, if not the literal text, of his message. The passage is revealing for its now familiar self-importance, refusal to countenance defeat, and glorified racism, and we can only wonder how White reacted as Semmes extolled the naval glory of "our race":

OFFICERS AND SEAMEN OF THE ALABAMA!—You have at length, another opportunity of meeting the enemy—the first that has been presented to you, since you sank the *Hatteras*! In the meantime, you have been all over the world, and it is not too much to say, that you have destroyed, and driven for protection under neutral flags, one half of the enemy's commerce, which, at the beginning of the war, covered every sea. This is an achievement of which you may well be proud; and a grateful country will not be unmindful of it. The name of your ship has become a household word wherever civilization extends. Shall that name be tarnished by defeat? The thing is impossible! Remember that you are in the English Channel, the theatre of so much of the naval glory of our race, and that the eyes of all Europe are at this moment, upon you. The flag that floats over you is that of a young Republic, who bids defiance to her enemies, whenever, and wherever found. Show the world that you know how to uphold it! Go to your quarters.[7]

About this time, Winslow was conducting a Sunday morning service and inspection. When, at 10:20, a lookout shouted, "She's coming out!" he immediately beat the drum to quarters and had the ship cleared for action.[8] Each captain had prepared his ship for battle by making sure there was plenty of water on hand to douse fires, and by spreading sawdust or sand on the decks to absorb the anticipated blood.

Both ships were roughly the same size: the *Kearsarge* was 1,031 tons; the *Alabama*, 1,040 tons. Both had roughly similar ordinance: the *Kearsarge* had four 32-pounders and the *Alabama* six. The *Kearsarge* had two 11-inch Dahlgren smooth-bore cannons mounted on pivots, each of which threw 135½-pound shells, with an effective range of about 900 yards. The *Alabama*, on the other hand, had one rifled 7-inch Blakely pivot gun amidships, which threw 100-pound shells, and one 8-inch smoothbore pivot gun aft (situated between the gun room and engine room skylights) that shot 68-pound shells. The *Kearsarge* had 163 officers and men; there were 149 on the *Alabama*.

Each captain had a battle plan based on his tactical advantage.

With its fouled bottom and leaky boilers, the *Alabama* was slower now, but its rifled Blakely pivot cannon had a greater range than the *Kearsarge*'s Dahlgrens, and Semmes therefore had a greater advantage at distance. Although unrifled, the Dahlgrens had a larger caliber and thus were more effective at close range, and Winslow understood that he would have to get close to press that advantage. He also understood that, if things didn't go well, Semmes would attempt to retreat into French territorial waters. Seeking to ensure that the battle remained in international waters, Winslow now steamed farther out into the Channel—a maneuver that also bought the *Kearsarge* time to build up a good head of steam.

Once again Semmes took the bait—now following the *Kearsarge* into the Channel—and at 7 miles out, forty-five minutes after the *Alabama* passed the breakwater (10:50 as recorded in the *Kearsarge*'s log), Winslow suddenly wheeled about and set a collision course straight for the *Alabama*. Understanding his disadvantage at distance, he piled on as much speed as he could. As Boykin put it, "Swift as a greyhound she closed, great streamers of smoke whirling from her funnel like the dark wings of an avenging angel."⁹ Winslow's hope was to either ram the *Alabama* or pass by it and rake it from its stern.

As opposed to a broadside, a "rake" is fire directed parallel to the long axis of an enemy ship. Although aimed at a smaller target, an individual rake shot can do more damage as it passes through more of the enemy's structure. A stern rake shot can be especially effective, as it can disable the enemy's rudder. Nelson used this technique to great effect in the Battle of Trafalgar in 1805, and both Winslow and Semmes would have been well versed in it.

About seven minutes later, when the ships were about a mile apart, Semmes sheered to port and fired the long-range Blakely with the shell passing high over the deck of the *Kearsarge* and causing only minor damage to the rigging. The *Alabama* got off two more bow rakes, also to little effect. Winslow avoided exposing his sides until he judged he was close enough for his own guns to count. Then, at 11:00, when the distance had closed to about 900 yards, the *Kearsarge* suddenly turned hard to port and delivered a shell from a small 30-pound rifled gun on the topgallant forecastle, and then a full broad-

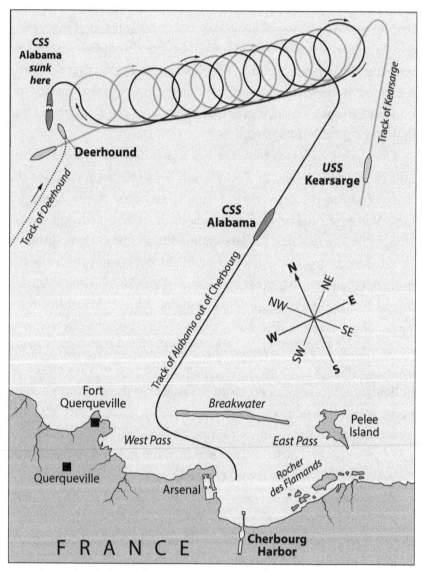

MAP 3. Battle of the *Alabama* and the *Kearsarge*. *Cartography by Jade Myers.*

side from the starboard battery. Both captains, understanding the paramount danger of a stern rake, then sought to protect their sterns and keep their starboard batteries aimed at the other. As a result, the two ships now began circling in a clockwise rotation, each firing constantly while they both drifted in the current toward the west (map 3). The *Alabama*'s crew averaged about one round a minute per gun, while the *Kearsarge*'s gunners paced themselves, reaching less than half that rate of fire but with much more care, deliberation, and effect.

Over the course of seven rotations through the battle, the *Kearsarge*'s shots sounded sharp and loud, having thin, clear vapor. In contrast, the *Alabama*'s shots were dull thuds, producing lots of blackish smoke. Over seventy minutes, the *Alabama* fired 300 shot and shells, with only twenty-eight (9.3 percent) striking the *Kearsarge* and none doing any significant damage to the ship itself. The lifeboats were another story.[10]

Chapter 22

≈

Demise

All the problems that had accumulated over the past year now became consequential. First, the *Alabama*'s gunners generally aimed too high and thus did little damage to the *Kearsarge*. In their haste, the gunners may have neglected to peel off the lead safety caps covering the fuses.[1] Even Commander Irvine Bulloch later wrote that the *Alabama*'s sailors "had not been trained to judge of distances, and were wholly without the skill, precision and coolness which come only with practice and the habit of firing at a visible object and noting the effect."[2] Second, the few shells that did hit the *Kearsarge*'s jury-rigged armor just bounced off. The third and most important problem was that many of the shells, having damp and unreliable powder and fuses, simply failed to explode. In one case, a shell hit the *Kearsarge*'s smokestack, tearing an enormous gash and sending down a shower of metal and sparks but doing little meaningful damage.

Another shell, it is said, might have changed the outcome: it landed in the *Kearsarge*'s sternpost but smoldered harmlessly. Had it exploded as designed, however, it would never have reached the sternpost at all.[3] In any event, the shell became so famous that even Lincoln expressed a desire to see it, and afterward, carpenters removed the sternpost with the shell and shipped it home. Over 150 years later, it can still be seen—at the National Museum of the US Navy in Washington, DC.

In contrast to the *Alabama*'s 300 shells, the *Kearsarge* fired only 173 shells, most with great precision. The *Kearsarge*'s 32-pounder's shells swept the *Alabama*'s deck, and the big Dahlgrens were aimed low, finding their mark at or near the waterline. Over the seven complete circles, the ships gradually drifted closer together, thereby only increasing the *Kearsarge*'s accuracy. Boykin described the effect of the *Kearsarge*'s Dahlgrens: "Their burly iron shells detonated like volcanoes, smashing, crashing, breaking into the hail of deadly fragments, spewing out clouds of sulphureous, stifling smoke, showering the deck with killing splinters. They ripped jagged holes in her side, tore off sections of her bulwarks. They crunched their way through wood and metal like paper. They were blasting the heart out of the *Alabama*."[4]

A single shell from one of the Dahlgrens leveled nearly the entire crew of the *Alabama*'s aft pivot cannon, killing and horrifically mangling several men. It passed through the entire gun's crew, piling up on the deck a mass of human fragments. "Such a ghastly sight," Sinclair wrote, "the writer never saw before."[5] Kell described the moment this way: "Our decks were now covered with the dead and the wounded, and the ship was careening heavily to starboard from the effects of the shot-holes on her water-line. . . . The port side of the quarter-deck was so encumbered with the mangled trunks of the dead that I had to have them thrown overboard, in order to fight the after pivot-gun."[6]

Two Dahlgren shells then pierced the *Alabama*'s side at the waterline, one of which tore through the bunkers at the very heart of the ship, and the water came pouring through. Sixty-five minutes after the first shot, it could take no more; the *Alabama* began to sink.

Now Semmes attempted to run for the shore. On the seventh rotation, with no steam left, he sent sailor John Roberts forward to set the ship's foresail and two jibs. As Roberts untethered the canvas, some shrapnel sliced open his belly, yet he held his guts in place with one hand as he finished his job with the other. He managed to work his way back to the forecastle deck before succumbing. It was all for naught, as Winslow anticipated the maneuver and blocked the escape.

At this point, Semmes sent Kell below to see how long the ship could float. In the wardroom, which served as an operating room, he was aghast to see a stunned Assistant Surgeon Llewellyn, his white apron saturated with blood. A Dahlgren shell had just swept through the room. "As I entered the ward-room the sight was indeed appalling. There stood Assistant Surgeon Llewellyn at his post, but the table and the patient upon it were swept away from him by an eleven-inch shell, which opened in the side of the ship an aperture that was fast filling the ship with water."[7]

Where was White? There is no indication he acted as a surgeon's assistant, so there is no reason to believe that he was with Llewellyn. If he was, Kell never mentioned him. Nor was he assisting Galt, who had got off in the quarter boat. According to secondhand accounts, he might have been on the deck with Bartelli, but Semmes never mentions him. Kell wrote, "Captain Semmes and I, his steward, Bartelli, and two of the men—the sailmaker, Alcott, and Michael Mars—we began to strip off all superfluous clothing."[8]

In another account, Kell reports Bartelli standing by Semmes: "I returned to the stern-port, where stood Captain Semmes with one or two of the men and his faithful steward, who, poor fellow! was doomed to a watery grave, as he could not swim. . . . The stern port was now almost to the water's edge . . . partly undressing, we plunged into the sea."[9] Boykin, who tended to embellish, wrote: "Where was little Dave the while? One moment he was standing with the group, around Semmes, smiling . . . confident as always that he was safe with those he had served so loyally. The next time someone looked, he was gone."[10] Although plausible, there is no known primary source supporting Boykin's assertion that White stuck close to Bartelli and Semmes or that, at this stage of the battle, he remained confident of being safe at all.

As the *Alabama*'s bow started to rise up out of the water, and with its stern awash, Semmes and Kell began to strip. It was now every man for himself. Two men pulled off Semmes's boots, and he took off his coat, which was "too well laden with buttons," and put on a lifebelt. However, it was said that "dignity balked" at removing his trousers.[11] Around this time, an unsuccessful effort was made to save Llewellyn: "It soon became known that Llewellyn could not swim, a couple of empty shell-boxes were procured, and secured on his person, one under each arm, to serve as an improvised life-preserver ... when last seen from the ship [he] was making good weather of it ... but his death was brought about by the shifting of the floats upon his person."[12]

After the *Alabama* was clearly understood to be sinking, a white flag finally appeared.[13] Semmes sent Master's Mate Fullam over to the *Kearsarge* in the dinghy to plead for help. About this time, Galt came on deck and was put in charge of a quarter boat with many of the wounded, which also struck out for the *Kearsarge*.

It is curious that Galt chose to accompany the wounded in the first quarter boat, while Llewellyn, facing a similar circumstance, remained behind. Presumably Galt's logic was that he could join forces with the *Kearsarge*'s surgeons to save as many lives as he could; this would have been common naval practice. According to the *Kearsarge*'s surgeon, Browne, however, Galt wasn't much help. Upon reaching the *Kearsarge*, Galt was so "prostrated with excitement and fatigue" that he was inadequate for duty and sent to rest in the surgeon's stateroom.[14] Llewellyn, on the other hand, made an affirmative decision to remain behind—even blocking other able sailors from entering a boat—so as not to take valuable space needed for the wounded.[15]

Once Fullam's dinghy reached the *Kearsarge*, he stated that the
Alabama had surrendered and was sinking, and asked for assistance.
According to Browne's firsthand account, when Fullam arrived, Captain Winslow demanded, "Does Captain Semmes surrender his ship?"
Given Semmes's history of deception—especially in the *Hatteras* incident—it was well for Winslow to put the direct question. "Yes," was
the reply.[16] Winslow at once commenced to lower his boats, when it
was discovered that only the two least accessible ones were usable;
the *Alabama*'s high shots had damaged all the others. Unaware of this
fact, and true to form, Semmes and Kell would later accuse Winslow
of tardiness in assisting the men in the water.[17] Fullam then asked
permission to return to the *Alabama* with the dinghy and crew to assist in rescuing the drowning, a request Winslow granted.

After Fullam departed, the *Deerhound* steamed under the *Kearsarge*'s stern, and Winslow implored Lancaster to help save the men
in the water. "For God's sake," he cried out, ". . . save who you can!"[18]
Altogether, three of the *Alabama*'s boats, two usable boats from the
Kearsarge, two from the *Deerhound*, and two French pilot boats were
engaged in picking up some hundred men struggling in the water.
Rather than return to the *Kearsarge*, however, Fullam proceeded to
the *Deerhound* and then, according to Surgeon Browne, "cast his boat
adrift."[19] According to Lancaster himself, after Fullam arrived at the
Deerhound, his boat was sunk "to prevent her falling into the hands of
the Federals."[20]

Then came the sequence of events that exposed Semmes to the
accusation of dishonor, if not cowardice. When one of the *Deerhound*'s lifeboat crewmen recognized Kell from his enormous beard,
he was rescued, and there Kell found Semmes lying down, pale and
exhausted. As a launch from the *Kearsarge* came near, Semmes remained prone in the bottom of the lifeboat and was covered with a
tarpaulin to avoid detection. Kell then donned a *Deerhound* crew cap

and grabbed an oar. On being asked about Semmes, Kell replied, "He is drowned!" and the ruse worked; both safely made it onto the *Deerhound*, along with thirty-nine other officers and crew.

Once aboard, Semmes implored Lancaster and Jones to head directly to the safety of British Southampton. In Kell's memoir, written some twenty years later, the *Deerhound* did not sail off until everyone had been saved. "When Mr. Lancaster approached Captain Semmes, and said, 'I think every man has been picked up; where shall I land you?' Captain Semmes replied, 'I am now under the English colors, and the sooner you put me with my officers and men on English soil, the better.'"[21]

It is worth scrutinizing this account, if only because it is at variance with more contemporaneous accounts and because the disinformation has recently resurfaced.[22] The captain of the *Deerhound*, Evan Jones, was more equivocal than Kell, writing only that, "when we saved all we could, we prepared to sail for Southampton."[23] Lancaster avoided the subject entirely in his indignant letter to the *London Daily News*.

Kell's contemporaneous firsthand account tells a different story. In a letter (included in an appendix to his memoir) written home on June 20, he inadvertently admitted that the *Deerhound* skipped the rescue: "We were in the water about half an hour when a boat from the English Steam Yacht Deerhound . . . picked us up, took us on board and kindly treated us—fifteen officers and about twenty-seven men—and steered away for this port. We left a French pilot boat and two boats from the Kearsarge picking up the remainder."[24]

The *Kearsarge*'s officers and crew had observed the *Deerhound* edging to leeward even though dozens of men were still struggling in the water. First Officer Thornton suggested to Winslow that it was making off, but Winslow at first refused to believe it. It was probably fundamentally at odds with his own concept of honor and responsibility that any vessel would sail off while sailors were struggling in the water. Then there was the matter of his prisoners escaping from a battle fairly fought and won. In his official report, he wrote:

> An English yacht, the *Deerhound*, had approached near the *Kear-sarge* at this time, when I hailed and begged the commander to run down to the *Alabama*, as she was fast sinking, and we had but two boats, and assist in picking up the men. He answered affirmatively, and steamed toward the *Alabama*, but the latter sank almost imme-diately. The *Deerhound*, however, sent her boats and was actively engaged, aided by several others, which had come from shore. These boats were busy in bringing the wounded and others to the *Kearsarge*, whom we were trying to make as comfortable as pos-sible, when it was reported to me that the *Deerhound* was moving off.... I could not believe that the commander of that vessel could be guilty of so disgraceful an act as taking our prisoners off, and therefore took no means to prevent it, but continued to keep our boats at work rescuing the men in the water. Sorry to say that I was mistaken.[25]

In another firsthand account, the *Kearsarge*'s boats continued to pick up prisoners for a full half an hour after the *Deerhound* sailed off:

> While we were picking up the men, the *Deerhound*, one of the Royal Yacht Squadron, steamed up to within hailing distance of the ship, and the Captain asked him if he would be kind enough to assist in picking up the men and deliver them up to him, as they were his prisoners. He said he would, and steamed in among them and picked up quite a number, and among them was Cap-tain Semmes. He then steamed off as fast as he could, taking ad-vantage while a good part of our men were off in the boats....

We spent about half an hour in picking up the prisoners, then we "stood in" for the land.[26]

In his formal report, Winslow put the matter bluntly to Welles: "My dispatch of the 21 ultimo informed the Department of the proceedings of the Deerhound yacht, her gradual edging to leeward, leading us to suppose she was seeking men who were drifting in the current, and then taking advantage of the hazy weather to make off while our boats were out, busy in rescuing the larger part of the prisoners, who were struggling in the water."[27]

After the battle, Secretary Welles roundly criticized Winslow for allowing Semmes to escape, but whether or not he knew Semmes was on board the *Deerhound*, it is unlikely Winslow would have chased it at the expense of the rescue or fired a shot at a vessel carrying women and children. As apparent from his letters and background, Winslow was an unusual amalgam of pacifist and warrior, all borne of a pious religiosity that would have had difficulty reconciling retribution at the expense of souls drowning in the water. Semmes remembered Winslow from the Mexican-American War as "a Christian gentleman" and may have counted on it.

In his review, Admiral Porter cut right to the chase: "While the confederate captain, as soon as he was safe on board the *Deerhound*, fearing that Winslow would demand his surrender, urged his friend to save HIM. The latter accordingly made off without further efforts at rescue; so that, if any one was drowned it was due more to the selfishness of Captain Semmes than any other cause."[28] While White, Bartelli, and Llewellyn, among others, were struggling in the water and in desperate need of assistance, Semmes and Kell *helped themselves.*

In an oral account years later, *Kearsarge* seaman James Magee reflected on the difficulty in saving some of the drowning men and their reluctance to accept help: "Some of the men we tried to save would throw up their hands and sink down, so we were obliged to take the boat-hook and reach down three or four feet and hook them up, and some were so far gone that they died in the boats. . . . Not 'til we had arrived [back in port] . . . did we learn how it was that the *Alabama*'s men were so willing to drown. The crew told us that Captain Semmes told them if they were taken prisoners by us that every man would hang to the yard arm."[29]

Once Semmes landed in Southampton and recovered his strength, he wrote a detailed official report to the Confederate agent James Murray Mason, dated June 21, 1864, which was published two days later in numerous British newspapers. The audacious dishonesty is breathtaking: "We now turned all our exertions toward saving the wounded, and such of the boys of the ship who were unable to swim. These were dispatched in my quarter-boats, the only boats remaining to me; the waist-boats having been torn to pieces."[30] In fact, none

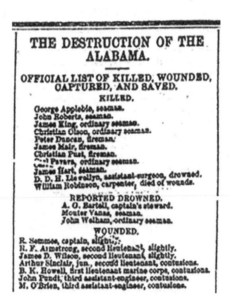

Figure 22.1. "Official List of Killed, Wounded, Captured and Saved," published in the *Liverpool Mercury*, June 27, 1864.

of those rescued by the *Deerhound* were Boys. The "Official List of Killed, Wounded, Captured and Saved," published on June 27 in the *Liverpool Mercury*, is revealing both for what it recorded and what it omitted (fig. 22.1). From this list, no Boys were rescued by the *Deerhound*, one by a French pilot boat, and three Boys by the *Kearsarge*.[31]

The same article is also revealing for a notable omission from the list of those killed and drowned.

Ever a ghost, in the last telling manifestation of the fate of the illiterate, and the racist world in which he lived and died, White remained at the end, invisible.[32]

Part III

AFTERMATH

Chapter 23

✍

Accounts

Having described what I can of David Henry White's actual life, it is now appropriate to read what Semmes and his officers had to say about him, and how they invented a false narrative to portray a Lost Cause caricature of the loyal Black factotum, happy and safe in servility. We have already encountered Semmes's entry in his daily log of Thursday, October 9, 1862, when the *Tonawanda* was captured: "The master having reported that one of the black waiters on board his ship was a slave, from Delaware, had him brought on board and entered as one of the crew, a waiter in the officers' messes."[1]

Semmes and Sinclair further discuss White in their postwar memoirs. These passages make discomforting reading in the original, and while they tell us almost nothing about White, they reveal a great deal about the writers.

Semmes's account includes the following:

I took from on board of her (THE TONAWANDA), one of her passengers. This was a likely negro lad of about seventeen years of age—a slave until he was twenty-one, under the laws of Delaware. This little State, all of whose sympathies were with us, had been ridden over, rough-shod, by the Vandals north of her, as Maryland afterward was, and was arrayed on the side of the enemy. I was obliged, therefore, to treat her as such.

The slave was on his way to Europe, in company with his master. He came necessarily under the laws of war, and I brought him on board the Alabama, where we were in want of good servants, and sent him to wait on the ward-room mess. The boy was a little alarmed at first, but, when he saw kindly faces beaming upon him, and heard from his new masters, and the servants of the mess, some words of encouragement, he became reassured, and, in the course of a few days, was not only at home, but congratulated himself on the exchange he had made. . . . He became, more especially, the servant of Dr. Galt, and there at once arose, between the Virginia gentleman and the slave boy, that sympathy of master and servant, which our ruder people of the North find it so impossible to comprehend. Faithful service, respect, and attachment followed protection and kind treatment, and the slave was as happy as the day was long. David soon became . . . indispensable . . . and was really . . . free, . . . except only in the circumstance that he could not change masters. I caused his name to be entered on the books of the ship, as one of the crew, and allowed him the pay of his grade. In short, no difference was made between him and the white waiters of the mess.

His condition was in every respect bettered; though, I doubt not, a howl went up over his capture, as soon as it became known to the pseudo-philanthropists of the North, who know as little about the negro and his nature, as they do about the people of the South.

It was pleasant to regard the affection which this boy conceived for Galt, and the pride he took in serving him. As he brought the doctor's camp-stool for him to the bridge, placed it in the coziest corner he could find, and ran off to bring him a light for his cigar, his eyes would dilate, and his ivories shine.

Dave served us during the whole cruise. He went on shore in all parts of the world, knew that the moment he touched the shore he was at liberty to depart, if he pleased, and was tampered with by sun-dry Yankee Consuls, but always came back to us. He seemed to have the instinct of deciding between his friends and his enemies.[2]

Sinclair also mentions White:

Among the prisoners shipping on the Alabama during the whaling-raid off the Azores, we will call your attention to little David H. White. He became quite a marked character on our vessel. Dave was a Delaware slave, a boy about seventeen or eighteen years old; and wanting in the ward-room mess of our ship an efficient waiter-boy, the lot fell to Dave. He was not only willing but anxious to ship. The natural instincts of the lad told him we would be his friends. He knew Southern gentlemen on sight. Dave became a great favorite with the officers, his willing, obliging manners, cheerful disposition, and untiring attention winning for him the affection of not only the officers, but of the entire ship's company. . . . It was his privilege to go on shore with the ward-room steward to market; and on all occasions the American consul or his satellites would use all their eloquence to persuade Dave to desert his ship, reminding him of his present condition of slavery and the chance presented of throwing off his shackles, but Dave remained loyal in face of all temptation.[3]

These passages are illuminating not just because of the obvious self-serving paternalism but even more so for the enduring trope they purposefully articulate: that of the happy servant that so dominated earlier, contemporaneous, and subsequent popular culture. In constructing this narrative, Semmes goes a step further in using White as an illustration of the entire Black population. He does this in two specific places—first, when he states that there arose "between the Virginia gentleman and the slave boy, that sympathy of master and servant, which our ruder people of the North find it so impossible to comprehend." Second, he complains that Northern "pseudo-philan-thropists" know "little about the negro and his nature." In explicitly using White as an illustration of the entire Black population, and in calling on their natural comfort, as a people, with servitude, this passage illustrates how Semmes invented a caricature and used it to articulate and promote his racist worldview to his audience. In this case, we can clearly see an enduring aspect of both individual and structural racism: a contempt for other members of the human race expressed not in epithets or color bars but in diminished expectations and opportunity.

Indeed, almost everything they had to say about White was demonstrably false. Before proceeding to a forensic dissection of the lies, it is of interest to note how these tropes were put to use. Part I presents the construction of the long-standing trope of the happy slave, of which Semmes's account was just one small part. But, more specifically, White's life has also been appropriated by various Confederacy-sympathizing websites to perpetuate the idea that Black Americans in the South somehow supported the Confederacy. Historian Kevin M. Levin points out that while the idea of Black Confederates originated in the Civil War, the trope was embraced in the twentieth century as a key component of the Lost Cause narrative because it "would make it easier for the descendants of Confederate soldiers and those who celebrate Confederate heritage to embrace their Lost Cause unapologetically without running the risk of being viewed as racially insensitive or worse."[4]

We see this happening specifically in the case of White. The numerous examples include his name being added to the Delaware Confederate Monument in May 2007; an editorial in the *Confederate*

Naval Historical Society Newsletter in 1990 celebrating White's loyalty to the Confederacy as a demonstration of racial and cultural harmony; and a website purporting to celebrate citizens of Delaware who served the Confederacy. White is described as "a popular wardroom mess steward, as well as a paid crew member of the ship. . . . David White repaid this action with faithful service. . . . Upon word of Lincoln's emancipation and while in port in Australia, David refused to return to Delaware against the wishes of [a] Federal loyalist."[5] Here it can be seen how the original falsehoods are not only propagated but embellished. Never mind that the *Alabama* was never closer to Australia than 900 miles (see map 1) or that Semmes received word of the Emancipation Proclamation on March 2, 1863, while the *Alabama* was in the North Atlantic. As far as I can document, the only effect the proclamation had on White was that Delaware changed its laws in such a way as to make it nearly impossible for him to return (chapter 16).

In more recent historical overviews of the Civil War at sea, White remains entirely invisible.[6] To be fair, such works stem from a paradigm focusing on global political conflict, as opposed to the one used here, which takes as its frame of reference one disempowered life. Where White has been mentioned, his appropriated life has entered the realm of accepted history.[7]

As time has gone by, successive writers have placed greater emphasis on Semmes's racism. Scholars such as Summersell, Spencer, Marvel, and Fox expose the gulf between Semmes's self-serving accounts and the external testimony of witnesses. Fox, in particular, judges Semmes severely and persuasively argues that the cruise of the *Alabama* deserved to end in defeat. The task at hand is for our understanding of White to catch up with our understanding of Semmes.

Chapter 24

⤗

An Ocean of Lies

It is now possible to summarize the original lies and perpetuated falsehoods that, together with the unattributed *New York Herald* account (chapter 12), are internally consistent—suggesting perhaps a prearranged story.[1] Notable falsehoods include: (1) White was a passenger on the *Tonawanda*; (2) White was a slave; (3) Semmes was told that White was a slave by the *Tonawanda*'s captain; (4) White was accompanying a Delaware businessman who was his master; (5) White was a slave until twenty-one under the laws of the state of Delaware; (6) White's condition on being transferred to the *Alabama* from the *Tonawanda* was "bettered" and he was "allowed the pay of his grade"; (7) "He became, more especially, the servant of Dr. Galt, and there at once arose, between the Virginia gentleman and the slave boy, that sympathy of master and servant, which our ruder people of the North find it so impossible to comprehend"; (8) "He went on shore in all parts of the world"; (9) White "knew that the moment he touched the shore he was at liberty to depart, if he pleased, and was tampered with by sun-dry Yankee Consuls, but always came back to us"; and, finally, (10) "We now turned all our exertions toward saving the wounded, and such of the boys of the ship who were unable to swim."

Each of these falsehoods can be refuted in turn.

1. "I took on board of her one of her passengers": The *Tonawanda* manifests make clear that White was demonstrably not a passenger on the *Tonawanda*; he was crew (chapter 4).

2. White was a slave: The description of White as "a slave" is conclusively disproven by reference to the US censuses of 1850 and 1860, in which he is listed under the category "Free Inhabitants of Lewes and Rehoboth Hundred" (chapter 3).

3. "The master [captain] having reported that one of the black waiters on board his ship was a slave, from Delaware": This is entirely disingenuous. Captain Julius certainly told Semmes that White was from Delaware, but it was Semmes's appropriation of Delaware law to describe White as enslaved. It is implausible that Julius would have said this to Semmes, inasmuch as Julius had signed White on, recorded the kidnapping in his logbook, and immediately reported the kidnapping of the free teenager to the American authorities in Liverpool (chapter 10). Moreover, Julius was a captain of a ship owned by a Quaker company that regularly couriered abolitionist literature and correspondence through an organized network of Black sailors with whom White sailed (chapter 4).

4. White was accompanying his Delaware master: On scrutiny, it is clear that this is another lie. For starters, the only posited white individual White might have accompanied was his former employer, Edward Watson. Watson does not appear on the *Tonawanda* manifest in any class—forward, cabin, or steerage. The definitive refutation of this canard, however, is the crew's manifest of

the *Tonawanda*, which documents that White joined the vessel as a paid cook and as part of a galley crew that signed on as a team (chapter 4). The contract, signed by both Captain Julius and White, explicitly stated "that for the due performance of . . . the abovementioned articles and agreements, and acknowledgement of their being voluntary, and without compulsion, or any other clandestine means being used, agreed to and signed by us."

5. A slave until twenty-one under the laws of Delaware: This was Semmes's sea-lawyerly incorrect interpretation—and appropriation—of Delaware law. Semmes was referring to Delaware's Act of 1797 and subsequent amendments "for the better regulation of servants and slaves within this government." Section 11 of the Act pertains to the children of "free Negroes" (chapter 2):

> And if any free Negro or Negroes having children, are not able to maintain or support them, it shall and may be lawful to and for the two next Justices of the Peace, and they are hereby required, together with the Overseers of the Poor of the hundred where the said Negro or Negroes shall dwell, to bind out to service such Negro children, the males until they shall come to the age of twenty-one years, the females until they shall come to the age of eighteen years.[2]

First, it is worth noting that this passage pertains to free families, not to slaves. Furthermore such "bindings to service" were recorded in the records of the justice of the peace or Trustees of the Poor. These apprenticeships were duly recorded, along with the age of the child bound out, but there is no such record for David Henry White of Sussex County.

There is no such record because White was not indigent; he

was gainfully employed, and this fact is well documented in his formal contract with the Cope Line. Finally, the law is clear that only justices of the peace or Overseers of the Poor "of the Hundred where said Negro or Negroes shall dwell" could bind out to service. Semmes had no such appointment, and it was a stretch—even in the convoluted world of maritime law—to argue, even in wartime, that the wide Atlantic Ocean had somehow become a legal hundred of Sussex County, Delaware.

In summary, as a gainfully employed teenager, White had never been subject to the penury sanctions of Delaware. As a legal matter, after April 1863, he was not even a resident of Delaware (chapter 15). According to an analysis by the late constitutional historian and associate justice of the Delaware Supreme Court, Randy J. Holland, from the viewpoint of contemporaneous Delaware law, White was free from the day he was born until the day he died.[3]

6. "His condition was in every respect bettered" and he was "allowed the pay of his grade": It is impossible to determine the degree to which White's condition was "bettered" in every respect. In two important respects by which we conventionally judge betterment—salary and station—his condition was demonstrably worsened. White's position on the *Tonawanda* was recorded in the manifest as that of "Passenger Cook," with a salary of $15 per month (chapter 4). Significantly, this was not the most junior position available on this or other vessels. As noted previously, in the nineteenth century it was common for males under the age of eighteen, irrespective of racial identity, to occupy the position of Boy. On the *Tonawanda*, Boys earned $6.00 a month.

Yet on the *Alabama*, in two separate manifests, White's position is recorded as that of Boy, once in Semmes's muster roll of

November 29, 1862, and again in the muster roll of July 7, 1863, with a monthly salary of $9.68 (chapter 18). When compared to his position on the *Tonawanda*, White's condition was "bettered" with a reduction in salary and a demotion.

7. "He became, more especially, the servant of Dr. Galt, and there at once arose, between the Virginia gentleman and the slave boy, that sympathy of master and servant, which our ruder people of the North find it so impossible to comprehend": The "sympathy of master and servant" notwithstanding, Galt got off on the first quarter boat with no apparent consideration for White.

8. "He went on shore in all parts of the world": One part of the world where White was certainly not permitted on shore was Singapore. Here, US consul Francis Stobb reported on December 22, "I endeavored to communicate with the crew of the *Alabama* but was prevented by no boats being permitted to approach her sides" (Chapter 19).[4]

9. He "knew that the moment he touched the shore he was at liberty to depart, if he pleased, and was tampered with by sun-dry Yankee Consuls, but always came back to us": As shown, Semmes may have had good reason to be irritated at the strident defense of American rights proffered by US consuls. A review of consular reports—by John W. Camps from Jamacia, Thomas Y. Wilson from Bahia, Walter Graham from Cape Town, and Francis D. Stobb from Singapore—provides no independent evidence that any of them ever encountered the teenager. Graham was especially meticulous in his reports, and one would think he would have made special mention of encountering White, whose kidnapping had been widely reported in the New York and Philadelphia newspapers. Perhaps the perils of a Black teenager weren't

worth mentioning, or just as likely, given Semmes's other fabrications, the encounters simply never happened.

Moreover, by April 1863, Delaware had changed its laws so that White was no longer considered a resident of the state and could no longer return home (chapter 16). Semmes neglects to mention that the *Alabama* visited only friendly ports and avoided unfriendly ones, such as Bombay. Furthermore in every location, White observed not only the fawning public reception by the local populations but also the gracious private receptions given to the *Alabama*'s officers by local authorities. He also regularly observed the local authorities helping the *Alabama*'s officers drag deserting sailors back to the ship in irons—and they were *white!* And then there is Sinclair's inadvertent admission that White was not allowed ashore alone, and his introduction of the word "shackles"—perhaps metaphorical, perhaps not.

White's "loyalty"—if it existed at all—is questionable given Semmes's description of his "loyal servant" Ned on the *Sumter*, who in reality had deserted (chapter 10). But what if we take Semmes at his word? It must then be considered that, having no other options, White may have ultimately accepted the bargain that Semmes, Kell, Galt, Low, the Bullochs, and Sinclair were offering: that from "faithful service, respect, and attachment . . . [would follow] protection and kind treatment." If so, White could not have known that he would be the victim of a lethal bait and switch, for at the moment he most needed protection—the moment impressionistically imagined from a distance in the Manet painting—Galt would hop on the first lifeboat, and Semmes, Kell, Sinclair, Low, Bulloch, and the other officers would just sail away.

Ever the sea lawyer, Semmes had chosen his words carefully. In exchange for his protection, he expected White's faithful service, but the captain never articulated a quid pro quo—that in return for White's faithful service, Semmes's protection would follow. Perhaps one followed the other—we will never know—but, if so, it was only a one-way proposition, entirely at the discretion of the captors.

10. "We now turned all our exertions toward saving the wounded, and such of the boys of the ship who were unable to swim. These were dispatched in my quarter-boats, the only boats remaining to me; the waist-boats having been torn to pieces": The record shows that the *Deerhound* left the scene while men were still floundering in the water, by Lancaster's account destroying a lifeboat on its way. According to the "Official List of the Killed, Wounded, Captured, and Saved" published in the *Liverpool Mercury*, no Boys were saved by the *Deerhound* at all (chapter 22).

To summarize White's position: He had grown up in poverty and illiteracy in Sussex County, Delaware—a place famous in his experience for the number of free Blacks who were under constant threat of kidnapping and being sold south (chapter 2). When kidnapped, he was "a little alarmed" (chapter 10). Days later, he experienced the terror of being lashed to the bulwark of an unfamiliar, unstable ship in a hurricane (chapter 11). He lived on a vessel with a dangerous cast of openly racist officers and alcoholic mercenaries. He understood that it wouldn't be easy to leave this ship, and he regularly watched sailors punished with irons, tricing, bread-and-water diets, spread-eagling, and dousing (chapters 12–20).

In conclusion, White's actual life has been obscured by a series of lies. In exposing these lies, his journey, while not conventionally heroic, belies the Lost Cause and takes on a significance worthy of further reflection.

Chapter 25

⤚

Aide toi et dieu t'aidera

In November 1984, the French minesweeper *Circe* discovered the wreck of the *Alabama* about seven nautical miles off the coast of Cherbourg. Four years later, 125 years after it plummeted with David White to the bottom of the Channel, French navy divers recovered the bronze casting affixed to the *Alabama*'s wheel; its engraved motto readily apparent in brutalist font. Artifacts we can recover; lives are not so easy.

An unofficial motto of the Confederacy, the phrase "Aide-toi et dieu t'aidera" was also famously engraved on Robert E. Lee's ceremonial sword, now on display at the American Civil War Museum in Richmond. The sentiment has a long and complex history that predates Christianity, appearing in several Greek tragedies as well as in Aesop's fables.[1] A favorite of French Bourbons, the adage may have crossed the Atlantic with Semmes's ancestors.

Although often mistaken as scriptural, it does not appear in the Bible. The English equivalent "God helps those who help themselves" was first coined in 1698 by the English political theorist Al-

Figure 25.1. *Alabama* ship's wheel. *Courtesy of National Museum of the U.S. Navy; Naval History and Heritage Command. Photo by Bryan R. Smith.*

gernon Sidney and became famously popularized in North America by Benjamin Franklin in the 1733 edition of *Poor Richard's Almanac*.

The phrase does not fit neatly within the range of ideas and expressions by which we familiarly hear a divine invocation. At one extreme is the passive form, such as the Yiddish expression *Gotenyu.*[2] "God Willing," "In God We Trust," and even the Confederacy's official motto, *Deo vindice*, "God is our defender," are also relatively passive. Prayer is a more active voice, in which God's intervention is faithfully requested.

"God helps those who help themselves" fits nowhere in this continuum. It exists completely outside the range of divine invocation, because it employs God's will ex post facto to justify human behavior, independently of any moral code. While not exactly a logical corollary, the phrase can be read as providing a permission structure for those who would deny help to others.

The phrase is viewed with suspicion by many Christians, as it could be interpreted as contrary to the Bible's message of God's grace. In this view, it is out of order to put individual agency before God as a source of help and strength.[3] It seems even more so in the French iteration: *Aide toi*, "help yourself," is at the beginning of the phrase. Another objection points out that the Bible says that God helps the *helpless*! Isaiah 25:4 declares, "For thou hast been a strength to the poor, a strength to the needy in his distress, a refuge from the storm, a shadow from the heat, when the blast of the terrible ones is as a storm against the wall."[4]

When taken out of context and stripped of its righteous and political applications, "God helps those who help themselves" is a benign, if not profound and powerful anthem for self-actualization, and we use it as such all the time. Who would deny that all other things being equal, we all bear a responsibility for determining our own fate? The difficulty is that all other things aren't equal, and the expression takes on a different meaning when applied to those who are experiencing, as the saying goes, the boot on the neck. It's no good saying "God helps those who help themselves" to a John McCain, who was held in a Vietnamese prison for over five years, or to the family of George Floyd, who did everything in his power over the space of nine minutes, to help himself.

In this sense, it is a rhetorical wolf in sheep's clothing. A benign-sounding expression, it carries undertones of Social Darwinism—the flawed Spencerian interpretation of the phrase "survival of the fittest" discussed in chapter 5. In this interpretation, "fittest" connotes strength and dominance, as opposed to the biological Darwinian meaning of differential reproduction.[5]

There is no question that Semmes, Kell, and Galt *helped themselves*. The issue is that they did it to the exclusion, if not at the expense, of those, such as White and Bartelli, who stripped of any other options, utterly depended on them, and to whom they had given false assurances of protection. Looters and thieves also *help themselves* to material goods not otherwise available to them under the law. When read in this way, "God helps those who help themselves" becomes a quasi-moral rationale for the law of the jungle.

To be clear, White did everything in his power to help himself. Born into a remote county at a time when poverty and denial of literacy were the norm, he found work by the age of fifteen and evaded antebellum Delaware's harsh Black Codes. When his employer's business faltered, he used one of the few avenues the Delaware legislature supplied and then snatched away, as an opportunity to earn a living, see the world, and return one day to his family. Despite being forcibly kidnapped, enduring the terror of being lashed to a bulwark on an unstable ship during a hurricane, and having to navigate tricky relationships with racist officers and a feral crew, he seems to have been well liked by just about everybody given the confining social conventions of his day. But none of that was good enough—because on the CSS *Alabama*, it was not the benign, self-actualizing meaning of the adage that applied, but that of the Social Darwinist.

In closing, the reference to Darwinism brings to mind a story germane to the issue of legacies. A famous debate was held at Oxford in 1870 on evolution between, among others, the Anglican bishop Samuel Wilberforce (son of the important British abolitionist William Wilberforce) and Thomas Huxley, one of Darwin's earliest and most articulate supporters. At one point, Wilberforce, so renowned an orator that he was popularly lampooned as "Soapy Sam," turned to Huxley and "begged to know, was it through his grandfather or his grandmother that he claimed his descent from a monkey?" Huxley's response was priceless: he would not be ashamed to have a monkey for an ancestor, he is reported to have said, but would be "ashamed to be connected with a man who used great gifts to obscure the truth."[6]

The expression applies well to Semmes, so that, it is possible after all to add something more than just an asterisk to his biography: he was a kidnapper, who used great gifts to obscure the truth.

As for White—whether he was forcibly restrained or a victim of a fraudulent scam—we can only hope that henceforth he will be remembered as a teenage Black life that mattered.

THE END

Acknowledgments

⚓

While the preface makes clear that I was sensitized to racism in South Africa, I was certainly prepared to engage on the subject given my own family background. My mother, Estelle Sillen Fuchs, an applied anthropologist, was deeply concerned with the issues faced by those struggling to navigate the modern world with traditional values, especially in the realm of education. My father, William Fuchs, a middle-school guidance counselor in Bushwick, Brooklyn, served on a panel for the US Civil Rights Commission that published a 1967 report on racial isolation in public schools. A captain in the US Army Air Corps during World War II, he moved with the 323rd Bomb Group to Augsburg, Bavaria, where, as an army officer fluent in Yiddish, he helped billet and resettle orphaned teenage survivors of Dachau. Both my parents were keenly aware of racism and anti-Semitism, and sensitized my brother and I accordingly.

Among the many wonderful professors I encountered as a doctoral student at the University of Pennsylvania in the 1970s, Anthony F. C. Wallace most influenced my approach to this material. Wallace was well known for his work on personality and culture, and I admired him for telling a good story and making the story tell. At the University of Cape Town, I was fortunate to work for and learn from Vice Chancellor Mamphela Ramphele, a cofounder of the Black Consciousness Movement. I also encountered an extraordinary cadre of scholars and writers in South Africa, from whom I learned, in one way or another, to read history as literature and to write it that way.

Over thirty-odd years of intermittent research, I have benefited from a number of archivists and librarians, among them Courtney Pinkard and Meredith McDonough at the Alabama Department of Archives and History; Joe Fodor, Judith Wild, and the librarians at Brooklyn College Interlibrary Loan; Dawne Slater at AncestryPro-Genealogists; Glynis Fobb, who viewed the HMS *Endymion* Logs at the British Archives; Cecily Dyer at the Center for Brooklyn History; Margaret Raubacher Dunham at the Delaware State Archives; Andrew Williams, Steve Smith, Sarah Heim, and the entire staff at the Historical Society of Pennsylvania; K. Edward Rice at the City of Philadelphia Department of Records; Megan Good, Sarah Augustine, and Craig Bruns at the Independence Seaport Museum in Philadelphia; Ashley Augustyniak at the Philadelphia Science History Museum; Maribeth Quinlan and Pat Schaefer at the Mystic Seaport Museum; Denise Clemons and Bill Hicks at the Lewes Historical Society; Denise Hibay, Tal Naden, and Deirdre E. Donahue at the New York Public Library; Debra Elfenbeim at the Pratt Library in Baltimore; Alexandra Villaseran at the Center for Legislative Archives in Washington, DC; Nathan Perry at the National Museums of Liverpool; Ervan L. Jordan Jr., Albert and Shirley Small Special Collections Library, University of Virginia; Matthew Guillen and Andrew Foster at the Virginia Museum of History and Culture; and the archivists at the Library of Congress and at the US, British, and South African National Archives. Among those who provided critical introductions, I thank Margaret Marshall, Florence and Admiral Robert Rosen, and Elliott Oldak.

A few key experts merit special appreciation, among them the late retired associate justice of the Delaware Supreme Court Randy J. Holland (in memoriam). Holland's expertise and imprimatur made it possible to state from a Delaware legal standpoint that White was free from the day he was born until the day he died.

I also benefited greatly from the generous time and informed expertise of Richard Du Moulin, chair of the Storm Trysail Foundation and former chair of the Seamen's Church Institute of New York and New Jersey, on all matters nautical. Douglas Stevenson conferred on the responsibilities of ship's surgeons in battle. Historian Jennie K. Williams provided key insight into middle ground history and historiography and asked tough, rigorous questions that continually challenged many of my earlier assumptions. Bruno Werz shared his unparalleled knowledge of Dutch East India shipwrecks at the Cape.

Becoming familiar with the relevant historiography beyond my home discipline was indeed a steep learning curve. In this case I also relied on the academic review process to help guide the way. Nadine Zimmerli and her team at the University of Virginia Press initially helped, and after the manuscript was taken up by Johns Hopkins University Press, Laura Davulis organized another round of review; together these reviews constituted a crash course in US naval and Civil War history. Anonymous reviewers' careful reading and detailed responses made it possible to tell White's story informed by relevant scholarship.

Primary sources pertaining to White are exceedingly rare, and so this project owes a special debt of gratitude to the Avil family, descendants of Captain Theodore Julius of the *Tonawanda*. In particular, Ted and Robert Avil and their late parents, Ted and Grace Avil, made available the *Tonawanda* log and Briscoe print, both of which the family has lovingly curated and preserved over the generations.

Lt. Ian McConnaughey, Public Affairs Officer, Communication and Outreach Division, graciously and efficiently facilitated Bryan R. Smith's photography of the *Alabama*'s wheel. Jade Myers did miraculous work on the illustrations, deftly working with my endless revisions and corrections. David Shire and Deniz Cordell transcribed "*Daar kom die Alibama.*" Devon Thomas expertly indexed the book.

On the subject of enduring endless revisions and corrections, special appreciation goes to Roxsana Patel Sussewell, a phenomenal editor who helped crystallize the narrative, provided an insightful sounding board as the manuscript took shape, and took on the herculean task of panel-beating the manuscript into *The Chicago Manual of Style.*

My agent, Christopher Rogers, encouraged me to expand my vision, understood the limited terrain of "crossover" book publishers, and found a home for the project at JHUP, where Laura Davulis, Ezra Rodriguez, Kyle Kretzer, and Ruth Chung made everything possible, promptly answering my endless queries and helping to provide critical resources and introductions.

I have relied on feedback from friends, colleagues, and relations who commented on early manuscripts or otherwise encouraged me. Among them are Robert Baron, Tina Barsby, Barry Feirstein, Ben Bernstein, Don and Maggie Buchwald, Teresa Clarke, Janet Graaff, Monica Graaff, Gunja San Gupta, Thomas Heffernan, Alan Hirsch, Hilary Ivory and Douglas Skinner, Ivan Jablonka, Gloria Levitas, Evan Lieberman, Margaret Marshall, Anthony Marx, Stephen Mulvain, Mamphela Ramphele, Charles Rudoy, Carmel Schrire; lifelong friends Didi Conn, Edward McCatty, Judy Rothman Rofé, David Wasserman, and Joshua Williams; my cousins Thomas and Robert Sillen; and my brother Jonathan M. Fuchs.

My children, Sam and Julia, remained enthusiastic and engaged, as I pursued this research literally over the course of their lives. Sam's GIS skills and Julia's close reading elevated the illustrations and narrative and were a deep source of pride and satisfaction. Finally, my heartfelt thanks to Annie Hauck, for all her encouragement, sustenance, and love in the final stretch.

Notes

Author's Note

1 Lori Tharp, "The Case for Black with a Capital B," *New York Times*, November 18, 2014, https://www.nytimes.com/2014/11/19/opinion /the-case-for-black-with-a-capital-b.html.

2 Tharp, "Black with Capital B."

3 Nancy Coleman, "Times Insider: Why We're Capitalizing Black," *New York Times*, July 5, 2020, https://www.nytimes.com/2020/07/05/insider /capitalized-black.html.

4 Neil Irvin Painter, "Opinion: Why 'White' Should Be Capitalized, Too." *Washington Post*, July 22, 2020, https://www.washingtonpost.com /opinions/2020/07/22/why-white-should-be-capitalized/.

Preface

1 A racially mixed population descended from enslaved people whom the Dutch brought from Indonesia, as well as from indigenous herders, and Afrikaners—themselves descended from both the Dutch and the French Huguenots.

2 In creating this index, the JSE employed a triple bottom-line methodology, an accounting framework that considers business value to include *people, planet,* and *profit.* See Tracy Burrows, "JSE Creates Social Responsibility Index," *ITWeb*, May 19, 2004, https://www.itweb.co.za /content/G98YdMLxl1yMX2PD.

3 In forcing public disclosure of "the depths of depravity" during the Apartheid years, the TRC was at once cathartic, emotionally traumatic,

and, for many, deeply unsatisfactory. Aaron Levin, "Tutu Praises Healing Power of Forgiveness," *Psychiatric News* 46, no. 12 (2011): 6–33, https://doi.org/10.1176/pn.46.12.psychnews_46_12_6. See also Lewis R. Gordon, foreword to *I Write What I Like*, by Steve Biko (Chicago: University of Chicago Press, 2002), vii–xiii. According to Charlayne Hunter-Gault, the TRC provided the foundation for "the messy work-in-progress called democracy." Quoted in Antjie Krog, *Country of My Skull: Guilt, Sorrow, and the Limits of Forgiveness in the New South Africa* (New York: Three Rivers Press, 1999), vii. Krog asserts "The goal is not to avoid pain or reality, but to deal with the never-ending quest for self-definition and negotiation required to transform differences into assets. Reconciliation is not only a process. It is a cycle that will be repeated many times" (386).

4   In flagging the importance of South African transformation, particularly for humanities scholarship, it should be noted that the South Africa of today still has a long way to go to catch up with the dreams and expectations of the transformational (immediate post-Apartheid) era. See John Eligon and Lynsey Chutel, "Has South Africa Truly Defeated Apartheid," New York Times, April 28, 2024, https://www.nytimes.com/interactive/2024/04/26/world/africa/south-africa-apartheid-freedom.html. These challenges have been well described by South Africans themselves. See Mamphela Ramphele, *Dreams, Betrayal and Hope* (Cape Town: Penguin Random House, 2017); Andrew Feinstein, *After the Party: A Personal and Political Journey inside the ANC* (Johannesburg: Jonathan Ball, 2007); Richard Calland, *The Zuma Years: South Africa's Changing Face of Power* (Johannesburg: Random House Struik, 2013); Jonathan Shapiro, *Zapiro: But Will It Stand Up in Court? Cartoons from Mail & Guardian, Sunday Times, and the Times* (Auckland Park, South Africa: Jacana, 2013); Hlumelo Biko, *The Great African Society: A Plan for a Nation Gone Astray* (Johannesburg: Jonathan Ball, 2013); and Sherylle Dass, Zimkhitha Mhlahlo, and Tsukudu Moroeng, "Broken Promises: Is South Africa on the Verge of Being a Failed State?" Friends of the LRC, Occasional Paper, 2001. In addition, Evan Lieberman, a political scientist at Princeton University, concluded in a detailed analysis that, while far from perfect, South African democracy has proved to be remarkably resilient and reasonably successful at limiting otherwise inherent ethnic tensions, and more notably, that in contrast to virtually all other failed or transitional democracies, it maintains a free press and fair elections. See Evan Lieberman, *Until We Have Won Our Liberty: South Africa after Apartheid* (Princeton, NJ: Princeton University Press, 2022).

5   See W. E. B. Du Bois, "Strivings of the Negro People," *The Atlantic,*August 1897, https://www.theatlantic.com/magazine/archive/1897/08/strivings-of-the-negro-people/305446/. In addition, Biko himself cited the Negritude movement, founded by opponents of French colonialism. See Zakes Mda, "BIKO: The Quest for a True Humanity," *paper* presented at the Steve Biko Memorial Lecture, 2001, https://www.apartheidmuseum.org/exhibitions/biko-the-quest-for-a-true-humanity. See also Steve Biko, *I Write What I Like: Selected Writings* (Chicago: University of Chicago Press, 1978); Mamphela Ramphele, *A Life* (Cape Town: David Philip, 1995). For further discussion of the origins of Black Consciousness, see Gordon, foreword.

6   Adam H. Domby, *The False Cause: Fraud, Fabrication, and White Supremacy in Confederate Memory* (Charlottesville: University of Virginia Press, 2020), 2.

7   Biko, *I Write What I Like*, 29.

8   See, for example, the District Six Museum, https://www.districtsix.co.za/; the Robben Island Museum, https://www.robben-island.org.za/; and the Apartheid Museum, https://www.apartheidmuseum.org/. See also Pippa Skotnes, ed., *Miscast: Negotiating the Presence of the Bushmen* (Cape Town: University of Cape Town Press, 1996); Pippa Skotnes, *Claim to the Country: The Archive of Lucy Lloyd and Wilhelm Bleek* (Johannesburg: Jacana, 2007).

9   John Maxwell Coetzee, *Dusklands* (New York: Penguin Books, 1974).

10   See, for example, Joel H. Silbey, *Storm over Texas: The Annexation Controversy and the Road to Civil War* (New York: Oxford University Press, 2007), xvii.

Chapter 1. David Henry White and the False Cause

1   In a letter to his son, Farragut wrote on July 20, 1864, "I would sooner have fought that fight than any ever fought on the ocean." Loyall Farragut, *The Life of David Glasgow Farragut, First Admiral of the United States Navy Embodying his Journal and Letters* (New York: D. Appleton and Company, 1882), 403.

2   Carl Sandburg, *Abraham Lincoln: The Prairie Years and the War Years* (New York: Harcourt Inc., 1954), 540.

3   See entry for July 6, 1864, in Gideon Welles, *Diary of Gideon Welles*, Vol. 2, *1864–1866* (New York: Houghton Mifflin, 1909), 67–68.

4 "The Alabama: Eighteen Men-of-War After Her—The Way Secretary
Wells Has Slept—The Work of the Navy-Yards." *New York Times*,
January 1, 1863, https://www.nytimes.com/1863/01/01/archives/the
-alabama-eighteen-menofwar-after-herthe-way-secretary-wells-has.
html. See also "Report of the Secretary of the Navy," *Sailor's Magazine
and Seamen's Friend* 35 (January 1863): 135, https://babel.hathitrust.org
/cgi/pt?id=hvd.ah6ggc&seq=7.

5 George W. Dalzell, *The Flight from the Flag: The Continuing Effect of the
Civil War upon the American Carrying Trade* (Chapel Hill: University
of North Carolina Press, 1940). For further analysis, see Charles M.
Robinson, *Shark of the Confederacy: The Story of the CSS* Alabama (London:
Leo Cooper, 1995), 156–57.

6 Even recent accounts, such as Craig L. Symonds, *The Civil War at Sea*
(New York: Oxford University Press, 2009); James M. McPherson,
War on the Waters: The Union and Confederate Navies, 1861–1865 (Chapel
Hill: University of North Carolina Press, 2012), and Phillip A. Keith
and Tom Clavin, *To the Uttermost Ends of the Earth: The Epic Hunt for
the South's Most Feared Ship-and the Greatest Sea Battle of the Civil War*
(Toronto: Hanover Square Press, 2022).

7 Foster reflects on whether the Lost Cause is best understood as
mythology, as "civil religion," or as a revitalization movement. See
Gaines M. Foster, *Ghosts of the Confederacy: Defeat, the Lost Cause, and the
Emergence of the New South* (New York: Oxford University Press, 1987).
7. For more on revitalization movements, see Anthony F. C. Wallace,
"Revitalization Movements.' *American Anthropologist* 58, no. 2 (April
1956), https://anthrosource.onlinelibrary.wiley.com/doi/epdf/10.1525
/aa.1956.58.2.02a00040.

8 For example, Caroline E. Janney, *Remembering the Civil War: Reunion and
the Limits of Reconciliation* (Chapel Hill: University of North Carolina
Press, 2013), 86.

9 Frank J. Wetta and Martin A. Novelli, *The Long Reconstruction: The
Post–Civil War South in History, Film, and Memory* (New York: Routledge,
2014), 68.

10 Raphael Semmes, *Service Afloat and Ashore during the Mexican War*
(Cincinnati: Wm. H. Moore and Co., 1851), 17.

11 Foster, *Ghosts of the Confederacy.*

12 Paul Quigley, *Shifting Grounds: Nationalism and the American South,
1848–1865* (New York: Oxford University Press, 2012).

13 Foster, *Ghosts of the Confederacy*, 25.

14 Janney, *Remembering the Civil War*, 142.

15 Alexander H. Stephens, *Constitutional View of the Late War between the States* (New York: National Publishing Company, 1870); Edward A. Pollard, *The Lost Cause; A New Southern History of the War of the Confederate.: Comprising a Full and Authentic Account of the Rise and Progress of the Late Southern Confederacy—The Campaigns, Battles, Incidents, and Adventures of the Most Gigantic Struggle of the World's History: Drawn from Official Sources, and Approved by the Most Distinguished Confederate Leaders* (New York: E. B. Treat & Co., 1866).

16 Semmes's 1869 memoir was influential in an unpredictable, orthogonal way: Kaiser Wilhelm II made it required reading among his senior naval officers, and among them was Erich Raeder, who would go on, with the aid of submarines, to adopt Confederate naval tactics in attacking Atlantic trade during World War II.

17 He refers to Great Britain's machinations to have slavery outlawed in Mexico as justification for the Mexican War. See Semmes, *Service Afloat and Ashore during the Mexican War*, 63.

18 The identical biblical justification was used one hundred years later by Hendrik Verwoerd to describe the "Bantu Education" policy of the Apartheid era.

19 Stephen R. Fox, *Wolf of the Deep: Raphael Semmes and the Notorious Confederate Raider CSS Alabama* (New York: Vintage Books, 2007), 201.

20 "Nobody who has read the letters, state papers, newspapers, and other surviving literature of the generation before 1861 can honestly deny that the one main, fundamental reason for secession . . . was to protect, expand, and perpetuate the slavery of the Negro race. In the official declaration by the seceding conventions in states which formed the Confederacy, there is no mention of any grievance unconnected with slavery." Samuel Eliot Morison, *The Oxford History of the American People* (New York: Oxford University Press, 1965), 608. The formative role of slavery in the development of Confederate identity and nationalism has been examined by Quigley, in *Shifting Grounds*.

21 Quigley, *Shifting Grounds*, 9.

22 "It so happened," he wrote, "that the slavery question was the issue which finally tore them asunder, but . . . this question was a mere means, to an end." Raphael Semmes, *Memoirs of Service Afloat During the War Between the States* (Baltimore: Kelly, Piet & Co., 1869), 69.

23 Semmes, *Memoirs of Service Afloat*, i.

24 In a similar vein, Semmes had written to his wife from Nassau on July 7, 1862, "The people of the South can never be made slaves of. Eight millions of people determined to be free will be sure to work out their ends." Raphael Semmes to Anne Semmes, July 7, 1862, Semmes Family Papers, Alabama Department of Archives and History, Montgomery.

25 James M. McPherson, *For Cause and Comrades: Why Men Fought in the Civil War* (New York: Oxford University Press, 1997), 20.

26 Domby, *False Cause*, 9.

27 "Illiteracy," Schrire argues, "is incontrovertible, and one price illiterates pay to history is prejudice. Ignorance of the other person's view brings with it a disinterest, a contempt for the history, and even for the sufferings of those who could not write." See Carmel Schrire, *Digging through Darkness: Chronicles of an Archaeologist* (Charlottesville: University Press of Virginia, 1995), 1

28 Schrire, *Digging through Darkness*, 1.

29 Saidiya V. Hartman, *Scenes of Subjection: Terror, Slavery, and Self-Making in Nineteenth-Century America* (Oxford, England: Oxford University Press, 1997).

30 Marisa J. Fuentes, *Dispossessed Lives; Enslaved Women, Violence, and the Archive* (Philadelphia: University of Pennsylvania Press, 2016), 6.

31 Cate Lineberry, *Be Free or Die: The Amazing Story of Robert Smalls' Escape from Slavery to Union Hero* (New York: St. Martin's Press, 2017).

32 See, for example, Michael Sokolow, *Charles Benson: Mariner of Color in the Age of Sail* (Amherst: University of Massachusetts Press, 2003).

33 Ivan Jablonka, "Historical Fiction and Intertextuality," presentation in panel discussion "Narrating the Past: Innovative Strategies for Writing History," La Maison Française, New York University, New York, February 26, 2020.

34 Joseph Campbell, *The Hero with a Thousand Faces* (New York: Pantheon Books, 1949). See also Christopher Vogler, *The Writer's Journey: Mythic Structure for Writers*, 3rd ed. (Studio City, CA: Michael Wiese Productions, 2007).

35 See Richard du Moulin, "Video: Maritime History, Technology, and Seamanship," gCaptain, May 6, 2018, https://gcaptain.com/maritime -history-technology-seamanship/.

36 "Forces of power . . . bore down on enslaved women, who sometimes survived in ways not typically heroic, and who sometimes succumbed to the violence inflected on them." Fuentes, *Dispossessed Lives*, 3.

37 I employ the approach, suggested elsewhere by Jablonka, that history, along with sociology and anthropology, can "achieve greater rigor and wider audiences by creating a literary text, written and experienced through a broad spectrum of narrative modes and rhetorical figures." Nathan Bracher, "Introduction: Writing History and the Social Sciences with Ivan Jablonka." *French Politics, Culture, and Society* 36, no. 3 (December 1, 2018): 3, https://doi.org/10.3167/fpcs.2018.360301. See also Ivan Jablonka, *History Is a Contemporary Literature: Manifesto for the Social Sciences*, trans. Nathan J. Bracher (Ithaca, NY: Cornell University Press, 2018).

38 This is not to say that archives themselves are not products of an unequal power dynamics, as has been explored in detail by Hartman, in *Scenes of Subjection*, and Fuentes, in *Dispossessed Lives*—but only that the archives considered here are exceptionally informative for what is essentially a forensic exercise.

39 Zack Stanton, "How Trumpism Is Becoming America's New 'Lost Cause,'" *Politico*, December 1, 2021, https://www.politico.com/news/magazine/2021/01/21/trump-civil-war-reconstruction-biden-lost-cause-461161. See also David W. Blight, "Europe in 1989, America in 2020, and the Death of the Lost Cause," *New Yorker*, July 1, 2020, https://www.newyorker.com/culture/cultural-comment/europe-in-1989-america-in-2020-and-the-death-of-the-lost-cause.

Chapter 2. Time and Place

1 Lawrence James, *Raj: The Making and Unmaking of British India* (London: Abacus, 1997).

2 The blight itself was an unintended consequence of global transportation; it seems the pathogen *Phytophthora infestans* originated in the New World and was transported via potatoes used to feed passengers on ships sailing from the United States to Ireland. See James S. Donnelly Jr., *The Great Irish Potato Famine* (Stroud, UK: History Press, 2001).

3 John O'Sullivan, "Annexation," *United States Magazine and Democratic Review*, 17 (1845): 5–6, 9–10.

4   Frederick Douglass, *Narrative of the Life of Frederick Douglass, an American Slave* (Boston: Anti-Slavery Office, 1845), 1.

5   "Letter from Wendell Phillips, Esq.," in Douglass, *Narrative of the Life*, xvi.

6   "Wesley to Wilberforce: John Wesley's Last Letter from His Deathbed," *Christianity Today* accessed 11/15/23, https://www.christianitytoday .com/history/issues/issue-2/wesley-to-wilberforce.html.

7   Barbara Jeanne Fields, *Slavery and Freedom on the Middle Ground: Maryland during the Nineteenth Century* (New Haven, CT: Yale University Press, 1985), xii.

8   Delaware rejected the amendment in 1865 and ratified it only in 1901.

9   Carole C. Marks, *A History of African Americans of Delaware and Maryland's Eastern Shore* (Wilmington: Delaware Heritage Commission, 1996).

10 The city's most famous abolitionist, Thomas Garrett, was probably the inspiration for the heroic Quaker Simeon Holliday in Harriet Beecher Stowe's *Uncle Tom's Cabin*. See Douglas Harper, "Slavery in Delaware," Slavery in the North, 2003, accessed November 15, 2023, http: //slavenorth.com/delaware.htm.

11 Patience Essah, *A House Divided: Slavery and Emancipation in Delaware, 1538–1865*, Carter G. Woodson Institute Series: Black Studies at Work in the World (Charlottesville: University Press of Virginia, 1997), 158.

12 That is, instability vacillating between one possible outcome and another; a term I have borrowed from physics. See "Metastability," Wikipedia, accessed October 5, 2022, https://en.wikipedia.org/wiki /Metastability.

13 For a table showing numbers of enslaved persons as a percentage of the Black population by state in 1850, see Fields, *Slavery and Freedom*, 2.

14 Petit Gulf was a hybrid cotton strain developed in 1833 that proved exceptionally well suited to the American South and contributed to the growth of the US cotton industry.

15 *Federal Reserve Bulletin* (Washington, DC: Government Printing Office, May 1923), 567.

16 Edwin G. Burrows and Mike Wallace, *Gotham: A History of New York City to 1898* (New York: Oxford University Press, 1999), 55.

17 That is, the European and African population; the indigenous population was unknown.

18 William Henry Williams, *Slavery and Freedom in Delaware, 1639–1865* (Wilmington, DE: SR Books, 1996), xii.

19 From Mary Parker Welch, George Theodore Welch, and Dorothy Welch White, *Memoirs of Mary Parker Welch, 1818–1912* (Brooklyn, NY: privately printed, 1947):

> The original house, now used for storage was of logs, erected in colonial days, weather-worn and moss-covered, with small windows, a big chimney and a five-fingered ivy climbing to the moldering roof; there was a modern attachment, itself of some age, and here in two big rooms and low lofts above lived the swarthy old farmer and his thin, dreary wife, eleven children and a maiden aunt. All worked hard, and lived scantily off the produce of one hundred and fifty acres of thin soil, which was mostly tilled for corn, and had a scraggy apple orchard on it, to which the children of the hamlet were welcome. . . . Besides the truck patches for family vegetables and a few acres of scanty pasturage for the oxen and cows, the balance of the land was yearly worked over and over for the crop of corn, as the unfertilized fields became more and more sterile. (101)

20 Harold B. Hancock, ed., *The History of Sussex County* (Rehoboth, DE: Sussex County Bicentennial Committee, 1976), 58.

21 Rebecca Sheppard and Kimberly Toney, *Reconstructing Delaware's Free Black Communities, 1800–1870* (Newark: University of Delaware Press, 2010).

22 See Marks, *History of African Americans of Delaware*, 17–18.

23 The historical archaeologist James Deetz explains the importance of probate records in illuminating the culture and values of early American households, in *In Small Things Forgotten: The Archaeology of Early American Life* (New York: Anchor Press, 1977), 8–10. According to Sheppard and Toney (*Reconstructing Delaware's Free Black Communities*, 27), in 1821, Sarah Hyatt left specific bequests to several of the persons she had enslaved. To Jacob Durham, she gave one good straw bed, one blanket, one good sheet, one coverlid, one cow, one hog, and fifteen dollars; to each of the two black women she owned, both named Rebecca, she gave "the beds and bedding they now have in use and my two worst feather beds, the old mesh chairs, one sheet, one blanket, one bed quilt, all the common crockeryware, old knifes and forks, one walnut table, and tubs, churns, pots and pails, wheel and reel."

In combination, these items would have allowed the three formerly enslaved to establish a minimally functioning household.

24 The memoir needs to be read from a nineteenth-century perspective. Welch, who was clearly opposed to slavery, provides a strong case, but to the contemporary reader, her paternalistic language and attitude in describing Blacks sounds at best anachronistic.

> When my father had concluded to abandon his business . . . and locate to Milton, he was sorely puzzled to know what to do with so many slaves. It was expensive to keep them under the most favorable conditions, but to take them to a town was utterly out of the question. He had never been an advocate of slavery, and had refused to accept any of the slaves on the old Parker plantation. . . . My mother did not approve of slavery either, but the slaves that she had inherited had long been fixtures in the family, and her attitude toward them was one of beneficence rather than any autocratic quality. . . . To set them free was like abandoning a helpless clan and, after many propositions had been discussed, and much mental suffering had been endured, it was resolved by my father and mother to dispose of most of them to their personal friends, with the proviso in the bill of sale that each was to be taught some useful trade whereby they could support themselves thereafter and each was to be manumitted when he or she had reached twenty-eight years of age. (Welch, Welch, and White, *Memoirs of Mary Parker Welch*, 139–51)

25 Jennie K. Williams, "Oceans of Kinfolk: The Coastwise Traffic of Enslaved People to New Orleans, 1820–1860" (PhD dissertation, John Hopkins University, 2020). See also https://www.kinfolkology. org/oceansofkinfolk. For anecdotal evidence of transport south in the interviews of formerly enslaved persons conducted in the 1930s, see US Work Projects Administration, *Slave Narratives: A Folk History of Slavery in the United States from Interviews with Former Slaves,* Volume 14, *South Carolina Narratives*, Part 3 (Washington, DC: Federal Writers' Project, 1941), 178.

26 More than 12,000 enslaved people were sent to New Orleans from Baltimore alone, and a portion of those individuals likely came from Delaware. See Michael Tadman, "The Interregional Slave Trade in the History and Myth-Making of the U.S. South," in *The Chattel Principle: Internal Slave Trades in the Americas*, edited by Walter Johnson, 117–64 (New Haven, CT: Yale University Press, 2004), 120. The matter was

a hot topic in Delaware at the time. The *Delaware Journal* carried a summary of the national agricultural situation:

> Most of our intelligent planters regard the cultivation of tobacco in Maryland as no longer profitable, and would almost universally abandon it, if they knew what to do with their slaves, for many reject the idea of selling them: others, however, are less scrupulous, and the consequence is, that great number of this unfortunate class are exported to other states, the cost of their subsistence being nearly or about equal to the whole value of their production. ("The Agriculture of the United States," *Delaware Journal* 1, no. 2 [April 27, 1827]: 1)

See also the oral history of Alice Brice Meadow, brought from Delaware to Virginia, in US Work Projects Administration, *Slave Narratives*, 18–19.

27 Emily West, *Family or Freedom: People of Color in the Antebellum South* (Lexington, KY: University Press of Kentucky, 2012), 26. See also Peter Kolchin, *American Slavery, 1619–1877* (London: Penguin Books, 1993), 241.

28 Fields, *Slavery and Freedom*, 2.

29 Williams, *Slavery and Freedom in Delaware*; Essah, *House Divided*.

30 Fields, *Slavery and Freedom*, 35.

31 Harold B. Hancock, "William Yates' Letter of 1837: Slavery and Colored People in Delaware," *Delaware History* 14, no. 3 (April 1971): 208.

32 Hancock, 208.

33 West, *Family or Freedom*; Fields, *Slavery and Freedom*.

34 An Act for the Better Regulation of Servants and Slaves within this Government, 77 *Del. Laws* 214 (1797).

35 An Act for the Better Regulation of Free Negroes and Free Mulattoes, 42 *Del. Laws* 108 (1807).

36 An Additional Supplement to the Act Entitled: An Act to Prohibit the Emigration of Free Negroes or Mulattoes into this State, and for Other Purposes, 324 *Del. Laws* 319 (1845).

37 The exception implicitly recognized the long-standing shortage of able seamen in the antebellum age of sail. During the Civil War, however, there was far less coastal traffic and less need for such labor.

38 "It is truly a deplorable fact," Yates wrote, "and but little creditable to the friends of the people of color of Delaware . . . that in all the state and among the 20,000 colored people who are found in it, there is but one little school in operation where the children can attend during the week." In addition to an 1821 law denying state aid to Black students, free Blacks were required, as were whites, to pay $2.00 for a marriage license, the revenue from which supported public school funding. Yet funds were distributed according to the number of white children, with Black children shut out of the equation. Hancock, "William Yates' Letter of 1837," 211.

39 Carol Wilson, *Freedom at Risk: The Kidnapping of Free Blacks in America, 1780–1865* (Lexington: University Press of Kentucky, 1994), 10.

40 Wilson, 20. see also Hancock, *History of Sussex County*, 65; and Robert Hazzard, "The History of Seaford," in Hancock, *History of Sussex County*, 114–18.

41 Hancock, "William Yates' Letter of 1837," 215.

42 From Williams, *Slavery and Freedom in Delaware.*

> When January 1 rolled around, the Black servant was given only thirty days to find new employment, or once again he would be sold into servitude until the next January 1. This procedure was to be repeated every year unless he found employment in January, or until he became too old or crippled to work. . . . Freedom in antebellum Delaware and Maryland was followed by an attempt by those in power to extract involuntary or coerced labor from those formerly enslaved.
>
> Once sold into this new form of servitude for a year it was very difficult to break out. Only by finding new employment in midwinter for their basically agrarian skills could Delaware's free Blacks liberate themselves from this annual cycle of state-coerced bondage. . . . More African-Americans than usual were hired for a season's work in January, but at very low wages wholly dictated by white employers because these laborers no longer had any negotiating clout. They could not reject job offers because rejection would only lead to their being sold into a form of labor that resembled temporary slavery, for up to a year at a time. (197–98)

Chapter 3. Childhood in Lewes

1 Sheppard and Toney, *Reconstructing Delaware's Free Communities.*

2 "Black Soldiers of Civil War Exhibit to Open Feb. 12," *Cape Gazette,* February 10, 2021, https://www.capegazette.com/article/black -soldiers-civil-war-exhibit-open-feb-12/215297.

3 George H. Mitchell, born in Georgetown, and George Watson, born in Sussex County in May 1845, were both enlisted by their slaveholders. Pvt. Theodore Tennant was born in the 1820s in Sussex County. He was a free man by 1830 and registered for the draft as a forty-year-old farmer in 1863. Prince Short, born in 1840 in Sussex County, and Bayard Sorden, also from Delaware, were free men. All trained near Philadelphia in Cheltenham Township at Camp William Penn, a Union Army camp dedicated to training African American troops from 1863 to 1865. See "Black Soldiers of Civil War Exhibit." See also Shayne Davidson, *Civil War Soldiers: Discovering the Men of the 25th United States Colored Troops* (Charleston: CreateSpace, 2013), 40, 42.

4 Williams, *Slavery and Freedom in Delaware;* Sellano L. Simmons, "Count Them Too: African Americans from Delaware and the United States Civil War Navy, 1861–1865," *Journal of Negro History* 85, no. 3 (2000): 183–90, https://doi.org/10.2307/2649075.

5 Simmons, "Count Them Too," 188.

6 Sheppard and Toney, *Reconstructing Delaware's Free Communities:*

> Shipbuilder Thomas Summers acquired a house and lot, probably on Pilottown Road, circa 1836. By 1840, his household included his wife, four children under age 10, and three young people between 10 and 24 years old. When he died three years later, he still owned the house and lot. His inventory demonstrated his investment in his shipbuilding business—$31 of his total $77 inventory value represented carpentry tools, and another $7 represented boats and equipment, for a total of 49 percent of his assets. Approximately $7 went towards agricultural implements and crops and the remaining $26 (33 percent) covered household goods and furniture. In order to settle the estate, his executors (son Cato and neighbor Noah Burton) held a sale of all the inventoried goods on October 11, 1843. . . . As a second-generation shipbuilder, Cato Summers purchased primarily carpentry and agricultural tools, as well as one boat and one bateau; he also selected a few other items for family use including a cradle, a table, and a gig. (17)

7   Sheppard and Toney, 70.

8   Sheppard and Toney, 76. See also Hancock, *History of Sussex County*, 65.

9   Sheppard and Toney, 70.

10 Hilda Belltown Norwood, "A Recollection," *Journal of the Lewes Historical Society* 4 (2001): 21–30.

11 Hancock, *History of Sussex County*, 68.

12 In the meaningful but not the literal sense. He did in fact leave behind $4.80 in unpaid wages.

13 US Census Bureau, Lewes & Rehoboth Hundred, Sussex County, Delaware, Dwelling 875, Family 875, John White household (1850), 116. http://www.ancestry.com.

14 In the first entry, his first name is omitted.

15 Lewes & Rehoboth Hundred, Sussex County, Delaware, Assessment Office, Assessment Records, Tax, John White (1860), 314, Family History Library, Microfilm 105634372. http://www.familysearch.org. This document further confirms the family's free status, as compared to corresponding records for whites in which enslaved persons were taxed as property.

16 This is confusing because in both 1852 and 1856 a Hanna Baily (yet another surname spelling variant) paid a tax for "own hous [*sic*] on public ground." The 1850 and 1860 censuses indicate that Hannah Baley (alternately spelled Bailey) was born between 1780 and 1785, also in Lewes & Rehoboth Hundred. The records searched so far do not make clear when she or her ancestors were manumitted, but it is likely to have occurred during the second half of the eighteenth century, certainly before 1830, as for the majority of Sussex County's free Black citizens. "Bailey" and its spelling variants was a common Black surname in the region; it was shared by Frederick Douglass's mother, Harriet. See US Census Bureau, Lewes & Rehoboth Hundred, Sussex County, Delaware, Dwelling 174, Family 167, John White household (1860), 26, http://www.ancestry.com.

17 Williams, *Slavery and Freedom in Delaware*, 103.

18 We don't know much about their home, but the census provides some insight into where exactly the family lived. The census taker numbered families in order of visitation; following this logic, we can surmise that the family lived near Savannah Road just outside Lewes's present city limits. In the 1860 census, the White family was recorded as number 167 in the order of visitation; the previous entry in the 1860 census,

166, was the family of Joel Prettyman, a white farmer whose "Value of Real Estate" was listed as $8,000 and "Value of Personal Estate" was listed as $2,000. Just above the Prettyman entry, there is another White family (number 164 in order of visitation) with another Sarah White, age 60, along with Henry, age 26; Elizabeth, age 28; and Hannah J., age 8. In all likelihood this family is related, though they are listed as "mulatto," while David H. White's household is labeled as Black. One hypothesis is that this Sarah was the widow of an older brother of John White; Henry and Elizabeth were her son and daughter-in-law; and Hannah was her granddaughter, named after Sarah's husband's mother, the Hannah Bailey in John White's household. See US Census Bureau, John White household (1860), 26.

19   E. D. Bryan, "The Confederate Raider *Alabama*: A Lewes Connection," *Journal of the Lewes Historical Society* 4 (2001): 50.

20   Eventually, the building, while it was owned by a Mr. S. Hazzard, was "consumed by fire" along with several other buildings in May 1870. See "Correspondence Lewes Fires and Serious Loss of Property, Etc. Lewes Del. May 17," *Delaware Tribune*, May 19, 1870, 1. The lot now holds a building occupied by a real estate office, uniform shop, and boutique. The former stable is now a parking lot.

21   Bryan, "Confederate Raider *Alabama*," 51.

22   "The War Turns Serious—1862," *Civil War Monitor* 2, no. 2 (Summer 2012): 1–80. For an overview of the period, see John Hope Franklin, *The Emancipation Proclamation* (Garden City, NY: Doubleday, 1963).

23   See Sheppard and Toney, *Reconstructing Delaware's Free Black Communities*.

24   Hancock, *History of Sussex County*, 80–81.

25   Marcie Schwartz, "Children of the Civil War: On the Battlefield— Youth in Wartime," American Battlefield Trust, April 6, 2017, https://www.battlefields.org/learn/articles/children-civil-war-battlefield.

Chapter 4. Passenger Cook

1   Gary B. Nash, *Forging Freedom: The Formation of Philadelphia's Black Community, 1720–1840* (Cambridge, MA: Harvard University Press, 1998), 136. See also Jeffrey W. Bolster, *Black Jacks: African American Seamen in the Age of Sail* (Cambridge, MA: Harvard University Press, 1997), 210–11.

2   An Act for the Better Regulation of Free Negroes and Free Mulattoes, 42 *Del. Laws* 108 (1807).

3 John Killick, "An Early Nineteenth-Century Shipping Line: The Cope Line of Philadelphia and Liverpool Packets, 1822–1872," *International Journal of Maritime History* 12, no. 1 (2000): 61–87, https://doi.org/10.1177/084387140001200104.

4 Andrew Sillen, "The Cope Line Voyages of David Henry White: Evidence from the Cope Family Archive," *Pennsylvania Magazine of History and Biography* 148 (January 2024).

5 Bolster, *Black Jacks*, 29

6 "Carriage of Passengers Act of 1855," Wikipedia, accessed November 24, 2023, https://en.wikipedia.org/wiki/Carriage_of_Passengers_Act_of_1855.

7 Killick, "Line."

8 Bolster, *Black Jacks*, 225.

9 Frank H. Taylor, *Philadelphia in the Civil War, 1861–1865: A Complete History Illustrated with Contemporary Prints and Photographs and from Drawings by the Author* (Philadelphia: Published by the City, 1913), 10.

10 Finding Aid, Cope Family Papers, Collection 1486, Historical Society of Pennsylvania, Philadelphia 2003. https://hsp.org/sites/default/files/mss/finding_aid_1486_cope.pdf.

11 John O'Brian Sr. sold to his son on October 22, 1863. Records of Deeds, Deeds Registry, ACH no. 123: 393, Philadelphia Department of Archives; K. Edward Price, personal communication, January, 10, 2023.

12 Maritime Records, Phila., V. Masters, Crews, Ships (vols. 73–75, 1862–1863), Independence Seaport Museum, Philadelphia.

13 Steven J. Ramold, *Slaves, Sailors, Citizens: African Americans in the Union Navy* (DeKalb: Northern Illinois University Press, 2002), 82, 63.

14 From "Condition and Care of Emigrants on Board Ship," letter to the editor, *New York Daily Times*, October 15, 1851:

> From Liverpool each passenger receives 5 lbs. of oatmeal, 2½ lbs. biscuit, 1 lb. flour, 2 lbs. rice, ½ lb. sugar, ½ lb. molasses, and 2 ounces of tea. He is obliged to cook it the best way he can in cook shop 12 feet by 6! This is the cause of so many quarrels and hard fighting, for might makes right there. Of course, many a poor women with her children can get but one meal done, and sometimes they get nothing warm for days and nights when a gale of wind is blowing, and the sea is mountains high and breaking over the ship in all directions. (4)

15 The steerage manifest includes 18 men, 11 women, and at least 3 families with children.

16 Philip Sheldon Foner, "William P. Powell: Militant Champion of Black Seamen," in *Essays in Afro-American History* (Philadelphia: Temple University Press, 1978), 88.

17 Foner, "William P. Powell."

18 "Owing to the prejudice against Color they could not acquire (an education) in their native country." Quoted in "Letters from the Colored Sailor's Home in the Mid-19th Century," Mystic Seaport Museum, Mystic, CT, February 11, 2022, https://www.mysticseaport.org/news/letters-from-the-colored-sailors-home/.

19 "Powell, William P., to Samuel May, Jr., Dec. 31, 1859," in *The Black Abolitionist Papers*, Vol. 1: *The British Isles 1830–1865*, ed. Peter C. Ripley, Jeffrey S Rossbach, Roy E. Finkenbine, Fiona E. Spiers, and Debra Sussie, 474–76 (Chapel Hill: University of North Carolina Press, 1985), 47.

20 "Powell, William P., to Samuel May, Jr." 474.

21 Powell's letter indicates that a Mr. Fisher, who regularly shipped on the *Saranak*, was a courier in an international network of Black sailors who carried abolitionist literature from Liverpool to Philadelphia. However, it turns out that *Joseph* Fisher is a different individual from the *Thomas C.* Fisher who sailed on the *Saranak*. "Powell, William P., to Samuel May, Jr."

22 Sillen, "Cope Line Voyages."

23 Charles Gilbert hid under a hotel, up a tree, under floorboards, in a thicket, and eventually on a steamer bound for Philadelphia. These individuals and others relied on dockworkers to assist them during their journey to freedom. Keshler Thibert, "On the Waterfront: Chronicling the Lives of Philly's Black Seamen," *Hidden City: Exploring Philadelphia's Landscape*, July 22, 2022, https://hiddencityphila.org/2022/07/on-the-waterfront-chronicling-the-lives-of-phillys-black-seamen/.

24 Anita Gonzalez, "Maritime Migrations: Stewards of the African Grove," *Theatre Research International* 44, no. 1 (2019): 64–70, https://doi.org/10.1017/s0307883318000962.

25 Powell, "Colored Seamen—Their Character and Condition," *National Anti-Slavery Standard*, November 12, 1846. See also Bolster, *Black Jacks*, 180; and Foner, "William P. Powell," 91.

26 William Burton to Cope, June, 27, 1862, Cape of Delaware, 48th Voyage of the *Wyoming*, Cope Family Papers.

27 Bolster provides a firsthand description of a New York–to–Liverpool packet galley as "a strange looking place . . . not more than five feet square, and about as many high, a mere box to hold the stove, the pipe of which stuck out of the roof. Within it was hung round with pots and pans." Bolster, *Black Jacks*, 82.

28 Sillen, "Cope Line Voyages."

29 Bolster, *Black Jacks*, 82.

30 Gibb Schreffler, *Boxing the Compass: A Century and a Half of Discourse about Sailor's Chanties*, Occasional Papers I, Folklore (Lansdale, PA: Loomis House Press, 2018). See also "Sea Chanteys and Other Nautical Songs," Calvert Marine Museum, accessed January 20, 2024, https:// www.calvertmarinemuseum.com/DocumentCenter/View/2281/Sea -Chanteys-and-other-Nautical-Songs?bidId=.

31 Great Britain Historical GIS Project, "Liverpool District" (population statistics, total population), A Vision of Britain through Time (University of Portsmouth), accessed November 24, 2023, https://www. visionofbritain.org.uk/unit/10105821/cube/TOT_POP.

32 "Liverpool and the American Civil War," Information Sheet 59, National Museums Liverpool, Archives Center, Maritime Museum, Liverpool, UK, accessed November 25, 2023, https://www. liverpoolmuseums.org.uk/archivesheet59.

33 Herman Melville, *Redburn: His First Voyage, Being the Sailor-Boy Confessions and Reminiscences of the Son-of-a-Gentleman, in the Merchant Service* (New York: Harper and Brothers, 1849), 203.

34 His son, William P. Powell Jr., was educated in Liverpool and went on to become one of the first Black physicians under contract with the Union Army. See Jill L. Newmark. "Face to Face with History," *Prologue Magazine* 41, no. 3 (Fall 2009), https://www.archives.gov/publications /prologue/2009/fall/face.html.

35 "The Sailors' Home," *Liverpool Daily Post*, April 22, 1862, 7.

36 According to one description,

    the houses appear to be crowded with people of a class neither good nor good looking. Sailors and fat frowsy women loll about. A black, with a red shirt and a blue cap, is gambolling for the amusement of a group of girls. Very unpleasant allusions to the eyes and limbs of passers-by are made . . . the houses are, for the most part, in a state of disorder—and the notion of Sabbath evening enjoyment, which the children have, is not flattering to those who claim to have them under their pastoral care. (Quoted in Ray Costello, *Black Salt: Seafarers of African Descent on British Ships* [Liverpool: Liverpool University Press, 2012], 61)

37 While Dickens's description of Liverpool's Black community was sympathetic for its time, the author "fell victim to the prevalent popular view of Black people as child-like figures." Dickens quoted in Costello, *Black Salt*, 61.

38 Dava Sobel, *Longitude: The True Story of a Lone Genius Who Solved the Greatest Scientific Problem of His Time* (London: Fourth Estate, 1998).

39 Burton from Liverpool, July 19, 1862, 48th Voyage of the *Wyoming*, Cope Family Papers.

40 Burton to Cope, August, 14, 1862, 48th Voyage of the *Wyoming*, Cope Family Papers.

41 "Comments of the Press Upon The President's Proclamation; The President's Proclamation," *Philadelphia Inquirer*, September 24, 1862, 2.

42 "Arrival of the 'Tonawanda,'" *Philadelphia Inquirer*, September 1, 1862, 8.

43 "In the health office at Liverpool, where sometimes 1000 emigrants are examined per day," a *New York Daily Times* article reported,

> they are merely required to show their tongue; but no other notice is taken of their filthy condition nor is the body which may be full of ulcers, itch, small pox, or other disagreeable diseases . . . so many deaths occur at sea and infectious diseases are spread throughout the vessel . . . it is well known that many (passenger) goes on board without a shirt and a bed, clothed in rags and full of vermin! (Signed Doctor). ("Condition and Care of Emigrants," 4)

44 From C. D. Miggs, untitled essay in *Summary of the Transactions of the College of Physicians of Philadelphia*, Vol. 2: *New Series* (Philadelphia: J. B. Lippincott & Co., 1856):

> The ships *Tuscarora* and *Tonawanda* . . . are large, and as well ventilated and provided with all appliances for health and comfort as are usually seen in the best emigrant vessels. Their captains are not only skillful sailors, but good disciplinarians,

and require all on board to observe cleanliness of person, and to ventilate their apartments to the fullest extent possible on board of vessels crowded with emigrants. These vessels, consequently, though carrying very nearly their full complement of passengers, are usually freer from those diseases which are caused by decomposing bodily emanations, than other vessels . . . whose captains are less careful to observe the means of preserving the health of their passengers. (280)

45 Crew Manifest, 36th Voyage of the *Tonawanda*, Cope Family Papers.

46 Semmes, *Memoirs of Service Afloat*; Bryan, Confederate Raider *Alabama*."

47 Another interesting entry is the address "Sailor's Home," listed as the place of surety for seaman Joseph Fisher, among others. This may refer to the Sailor's Home in Liverpool.

48 "Portage Bill of Ship *Tonawanda* from Liverpool 36th Voyage of the *Tonawanda*," Cope Family Papers.

49 Sillen, "Cope Line Voyages."

Chapter 5. Manifest Destiny

1 Notably, by Charles Grayson Summersell, in "The Career of Raphael Semmes Prior to the Cruise of the *Alabama*," PhD dissertation, Vanderbilt University, Nashville, 1940; and by Warren F. Spencer, in *Raphael Semmes: The Philosophical Mariner* (Tuscaloosa: University of Alabama Press, 1997); and Fox, in *Wolf of the Deep*.

2 The error of applying contemporary values to past subjects is called presentism by historians. See, for example, Adaobi Tricia Nwaubani, "My Nigerian Great-Grandfather Sold Slaves," *BBC News*, July 19, 2020, https://www.bbc.co.uk/news/world-africa-53444752.

3 John M Taylor, *Confederate Raider: Raphael Semmes of the Alabama* (Washington, DC: Brassey's Inc, 1994), 31–32.

4 Leonard Calvert was the second son of the First Baron Baltimore and first proprietary governor of the province of Maryland. Farnum places Semmes's ancestor on the *Ark*, one of the two original vessels (along with the *Dove*) sent by Baltimore. See George R. Farnum, "Raphael Semmes: Lawyer and Falcon of the Seas," *American Bar Association Journal* 30, no. 11 (1944): 363–69, 665–66.

5 Solomon Northup, *Twelve Years a Slave*, edited by Kevin M. Burke and Henry Louis Gates Jr., Norton Critical Edition (New York: W. W. Norton, 2016).

6   A classified advertisement placed in the *Daily National Intelligencer* of
     December 8, 1823, by Raphael Semmes (uncle to Raphael Semmes,
     captain of the *Alabama*) read:

> TWENTY DOLLARS REWARD. ABSCONDED from the
> subscriber, in Georgetown, D.C. on the 22d inst a negro girl,
> named HARRIET, about 18 years of age, a bright mulatto,
> very sprightly, about the common height, and rather stout,
> has grey eyes, and a scar under her throat; her hair is not so
> black as is usual for negroes, which she wears long, and turns
> up with a comb; she had on, when she absconded, a blue and
> white domestic frock, an[d] took with her a pale blue stuff,
> a black . . . shawl, and a pair of high heeled black Morocco
> shoes, with a variety of other clothing not recollected. Harriet
> belonged to the estate of the late Captain Thomas Jenkins, of
> Cobb Neck, Charles County, Maryland, but has resided for
> the last two or three years in Baltimore, so that it is uncertain
> whither she may go if she leaves the District of Columbia. The
> above reward will be given to any person who may apprehend
> the above described girl, or secure her in ay jail so that I get
> her again.

7   Ian W. Toll, *Six Frigates: The Epic History of the Founding of the U.S. Navy*
     (New York: W. W. Norton, 2006), 434. See also Herman Melville,
     White Jacket: Or the World of a Man-of-War (London: Richard Bentley,
     1850). Similarly, Christopher McKee discusses *deference* as the key
     organizing principle of the early American navy, in *A Gentlemanly and
     Honorable Profession: The Creation of the U.S. Naval Officer Corps, 1794–1815*
     (Annapolis, MD: Naval Institute Press, 1991), 28.

8   Harold D. Langley, *Social Reform in the United States Navy, 1798–1862*
     (Annapolis, MD: Naval Institute Press, 1967); McKee, *Gentlemanly and
     Honorable Profession*; Toll, *Six Frigates*.

9   Robert Smith to De Witt Clinton, November 1, 1805, quoted in McKee,
     Creation of U.S. Naval Corps, 46.

10   Toll, *Six Frigates*, 223.

11   Toll, 247.

12   See Howard Zinn, *A People's History of the United States, 1492–2001* (New
     York: Harper Collins, 1999), 139–46.

13   According to historian George E. Buker, Semmes departed Camp Call
     on October 2, 1836, bound for the Withlacoochee, with Gen. Leigh
     Read of the Florida militia and his command on board. The *Lt. Izard*

had to remain six to eight miles off the mouth of the river until the channel could be found. Once he found the channel, Semmes doubted a vessel the size of the *Lt. Izard* could navigate the intricate route to the river; however, General Read was impatient to get upstream and establish his depot, and he convinced Semmes of the urgency of the situation. Lieutenant Semmes began warping his ship up the channel by sending boats up ahead with anchors that were dropped at strategic positions, and then the *Izard* hauled itself up to the anchor. Near the shore, the lines could also be attached to fixed objects. It was a rather delicate feat requiring top-notch seamen. Although Semmes realized many of his crew were militiamen, he committed himself. When he had maneuvered the *Lt. Izard* into a particularly difficult position among some small oyster banks, the tide caught the steamer and swung her about so that the bow and stern rested on two of the banks on opposite sides of the channel. The tide was running out, and before Semmes could get the *Lt. Izard* off, it "gave way amidships, filled with water and sunk." Buker, *Swamp Sailors in the Second Seminole War* (Gainesville: Library Press at University of Florida, 1997).

14 Buker.

15 Fox, *Wolf of the Deep*, 23.

16 Fox, 23.

17 Fox, 23.

18 Herbert Spencer, *Social Statics; Or, The Conditions Essential to Human Happiness Specified, and the First of Them Delivered* (London: John Chapman, 1851), 416.

19 Of course, this notion of fitness is at variance with evolutionary Darwinism, according to which "fitness" refers only to differential reproduction.

20 Semmes, *Service Afloat and Ashore*. The Alani were an ancient nomadic pastoral people who occupied the steppe region northeast of the Black Sea. *Alan* represents an Iranian dialectal form of the more familiar term *Aryan*.

21 Coincidentally, the same day of the year as the *Alabama-Kearsarge* battle and White's demise, a year earlier.

22 Silbey, *Storm over Texas*, 41 (citing John C. Calhoun to Richard Pakenham, April 18, 1844).

23 Silbey, 113.

24 Silbey, 113.

25 G. Rathbun, "The Wilmot Proviso: Speech of Mr. G. Rathbun of New York in the House of Representatives, February 9, 1847." Cong. Globe, 29th Cong., 2d Sess., New Series, no. 12, 179, online at American Memory, Library of Congress, https://memory.loc.gov/cgi-bin/ampage?collId=llcg&fileName=018/llcg018.db&recNum=786.

26 Morison, *Oxford History of the American People*, 560.

27 Jean West Mueller and Wynell B. Schamel, "Lincoln's Spot Resolutions," *Social Education* 52, no. 6 (October 1988): 455–57, 466, online at "Educator Resources: Lincoln's Spot Resolutions," National Archives, accessed November 27, 2023, https://www.archives.gov/education/lessons/lincoln-resolutions.

28 Henry David Thoreau, *Walden; and, Civil Disobedience: Complete Texts with Introduction, Historical Contexts, Critical Essays*, edited by Paul Lauter (Boston: Houghton Mifflin, 2000).

29 Abiel Abbot Livermore, *The War with Mexico Reviewed* (Boston: American Peace Society, 1850), 40.

30 See Jane Grey Swisshelm, *Half a Century*, 3rd ed. (Chicago: Jansen, McClurg and Co., 1880), 96. An articulate and passionate abolitionist and feminist, Swisshelm nevertheless remained racist in her characterization of the Sioux of Minnesota where she lived in the 1860s. The Dakota War of 1862 between the native Sioux and the expanding United States resulted in atrocities and bitter enmity on both sides of the conflict. See also Jane Grey Swisshelm, *Crusader and Feminist: Letters of Jane Grey Swisshelm, 1858–1865*, ed. Arthur J. Larsen (St. Paul: Minnesota Historical Society, 1934).

Chapter 6. Gulf of Mexico

1 Various Purses to [names indecipherable] to Commodore David Conner, USS *Potomac* off Vera Cruz, May 20, 1845, David Conner Papers, Manuscripts and Archives Division, Astor, Lenox, and Tilden Foundations, New York Public Library.

2 "In obedience to your order today we have held a strict and careful survey on the Beans therein mentioned and find one hundred ten gallons wholly unfit for food, being worm eaten and smelling badly—we condemn them to be thrown overboard which has been done in our presence." Various Purses to . . . Conner, May 20, 1845.

3   Ship's Surgeon [name indecipherable] to Conner, USS *Raritan* off Vera Cruz, May 29, 1846, David Conner Papers:

> Sir,
> Since the visit of this ship to Point Isabel, we have had a number of severe cases of dysentery. At this time there are several very bad cases on the sick report in one of which I have not the slightest hopes of a recovery. Among the number sick are Assistant Surgeon Thomas Potter and the Hospital steward . . . Bruce. From the number of sick at this time the services of an assistant surgeon are very much required; and should this disease increase, or any epidemic appear, to which this port is peculiarly obnoxious, the sick on board this ship would suffer for the want of medical attendance.

4   Quigley, *Shifting Grounds*, 37.

5   Semmes, *Service Afloat and Ashore*, 79.

6   Semmes, *Service Afloat and Ashore*, 76.

7   Peter Karsten *The Naval Aristocracy: The Golden Age of Annapolis and the Emergence of Modern American Navalism* (Annapolis, MD: Naval Institute Press, 1972), 27.

8   John V. Quarstein, "Mutiny at Sea: Death and Destruction on USS *Somers*," Mariners' Museum and Park (Newport News, VA) December 15, 2022, https://www.marinersmuseum.org/2022/12/mutiny-at-sea-death-and-destruction-on-uss-somers/.

9   Commander James Gerry to David Conner, US Brig *Somers* off Vera Cruz, June 2, 1845, David Conner Papers.

10   See Langley, *Social Reform in the United States Navy*, 172.

11   M. L. Claiborne to David Connor, October 24, 1846, David Conner Papers.

12   For the impact of wireless on naval command, see Du Moulin, "Video: Maritime History, Technology, and Seamanship.

13   See Spencer, *Raphael Semmes*, 32.

14   Captain Lambert wrote:

> AM. Daylight observed a strange sail in the offing and the American Brig Somers proceed to sea. . . . Stranger proved to be the American Corvette *John Adams* and passed by Anton Lizardo. 9:00 Observed a strange sail in the offing. . . . 9:45

Observed the United States Brig *Somers* off the North end of [——] Islands reef capsizing in a heavy squall of wind . . . and sink. Out boats and struck to the assistance of the crew. Down Top Gallant Yards. 10:15 Recalled the boats it blowing too heavy for them to . . . render assistance. 10:30 In and up Boats, down top gallant . . . 11:30 [——] and Tarleton [working?] the gig to take two of the Somers crew off the Paxaros Reef. ("Captain's Logs Including Endymion, 6 November 1840 to 18 January 1848," ADM 51/3603, National Archives, 1846, Kew, London)

15 "Lieutenant Claiborne saved himself on a small hatch, about 2 feet square, used for covering the pump well, and which he found floating near the wreck." Semmes, in J. Y. Mason, "Report of the Secretary of the Navy in Answer to a Resolution of the Senate Calling for Information in Relation to the Loss of the United States Brig *Somers*, and to the Assistance Rendered by the Officers and Crews of the French, Spanish, and British Ships-of-War Lying off Vera Cruz, in the Rescue of the Officers and Crew of the Somers," 29th Cong., 2d sess., H.R. Rep. no. 43 (January 7, 1847), 4. As Spencer explained, "Some reached a grating, some an oar, some a boat's mast, some a hen coop . . . 'an arm-chest grating' . . . 'an upper half-port.' . . . Midshipman Francis G. Clarke was in charge of the only boat, who picked up Semmes." *Raphael Semmes*, 34.

16 Summersell, "Career of Raphael Semmes," 33.

17 William H. Parker, *Recollections of a Naval Officer, 1841–1865* (New York: Charles Scribner's Sons, 1883), 60.

18 Specifically, Claiborne testified that the vessel carried "about six hundred gallons of water; scarce anything in her store rooms—her compliment of water is about 5,600 gallons." "Proceedings of a Naval Court of Enquiry held on board of the U.S. frigate *Potomac* on the 16th day of December 1846," Records of General Courts Martial and Courts of Enquiry of the Navy Department, 1799–1867, Records of the Office of the Judge Advocate General (Navy) (Record Group 125), NARA Microfilm M273, Case 96A/61, vol. 55, March 4, 1846–February 6, 1847.

19 See "Proceedings of a Naval Court of Enquiry."

20 See "Proceedings of a Naval Court of Enquiry."

21 See Mason, "Report of the Secretary of the Navy," 1–7.

22   Spencer, *Raphael Semmes*, 33–35. See also Taylor, *Confederate Raider*, 25.

23   As Semmes remembered:

> I feel that I should not be doing justice to the officers and men if I were to close this report, without bearing the testimony to their uniform coolness and self-possession, under the trying circumstances in which we were placed; the alacrity with which they obeyed my orders, and when all was over, the generosity with which they behaved toward each other in the water, where the struggle was one of life and death. . . . Those men who could not swim, were selected to go in the boat. A large man, by the name of Seymour, the ship's cook, having got into her, he was commanded by Lieutenant Parker to come out, in order that he might make from for two smaller men, and he obeyed the order. He was afterward permitted to return to her, however, when it was discovered that he could not swim. Passed Midshipman Hynson, a promising young officer, who had been partially disabled by a bad burn, received in firing the Creole, a few days previously, was particularly implored to go into the boat. A lad by the name of Nutter, jumped out of the boat and offered his place to Hynson, and a man by the name of Powers did the same thing. Hynson refusing both offers, these men declared that then others might take their places, as they were resolved to abide the wreck with him. Hynson and Powers were drowned. Nutter was saved. When the plunge was made into the sea, Sailing-Master Clemson seized a studding-sail boom, in company with five of the seamen. Being a swimmer, and perceiving that the boom was not sufficiently buoyant to support them all, he left it, and struck out alone. He perished—the five men were saved." (*Service Afloat and Ashore*, 98)

24   Christopher Cameron, "The Puritan Origins of Black Abolitionism in Massachusetts," *Historical Journal of Massachusetts* 39, nos. 1–2 (Summer 2011): 78–107, https://www.westfield.ma.edu/historical-journal/wp-content/uploads/2018/06/Puritan-Origins-of-Black-Abolitionism.pdf.

25   Nikole Hanna-Jones, *The 1619 Project: A New Origin Story* (New York: One World, 2021).

26   Peter W. Wood, *1620: A Critical Response to the 1619 Project* (New York: Encounter Books, 2022).

27 As does the story of Genesis by evangelical Christians. See Henry Ward Beecher, *Evolution and Religion*, Part 1: *Eight Sermons, Discussing the Bearing of the Evolutionary Philosophy on the Fundamental Doctrines of Evangelical Christianity* (New York: Fords, Howard and Hulbert, 1885), 61–62, 90. As also does Darwinism by evolutionary biologists, see Stanley N. Salthe, "Analysis and Critique of the Concept of Natural Selection (and of the NeoDarwinian Theory of Evolution) in Respect (Part 1) to Its Suitability as Part of Modernism's Origination Myth, as Well as (Part 2) of Its Ability to Explain Organic Evolution," Niels Bohr Institute, updated 2006, https://www.nbi.dk/~natphil/salthe/Critique_of_Natural_Select_.pdf.

28 John W. Weeks, Address, In *Record of the Dedication of the Statue of Rear Admiral John Ancrum Winslow: May 8, 1909* (Boston: State Printers, 1909), 25–59.

29 Weeks, 29.

30 Quoted in John M. Ellicott, *The Life of John Ancrum Winslow: Rear-Admiral, United States Navy, who Commanded the U.S. steamer "Kearsarge" in her Action with the Confederate Cruiser "Alabama"* (New York: G. P. Putnam's Sons, 1902), 31.

31 Quoted in Ellicott, 38.

32 Letter from Vera Cruz, November 4, 1846, quoted in Ellicott, *Life of John Ancrum Winslow*, 43.

33 Ellicott, *Life of John Ancrum Winslow*, 45.

34 There was no *Morris* court of inquiry, even though on January 18, 1847, another court of inquiry charged that Edward W. Carpenter of the USS *Truxton*, "in or about 16th day of August, 1846, did through inattention suffer the said brig to be run upon a shoal near the town of Tuxpan in Mexico." See Records of Courts of Enquiry.

35 "Proceedings of a Naval Court of Enquiry." In this respect, it is of interest that Semmes regularly railed against Puritans. See Ellicott, *Life of John Ancrum Winslow*, 46. Given their familiarity with each other, it is tempting to think that Semmes specifically had Winslow in mind when he wrote:

> The Puritan leaven had at last "leavened the whole loaf," and the descendants of those immigrants who had come over to America, in the May Flower, feeling that they had the power to crush a race of men, who had dared to differ with them in opinion, and to have interests separate and apart from them,

were resolved to use that power in a way to do no discredit to their ancestry. Rebels, when in a minority, they had become tyrants, now that they were in a majority. (Semmes, *Memoirs of Service Afloat*, 69)

36 See "USS *Chesapeake*–HMS *Leopard* Affair," Naval History and Heritage Command, accessed December 3, 2023, https://www.history.navy.mil /content/history/nhhc/our-collections/art/exhibits/conflicts-and -operations/the-war-of-1812/uss-chesapeake--hms-leopard-affair.html.

37 Nor did the officers on board bear the burden of loss well. Lt. William Henry Allen wrote home to his father: "Oh! That some one of their murderous balls had deprived me of the power of recollection. . . . My god is it possible? My country's flag disgraced. You cannot appreciate, you cannot conceive of my feeling at this moment . . . to be so mortified, humbled—cut to the soul. Yes to have the finger of scorn pointing me out as one of the Chesapeake." Quoted in Toll, *Six Frigates*, 299.

Chapter 7. Secession

1 McPherson, *For Cause and Comrades*, 16–17.

2 James M. Morgan, *Recollections of a Rebel Reefer* (Boston: Houghton Mifflin Company, 1917), 40.

3 Ambivalent about secession or not, Lee's unsavory behavior with regard to those he enslaved has led to a fundamental reevaluation of his legacy and the removal of his statue from Richmond in 2021. See Gillian Brockell, "Let's Get Real about Robert E. Lee and Slavery," *Washington Post*, September 10, 2021, https://www.washingtonpost. com/history/2021/09/10/robert-e-lee-slavery/; see also Brent Staples, "Confederate Tributes Are Losing Their Patron Saint," *New York Times*, April 27, 2023, Opinion, https://www.nytimes.com/2023/04/27 /opinion/fort-lee-renaming.html?searchResultPosition=1.

4 William S. Dudley. *Going South: U.S. Navy Officer Resignations and Dismissals on the Eve of the Civil War* (Washington, DC: Naval Historical Foundation, 1981).

5 William N. Still, ed., *The Confederate Navy: The Ships, Men, and Organization, 1861–65* (Annapolis, MA: Naval Institute Press, 1997), 7.

6 Toll, *Six Frigates*, 408

7 Raimondo Luraghi, "Background," in Still, *Confederate Navy*, 16.

8 Luraghi, 13.

9   Shelby Foote, *The Civil War, a Narrative*, Vol. 1: *Fort Sumter to Perryville* (New York: Vintage Books, 1958), 793.

10 These lists are taken from Dalzell, *Flight from the Flag*, 3–4; and Toll, *Six Frigates*, 12–13.

11 See Dalzell, *Flight from Flag*, 3–4; and Toll, *Six Frigates*, 12–13.

12 "The Norie Atlas and the Guano Trade," National Museum of American History, exhibited February 16, 2016, to January 29, 2017, archived at Archive It, accessed January 21, 2024, https://wayback. archive-it.org/3340/20231013213836/https://americanhistory.si.edu /norie-atlas/. See also Paul F. Johnston, "The Smithsonian and the 19th Century Guano Trade: This Poop Is Crap" National Museum of American History, May 31, 2017, https://americanhistory.si.edu/blog /smithsonian-and-guano.

13 Stephen Chapin Kinnaman, *The Most Perfect Cruiser: How James Dunwoody Bulloch Constructed and Equipped the Confederate States Steamer Alabama* (Indianapolis: Dog Ear, 2009), 158. Bulloch's half-sister Martha married businessman Theodore Roosevelt Sr.; their son Theodore Roosevelt Jr., who became the twenty-sixth president, regularly celebrated his family's *Alabama* connection to curry favor with southern voters.

14 McPherson, *For Cause and Comrades*.

15 Kinnaman, *Most Perfect Cruiser*, 31; Amanda Foreman, *A World on Fire: Britain's Crucial Role in the American Civil War* (New York: Random House, 2010).

16 Raphael Semmes to Secretary of the Navy Stephen R. Mallory, June 15, 1862, Semmes Family Papers, Alabama Department of Archives and History, Montgomery.

17 Kinnaman, *Most Perfect Cruiser*, 158.

18 Kinnaman, 160–61.

19 A key spy has been identified as Victor Buckley, a junior official in the Foreign Office, the son of a veteran of the Battle of Waterloo, and a godson of Queen Victoria, described by Alexander Rose as an "aristocratic, if penurious, boulevardier." Rose, *The Lion and the Fox: Two Rival Spies and the Secret Plot to Build a Confederate Navy* (New York: W. W. Norton, 2023), 119.

20 G. H. Carleton, "Semmes and the *Alabama*; The Infamous Career of the Privateer, as Described by Himself [. . .]," *New York Times*, September 2,

1864, https://www.nytimes.com/1864/09/02/archives/semmes-and
-the-alabama-the-infamous-career-of-the-privateer-as.html.

21 Kinnaman, *Most Perfect Cruiser*, 178.

Chapter 8. The *Alabama*

1 Kinnaman, *Most Perfect Cruiser*, 198–99.

2 The official motto of the Confederacy was *Deo vindice* (God is our
defender/protector/vindicator).

3 Library of Congress Print 48027/24070, quoted in Charles Grayson
Summersell, *CSS* Alabama: *Builder, Captain, and Plans* (Tuscaloosa:
University of Alabama Press, 1985), 13.

4 As described by Matthew Maguire in an internal memo to Consul
Dudley:

> Passing from this to a little more forward, is a large saloon,
> where the chief officers' and chief engineers' cabins are
> situated on each side, fitted up with chart and book cases. From
> this you pass through a doorway into the engine room. There
> is a platform over the engines (which are two in number) and
> which are most complete and handsome pieces of machinery,
> only occupying a small space and lying entirely at the bottom.
> . . . From here also you can pass in-to [*sic*] the stoke holes.
> Forward of this, but no communication, are the men's berths,
> which are quite open and spacious and run entirely forward, in
> the center is the cooking apparatus. The hooks are slung to the
> deck for the men's hammocks. . . . Forward of the mizen mast
> is a skylight to the small saloon and forward of this skylight
> is a larger one, which gives light to the larger saloon. These
> skylights do not stand more than a foot high on deck and
> which have iron bars across. Forward of this skylight and abaft
> the funnel, is a skylight five or six feet long, which gives light
> to the engine room. The base of the funnel forms a square,
> about two feet high; each corner is latticed with iron rails, to
> throw light and air into the stoke room. Each side abaft the
> funnel, are two ventilators with round bell mouth and which
> stand about five or six feet high; more forward of the mainmast
> are two more ventilators of the same description. . . . The
> entrance to the men's sleeping apartment, is raised, about 2
> feet high. A small chimney, or brass or copper funnel rises here

from the cooking apparatus. (Quoted in Robinson, *Shark of the Confederacy*, 169–70)

5 See Deposition of Theodore Julius, in *Correspondence Concerning Claims against Great Britain, Transmitted to the Senate of the United States in Answer to the Resolutions of December 4 and 10, 1867, and of May 27–1868*, Vol. 3: *Rebel Cruisers* (Washington, DC: Government Printing Office, 1870), 79.

6 John McIntosh Kell, *1886 Cruise and Combats of the "Alabama"* 31 (April 1886): 911.

7 Rick Spillman, "Are Modern Ships Slower than Sailing Ships? Probably Not." *The Old Salt Blog*, September 17, 2012, https://www.oldsaltblog .com/2012/09/are-modern-ships-slower-than-sailing-ships-probably -not/.

8 John McIntosh Kell, *Recollections of a Naval Life—As Executive Officer of the CSS Warships* Sumter *and* Alabama (Washington, DC: The Neale Company, 1900); William M. Robinson. *The* Alabama-Kearsarge *Battle: A Study in Original Sources* (Salem, MA: Essex Institute, 1924).

9 William Marvel, *The Alabama and the Kearsarge—The Sailor's Civil War* (Chapel Hill: University of North Carolina Press, 1996), 64.

10 *Alabama* Log, entry for Monday, August 25, 1862, Semmes Family Papers.

11 Park Benjamin, *United States Naval Academy, Being the Yarn of the American Midshipman* (New York: G. P. Putnam's Sons, 1900).

12 Langley, *Social Reform in the United States Navy*, 25.

13 Over one hundred years later, the psychologist Kenneth B. Clark expressed the corollary when he wrote that "contemporary problems inherent in segregated education involve the degree to which stereotyped assumptions concerning the inferiority or limited intellectual potentialities of large groups of children lead to the lowering of educational standards in the schools which they are required to attend, the degree to which these conditions, in fact, depress the educational aspirations and level of performance of these children thereby permanently impairing their ability to learn." Clark, "Segregated Schools in New York City," *Journal of Educational Sociology* 36, no. 6 (1963): 249.

14 Kell, *Recollections of a Naval Life*, 140.

15 Also referred to as Fullam's Navigation School, G. T. Fullam's Trade Civil Service and Naval School, and G. T. Fullam's Nautical and Steam School.

16 Charles Grayson Summersell, ed., *The Journal of George Townley Fullam: Boarding Officer of the Confederate Sea Raider* Alabama (Tuscaloosa: University of Alabama Press, 1973), viii.

17 Stephanie K. Koenig, "Common Men in Uncommon Times: Analyzing the Daily Lives of American Civil War Sailors Using Personal Narratives" (MA thesis, Texas A&M University, 2016), 94–104. As Sinclair put it in his introductory statement:

> Captain Raphael Semmes's account of the service of the *Alabama*, as the public probably observed, was most carefully confined within the limits of legal and professional statement. It was no part of his purpose to enter into the details of life on board, or to make any unnecessary confidences respecting himself or the officers and crew who shared his labors and successes. . . . It will not be doubted that a cruise so unique and remarkable had its share of daily and hourly interests, and of manifestations of that human nature which is of the first consequence in all narrative." (*Two Years on the Alabama* [Boston: Lee and Shepard, 1895], 1)

18 Morgan, *Recollections of a Rebel Reefer,* 40.

19 Edward T. Green Sr., Finding Aid (2008), Francis L. Galt Papers, Manuscript Division, Library of Congress.

20 Warren F. Spencer, *The Confederate Navy in Europe.* (Montgomery: University of Alabama Press, 1983), 189. An Adam Shilland is listed in the muster roll of July 7, 1863, but not identified as Black, enslaved, or deceased (*Alabama* log cited in chapter 17). Similarly, a fireman Andrew Shilland listed in an undated muster roll is not identified as Black, enslaved, or deceased (*A General Muster-Roll of the Officers, Petty Officers, and Firemen of the* C. S. Steamer Alabama, *from the Day She Was Commissioned August 24th, 1862, to the Day She Was Sunk, June 19th, 1864.* See Confederate States Navy Misc. Manuscripts, 1885–2001, from the holdings of the Museum of the Confederacy. Mss3 M9722 f 265–269). Finally, in a *Schedule of Officers and Crew of the Steamer Alabama,* there is no Adam or Andrew Shilland, but there is an entry for "Andrew Shilling, Scotchman; resides at Athel street, Liverpool has a wife; enlisted at Liverpool; is a fireman." See *Correspondence Concerning Claims against Great Britain Transmitted to the Senate of the United States in Answer to the Resolutions of December 4th and 10th, 1867, and of May 27, 1868,* Vol. 3: *Rebel Cruisers* (Washington, DC: Government Printing Office, 1870), 215.

21 Melville, *Redburn,* 155.

22 Semmes, *Alabama* log, entry for Saturday, August 23, 1862, 5, Semmes Family Papers.

23 Nathan Perl-Rosenthal, *Citizen Sailors: Becoming American in the Age of Revolution* (Cambridge, MA: Belknap Press of Harvard University Press, 2015), 30–33.

24 Semmes, *Alabama* log, entry for Monday, December 29, 1862, Semmes Family Papers.

Chapter 9. Prelude

1 Semmes, *Memoirs of Service Afloat*, 409.

2 This is Kell's recollection, quoted in Norman C. Delaney, *John McIntosh Kell of the Raider* Alabama (Tuscaloosa: University of Alabama Press, 1973), 130.

3 Morgan, *Recollections of a Rebel Reefer*, 129.

4 Naval historians of the period repeatedly stress the ambiguous status of engineers. See Royce Shingleton, "Seamen, Landsmen, Firemen, and Coal Heavers," in Still, *The Confederate Navy*, 131. see also Karsten, *Naval Aristocracy*, 65.

5 Marvel, *The* Alabama *and the* Kearsarge, 66. See also Delaney, *John McIntosh Kell*, 132.

6 Summersell, *CSS* Alabama, 24.

7 The approach set the stage for naval warfare for a century. Kaiser Wilhelm made Semmes's memoir mandatory reading for his officers.

8 The long history of trophy collecting has been described by the South African physical anthropologist Alan G. Morris, in "Trophy Skulls, Museums, and the San," In Skotnes, *Miscast*, 67–80.

9 The custom was described graphically by Ammianus Marcellinus, a Roman soldier and historian:

> And as ease is a delightful thing to men of a quiet and placid disposition, so danger and war are a pleasure to the Alani, and among them that man is called happy who has lost his life in battle . . . nor is there anything of which they boast with more pride than of having killed a man: and the most glorious spoils they esteem [are] the scalps which they have torn from the heads of those whom they have slain, which they put as trappings and ornaments on their war horses. (Marcellinus

Ammianus, essay, in *The Roman History of Ammianus Marcellinus During the Reigns of The Emperors Constantius, Julian, Jovianus, Valentinian, and Valens*, trans. C. D. Yonge, Book 31, Section 2: *Roman History* [London: G. Bell and Sons, 1911], para. 22, 582)

Fox, in *Wolf of the Deep*, 55, describes the chronometers as scalps.

10 Charles W. Morgan, "Edgartown Whaling Ship Ocmulgee, Sunk by Confederate Raider," Charles W. Morgan Blog, June 23, 2014, *Vineyard Gazette*, https://vineyardgazette.com/blog/charles-w-morgan.

11 Marvel, *The* Alabama *and the* Kearsarge, 67

12 Sinclair, *Two Years on the* Alabama, 26.

13 Edward Boykin, *Ghost Ship of the Confederacy* (New York: Funk and Wagnalls, 1957), 203.

14 Semmes, *Memoirs of Service Afloat*, 444.

15 "The Depredations of the Rebel Steamer '290,' Alias the 'Alabama,'" *Philadelphia Inquirer*, October 17, 1862, https://www.newspapers.com/image/167475746/?terms=elisha%20dunbar&match=1.

Chapter 10. Capture

1 Theodore Julius to Cope, October 1, 1862, 36th Voyage of the *Tonawanda*, Cope Family Papers.

2 From Theodore Julius, *Tonawanda* Log, entry for October 9, 1862, Avil Family Papers, courtesy of Avil Family:

Commences moderate breeze clear & pleasant. At 4h PM, made a large Bark rigged steamer on the Starboard Quarter under Canvas proved to be the Privateer Alabama alias 290. She run up the St. Georges Cross and we run the Ensign she then fired a gun for us to heave to and hauled down the English Colors and run up the Rebel Flag we Hove to & she sent a boat on board which took Capt T. Julius on board of the 290 leaving 2 of their officers in charge, they then gave chase to a Brig. Hove her to, sent a boat on board and let her proceed at 9:30 PM, Capt Julius carried on board with orders to keep close to the 290. All night. During the night Fresh Breeze and cloudy. At 11:30 AM the 290 sent a boat on board. Taking Capt. Julius on board of them as a hostage ordering me to keep after them or they would fire into me. She sent 19 prisoners on board crews of the Bark Wave Crest, Capt. Harmon & Brig Dunkirk Capt. Johnson. Both of New York and Both of these vessels had been burned by the 290.

3   Theodore Julius, deposition to Thomas H. Dudley, Liverpool, October 30, 1862, in *Correspondence Concerning Claims Against Great Britain*, 3:77–79.

4   From Theodore Julius, deposition to Thomas H. Dudley:

> I am held and firmly bound, and I do hereby bind the said Thomas P. Cope and Francis R. Cope, their and my heirs, executors, and assigns, well and truly to pay unto the president of the Confederate States of America, for the time being, at the conclusion of the war, the amount of $80,000 current money of the said Confederate States; and the ship Tonawanda, her tackle and apparel, are hereby mortgaged for the payment of this bond. (3:78)

5   Theodore Julius, deposition to Thomas H. Dudley, 3:78.

6   Julius Jr.'s identification of White as "Henry White of Lewistown Delaware" confirms that the name "David Henry" in the ship's manifest is the same individual as David Henry White. Theodore Julius, *Tonawanda* Log, entry for October 9, 1862, Avil Family Papers, courtesy of Avil Family.

7   Semmes, *Memoirs of Service Afloat*, 469.

8   David D. Porter, *The Naval History of the Civil War* (New York: Sherman Publishing Company, 1886), 635.

9   *Tonawanda* Log, entry for Saturday, October 17, 1862, Avil Family Papers.

10   *Tonawanda* Log, entry for Sunday, October 18, 1862, Avil Family Papers.

11   See Marvel, *The* Alabama *and the* Kearsarge, 75. Similarly, Frank H. Taylor wrote that "inasmuch as the North was treating enemy-owned slaves as contraband of war, Semmes did the same. He appropriated White from his owner [and] pronounced him free." *Confederate Raider*, 123.

12   *Official Records of the Union and Confederate Navies in the War of the Rebellion* (hereafter cited as *O.R. Navy*), Ser. I, Vol. 16 (Washington, DC: Government Printing Office, 1903), 689.

13   Ramold, *Slaves, Sailors, Citizens*, 41.

14 "The Second Confiscation Act" (*US Statutes at Large, Treaties, and Proclamations of the United States of America*, vol. 12, 589–92), Freedmen and Southern Society Project, accessed December 9, 2023, http://www.freedmen.umd.edu/conact2.htm. See also Franklin, *Emancipation Proclamation*.

15 Semmes, *Memoirs of Service Afloat*, 2.

16 Fox, *Wolf of the Deep*, 201–2; Semmes, *Memoirs of Service Afloat*, 201.

17 Semmes, *Memoirs of Service Afloat*, 465.

18 Kell, *Recollections of a Naval Life*, 10.

19 Semmes, *Alabama* Log, entry for October, 9, 1862, Semmes Family Papers.

20 Sarah Agnes Wallace and Frances Elma Gillespie, eds., *The Journal of Benjamin Moran 1857–1865* (Chicago: University of Chicago Press, 1949), 2:1085.

21 For more on "seasoning," see Steven Mintz, ed., "Introduction," *African American Voices: A Documentary Reader, 1619–1877.* (Oxford: Wiley-Blackwell, 2009), 11. Also see Michael Gomez, *Reversing Sail: A History of the African Diaspora* (Cambridge: Cambridge University Press, 2005), 100.

22 Richard Henry Dana Jr., *Two Years Before the Mast: A Personal Narrative of Life at Sea* (New York: Harper and Brothers, 1840).

23 Semmes, *Memoirs of Service Afloat*, 465.

Chapter 11. Storms

1 The Confederacy had kept to the 1850 ban on flogging, but continued to employ corporal punishment in the form of *tricing*. In this practice, the unfortunate seaman's thumbs or hands were chained together around an overhead beam, so that his feet scarcely reached the deck. It was said to be excruciatingly painful, particularly as the hanging chain was made ever shorter.

2 Tom Chaffin, *Sea of Gray: The Around-the-World Odyssey of the Confederate Raider* Shenandoah (New York: Hill and Wang, 2007), 100.

3 Chaffin, *Sea of Gray*, 100.

4 By Semmes's estimation, he encountered the storm more than three hundred miles east of the track much later reconstructed by the National Oceanic and Atmospheric Administration. See Jose J.

Fernandez-Partagas, "Year 1862," in "Storms of 1858–1864," Atlantic Oceanographic and Meteorological Laboratory, National Oceanic and Atmospheric Administration, accessed December 10, 2023, https://www.aoml.noaa.gov/hrd/Landsea/Partagas/1858-1864/1862.pdf, 40–44.

5   Although Julius didn't plan it this way, the *Tonawanda*, by comparison, enjoyed moderate weather and clear sailing on its continued voyage east to Liverpool. In contrast, over days of worsening weather, Semmes doggedly held to a westerly course, thereby steering directly toward the eye of the storm from the worst possible angle.

6   See Stuart B. Schwartz, *Sea of Storms: A History of Hurricanes in the Greater Caribbean from Columbus to Katrina*, Lawrence Stone Lectures 6 (Princeton, NJ: Princeton University Press, 2015). See also Rachel Slade, *Into the Raging Sea: Thirty-Three Mariners, One Megastorm, and the Sinking of the* El Faro (New York: HarperCollins, 2018), 45.

7   Semmes, *Alabama* Log, entry for Monday, October 13, 1862, Semmes Family Papers.

8   Rachel Oblack, "How to Read a Barometer: Use Rising and Falling Air Pressure to Predict the Weather," *ThoughtCo.*, update March 4, 2020, https://www.thoughtco.com/how-to-read-a-barometer-3444043.

9   William Stanley Hoole, *Four Years in the Confederate Navy: The Career of Captain John Low on the C.S.S.* Fingal, Florida, Alabama, Tuscaloosa, *and* Ajax (Athens: University of Georgia Press, 1964), 63.

10 Oblack, "How to Read a Barometer."

11 Semmes, *Alabama* Log, entry for Monday, October 16, 1862. Semmes Family Papers.

12 Slade, *Into the Raging Sea.*

13 See William Falconer, *Shipwreck: A Sentimental and Descriptive Poem, in Three Cantos* (1762), online at Evans Early American Imprint Collection, accessed December 10, 2023, https://quod.lib.umich.edu/e/evans/N16417.0001.001/1:3?rgn=div1;view=fulltext.

14 George Townley Fullam, entry for October 16, 1862, in Summersell, *Journal of George Townley Fullam,* 37.

15 From Hoole, *Four Years in the Confederate Navy:*

   Within thirty minutes, the winds struck again, this time from the northwest, butt end foremost, a mighty roaring, spewing engine. Instantly, the gallant little cruiser toppled over, for all the world like a toy boat, dashing her lee guns under water, her timbers fairly groaning and cracking, her larboard deck awash to the stack. Lieutenant Low, experienced seaman that he was, grasped the helm—without Captain Semmes' orders. Slowly, ever so slowly, he wore the ship from the port tack, at last righting her, giving her a second chance. Had he hesitated, even for five minutes, his skilled maneuver would have been impossible. (64)

16 Marvel, *The* Alabama *and the* Kearsarge, 77. Semmes says "all hands were on deck," in *Memoirs of Service Afloat*, 474.

17 Semmes, *Memoirs of Service Afloat*, 474.

18 Sinclair, *Two Years on the Alabama*, 44.

19 Hoole, *Four Years in the Confederate Navy*, 64–65.

20 Semmes, *Alabama* log, entry for Monday, October 16, 1862, Semmes Family Papers.

Chapter 12. Reports

1 Depredations letter from Capt. Theodore Julius, *New York Times*, November 16, 1862.

2 "The Pirate Alabama," *New York Daily Herald*, November 13, 1862, 5.

3 Theodore Julius, deposition to Thomas H. Dudley, 3: 77–79. Indeed, the original typescript of the *Philadelphia Public Ledger* of November 14, 1862, says, "being without protection *or* free papers"; the *New York Times'* November 16, 1862, transcriptions were incorrect.

4 Mark Lieberman, "Egg Corns: Folk Etymology, Malapropism, Mondegreen, ???," *Language Log* (blog), April 4, 2004, http://itre.cis.upenn.edu/~myl/languagelog/archives/000018.html.

5 For example, the frigate HMS *Hermione*, with a regular complement of 180 men, had 129 desertions between 1793 and 1797. Desertion rates for Dutch and French warships was even higher, with annual rates of up to 90 percent not uncommon. In 1795, the Dutch vessel *Staaten Generaal*, with a complement of 550, lost 428 to desertion; the *Delft*, with 350 men, lost 340. See Niklas Frykman, "Seamen on Late-Eighteenth-Century European Warships," *International Review of Social History* 54, no. 1 (2009): 67–93, https://doi.org/10.1017/s0020859009000030.

6 Theodore Julius, deposition to Thomas H. Dudley, 77–79.

CHAPTER 13. MUTINY

1   Boykin, *Ghost Ship of the Confederacy*, 226.

2   Porter, *Naval History of the Civil War*, 635.

3   Spencer, *Raphael Semmes*, 145.

4   Memorial of the New York Chamber of Commerce to the Secretary of the Navy regarding protection of shipping interests of the United States, New York, July 22, 1863, in *O.R. Navy* (1895), Ser. I: Vol. 2, 402–3.

5   Semmes, *Memoirs of Service Afloat*, 467.

6   No one knows Winslow Homer's exact inspiration for the illustration, as his correspondence with *Harper's Weekly* of the period has been lost (William R. Cross, personal communication). See also William R. Cross, *Winslow Homer: American Passage* (New York: Farrar, Straus and Giroux, 2022), and Barbara Brooks Tomblin, *Life in Jefferson Davis' Navy* (Annapolis, MD: Naval Institute Press, 2019).

7   Sokolow, *Charles Benson*, 64.

8   Sokolow, 64.

9   Davenport Dinnerware. CSS *Alabama* Artifact Photo Collection. Naval History and Heritage Command. https://www.history.navy.mil /research/underwater-archaeology/conservation-and-curation /ua-artifact-collections/css-alabama-artifact-collection/css-alabama -artifact-photo-collection/css-alabama-davenport-dinnerware.html.

10   Bowcock, *Anatomy of a Confederate Raider*, 10.

11   Morgan, *Recollections of a Rebel Reefer*, 129.

12   Sinclair, *Two Years on the* Alabama, 93.

13   See Sinclair, 93. As a midshipman on the *Georgia*, James M. Morgan was afforded a few opportunities to improve his diet. He was offered a glass of sherry and a brown bag full of cakes from various visitors to the ship. Provisions were taken from prize vessels, which usually included coal or luxury items such as champagne or, in one instance, several bottles of eau-de-vie de Danzig with gold dust floating in it. Morgan, *Recollections of a Rebel Reefer*, 145, 156, 162.

14   Morgan, *Recollections of a Rebel Reefer*, 76.

15   Costello, *Black Salt*.

16   Bolster, *Black Jacks*, 81.

17 Summersell, *Journal of George Townley Fullam*, 54. See also Sinclair, *Two Years on the* Alabama, 50.

18 Langley, *Social Reform in the United States Navy*, 142.

19 Kell, *Recollections of a Naval Life*, 197. See also Robinson, *Shark of the Confederacy*, 59.

20 Kell, *Recollections of a Naval Life*, 198.

21 Summersell, *Journal of George Townley Fullam*, 53–54; Fox, *Wolf of the Deep*, 135.

Chapter 14. South to Galveston

1 By September 1861, however, Navy secretary Gideon Welles had received so many requests to enlist fugitive slaves in the navy that he permitted the enlistment of former slaves whose "services can be useful," stipulating that the "contrabands" be classified as Boys irrespective of age. Order of September 25, 1861, Naval Personnel, Recruitment, and Enlistment, 1860–1870, Naval Records Collection of the Office of Naval Records and Library (Record Group 45), National Archives. In December 1862, Welles removed the restriction that contraband enlistees be rated exclusively as Boys, but the practice continued in the Confederate Navy.

2 Marvel, *The* Alabama *and the* Kearsarge, 106.

3 Sinclair, *Two Years on the Alabama*, 28.

4 Marvel, *The* Alabama *and the* Kearsarge, 106.

5 Semmes, *Memoirs of Service Afloat*, 418.

6 Semmes, 419.

7 Porter, *Naval History of the Civil War*, 639.

8 According to Lieutenant Low, "We informed them that we were the Confederate States Steamer *Alabama*, and upon saying so fired a broadside which she instantly replied to, whereon the action became general. . . . At this time I suppose we were about two hundred yards from each other and the rifle shot & shells she was throwing pretty rapidly at us but generally going too high." John Low, quoted in Hoole, *Four Years in the Confederate Navy*, 73.

9 James Morgan singled out Blake for his heroism and for keeping the *Hatteras*'s guns firing until they were level with the water. Morgan, *Recollections of a Rebel Reefer*, 127.

10 See Summersell, *Alabama*, 48.

11 From Porter, *Naval History of the Civil War.*

> The course pursued by the Confederate commander in this action cannot be justified by the rules of war. In answer to a hail from the *Hatteras*, he declared his vessel to be Her Britannic Majesty's steamer *Petrel* and when Lt. Commander Blake proposed to send a boat alongside of him, expressed his willingness to receive the offers in a friendly manner. . . . If it had been simply a ruse to escape while the boat was being lowered, it might have passed. But when, as in this case, it was to gain time in which to train the guns upon the vital parts of an enemy, and make preparations for taking human life, it was simply perfidy. . . . When two men-of-war meet in the day-time their nationality is shown by their flag; but when, under cover of darkness, a false nationality is given, and willingness to receive a friendly visit expressed, it is the same as violating a flag of truce, for the visitor goes on board with the full expectation of meeting a kind of reception and does not anticipate treachery. (640)

12 Hoole, *Four Years in the Confederate Navy*, 73. In a similar hagiographic vein, Robinson misleadingly reported that the *Alabama* "did not sacrifice the life of a single captive—even in her night engagement with the *Hatteras* [from which] every man of the enemy crew was saved." Alabama-Kearsarge *Battle*, 34. In fact, two Hatteras crewman were lost in the engagement.

CHAPTER 15. PORT ROYAL, THE *OLIVE JANE*, AND THE *JOHN A. PARKS*

1 Semmes, *Memoirs of Service Afloat*, 562.

2 Porter, *Naval History of the Civil War*, 640.

3 See Joel Lewis Headley, *Farragut and Our Naval Commanders* (New York: E. B. Treat and Co., 1867), 282 and 283, respectively, for the following two letters:

> To the Commander H.B.M. ship Greyhound:
>
> January 24, 1863,
>
> Lieutenant-Commander H. C. Blake, of the United States Navy, presents his compliments to the Commander of H.B.M. ship Greyhound, and desires to learn whether or not he may consider the playing of "Dixie's Land" by the band of the Greyhound upon arrival of the Confederate steamer Alabama, on the evening of the 21st instant, as a mark of disrespect to

the United States Government, or its officers who were prisoners on board the Alabama, at the period indicated.

Lieutenant-Commander H. C. Blake
respectfully requests an early response,
US Consulate, Jamacia.

Commander Hickley, R.N., presents his compliments to Lieutenant-Commander Blake, U.S.N., and has to acquaint him that on the evening in question he was on board the A— dining with Captain Crocroft. Shortly after the time of the officer of the guard reporting the Alabama's arrival, he heard the drums and fifes of H.M.S. Greyhound playing, among other tunes, the tune of "Dixie's Land." He immediately repaired on board, causing other national tunes to be played, among which was the United States national air, and severely reprimanded the inconsiderate young officer who had ordered "Dixie's Land" to be played, calling for his reasons, and writing and forwarding them forthwith, with his report to Commodore Hugh Dunlop, C.B., who severely reprimanded the officer.

As the officer in question had no idea that any U.S. officer or man was on board the Alabama, it must be evident to Lieutenant-Commander Blake that no insult was intended.

HMS Greyhound,
Port Royal, Jamaica,
January 24, 1863.

4   Semmes, *Memoirs of Service Afloat*, 562.

5   Dispatches from US consul John W. Camps to US secretary of state William Seward, Kingston, Jamaica, February 4, 1863, United States Consular Despatches, Records of the Foreign Service Posts of the Department of State, 1788–1990 (Record Group 84), National Archives.

6   See "Flamstead, Jamacia, Port Royal," Centre for the Study of the Legacies of British Slavery, University College London, accessed December 12, 2023, https://www.ucl.ac.uk/lbs/estate/view/2965.

7   Semmes, *Memoirs of Service Afloat*, 557.

8   Consul Camps to Secretary of State Seward, February 4, 1863.

9   Boykin, *Ghost Ship of the Confederacy*, 277. Boykin adds another part to this story, but it is unattributed: "'But what about the sharks?' Semmes

asked. 'The harbor was full of them. They might have eaten the boys up.' 'Sharks don't eat them black boys, your honor'" (277). Semmes does indeed mention the shark-infested waters of Port Royal Bay, but in his memoirs does not relate the Q&A specifically about sharks.

10 Semmes, *Memoirs of Service Afloat*, 565.

11 Semmes, 575.

12 Sinclair, *Two Years the on Alabama*, 94–95.

13 Semmes later recalled:

> I was grieved to find that our most serious loss among the deserters, was our Irish fiddler. This fellow had been remarkably diligent, in his vocation, and had fiddled the crew over half the world. It was a pity to lose him, now that we were going over the other half. When the evening's amusements began, Michael Mahoney's vacant camp-stool cast a gloom over the ship. There was no one who could make his violin "talk" like himself, and it was a long time before his place was supplied. (*Memoirs of Service Afloat*, 675)

14 Semmes, 453.

15 See also John Townley, "Music in the Confederate Navy," *Confederate Naval Historical Society Newsletter*, no. 5 (October 5, 1990): 3–5.

16 At latitude 29°25' N, longitude 37°47' W.

17 Semmes wrote in his memoir:

> On the second day after burning the *Kingfisher*, we made two more captures. . . . They came along lovingly, arm-in-arm, as it were, as though in the light airs and calms that were prevailing, they had been having a friendly chat, or one of the masters had been dining on board of the other. They were evidently American ships, and had most likely been having a cozy talk about the war. The "sainted" Abraham's Emancipation Proclamation was the favorite topic of the day, as we had learned from the mail-bags of the Parks, and perchance they had been discussing that. (*Memoirs of Service Afloat*, 588)

18 "An Act in Relation to Free Negroes and Mulattoes." *Georgetown Messenger*, April 15, 1863, 4.

19 An Act in Relation to Free Negroes and Mulattoes, 305 *Del. Laws* 330 (1863).

20 The 1863 law applied to White henceforth because the general rule
in Delaware was (and is) that new law is effective immediately as to
all actions taken after its enactment unless the effective date is later or
there is a grandfather clause. The 1863 law was effective immediately
and contained no grandfather clause. The ex post facto principle
applies only to criminal laws, not to civil law. Randy J. Holland,
personal communication, August 10, 2021.

Chapter 16. Brazil and the South Atlantic

1 Kell, *Recollections of a Naval Life*, 109–10. The Neptune ritual may be
characterized as an example of what anthropologists call liminal space,
that is rituals in which individuals transition from one socially defined
category to another are often characterized by a suspension of the
normal rules of social interaction. Victor Turner, *The Ritual Process;
Structure and Anti-Structure* (London: Aldine, 1969).

2 Koenig, "Common Men in Uncommon Times," 77–78.

3 Fox, *Wolf of the Deep*, 143.

4 Fox, 143–44.

5 Delaney, *John McIntosh Kell*, 148.

6 Boykin, *Ghost Ship of the Confederacy*, 291.

7 "Our Relations with Great Britain." *Harper's Weekly* 7, no. 330 (April 25,
1863): 258, online at Daily Observations from the Civil War, March 27,
2013, https://dotcw.com/our-relations-with-great-britain/.

8 Boykin, *Ghost Ship of the Confederacy*, 296.

9 See also Summersell, *Journal of George Townley Fullam*, 110.

10 Boykin provides a more colorful account, but it is unattributed. See
Ghost Ship of the Confederacy, 297.

11 Dispatches from Thomas Y. Wilson to U.S. Secretary of State William
Seward, Bahia, December 22–23, 1863, United States Consular
Despatches, Records of the Foreign Service Posts of the Department of
State, 1788–1990 (Record Group 84), National Archives.

12 See Semmes, *Memoirs of Service Afloat*, 617. For a description of the
evening, see Morgan, *Recollections of a Rebel Reefer*, 128–29.

13 Semmes, *Memoirs of Service Afloat*, 617. Porter, in *Naval History of the Civil
War*, 644, put it this way: "He was finally permitted to remain and give
his men liberty on shore, where they turned the town upside down
generally."

14 McCallum, quoted in Fox, *Wolf of the Deep*, 143.

15 Loveland, quoted in Fox, 144.

16 Sinclair, *Two Years on the Alabama*, 148.

17 Semmes, *Alabama* log, entry for June 15, 1863, Semmes Family Papers.

18 Semmes, *Alabama* log, entry for June 29, 1863.

19 McKee, *Gentlemanly and Honorable Profession*, 148.

20 Powell to James Demarest, Chairman of the Sailor's Home Committee, March 30, 1864, Correspondence and Reports, 1864–1868, Manuscript Collection, Maritime Historical Association, American Seamen's Friend Society, Mystic Seaport Museum, Mystic, CT.

21 See Foner, "William P. Powell," 104–10 (Powell quote on 104–5). See also *Thirty-sixth Annual Report of the American Seaman's Friend Society* (New York: S. Halle, Book and Job Printer, 1864), 42–43.

22 Semmes, *Memoirs of Service Afloat*, 636; Boykin, *Ghost Ship of the Confederacy*, 306.

CHAPTER 17. CAPE OF GOOD HOPE

1 Semmes, *Alabama* log, entry for July, 7, 1863, Semmes Family Papers.

2 Semmes, *Memoirs of Service Afloat*, 638.

3 A century later, Nelson Mandela and his comrades on Robben Island would frequently argue the point:

> One subject we hearkened back to again and again was the question of whether there were tigers in Africa. Some argued that although it was popularly assumed that tigers lived in Africa, this was a myth and they were native to Asia and the Indian subcontinent. Africa had leopards in abundance, but no tigers. The other side argued that tigers were native to Africa and some still lived there. Some claimed to have seen with their own eyes this most powerful and beautiful of cats in the jungles of Africa. I maintained that while there were no tigers to be found in contemporary Africa, there was a Xhosa word for tiger, a word different from the one for leopard, and that if the word existed in our language, the creature must once have existed in Africa. Otherwise, why would there be a name for it? (Mandela, *Long Walk to Freedom: The Autobiography of Nelson Mandela* [New York: Little, Brown, 1994], 430)

See also Carmel Schrire, *Tigers in Africa: Stalking the Past at the Cape of Good Hope* (Charlottesville: University Press of Virginia, 2002). 430.

4   Semmes, *Memoirs of Service Afloat*, 639.

5   Walter Graham to William Seward, August 4, 1863, United States Consular Despatches, Records of the Foreign Service Posts of the Department of State, 1788–1990 (Record Group 84), National Archives.

6   "*Daar kom die Alibama*" (There Comes the *Alibama*), translated:

> There comes the *Alibama*,
> The *Alibama* comes over the sea,
> There comes the *Alibama*,
> The *Alibama* comes over the sea.
>
> Girl, girl, the reed bed,
> Girl, the reed bed is made,
> The reed bed is made
> for you to sleep on.
>
> Girl, girl, the reed bed,
> The reed bed is made,
> The reed bed is made
> for you to sleep on.
>
> The *Alibama*, the *Alibama*,
> The *Alibama* comes over the sea,
> The *Alibama*, the *Alibama*,
> The *Alibama* comes over the sea.

7   Bruno Werz, *The Shipwrecks of the* Oosterland *and* Waddinxveen, *1697, Table Bay* (Johannesburg: Zulu Planet, 2009), 75.

8   That is, between 1652, when the Dutch East India Company planted the first seeds in the Company Gardens, and 1870, when the Suez Canal opened.

9   Lauren Beukes and Nechama Brodie, *Maverick: Extraordinary Women from South Africa's Past* (Century City, South Africa: Umuzi, 2015).

10   The *Tuscaloosa* had been converted from the bark *Conrad*, captured off Brazil on June 20.

11   Sinclair, *Two Years on the* Alabama, 153.

12   "The Rebel Pirates; The Alabama, Georgia, and the Tuscaloosa at the Cape of Good Hope. Enthusiastic Reception Extended

to the Confederates. More American Vessels Captured and Destroyed. Proceedings of Capt. Semmes's Admiralty Court. Spicy Correspondence Between U.S. Consul Graham and Gov. Wodehouse," *New York Times*, October 8, 1863, https://www.nytimes .com/1863/10/08/archives/the-rebel-pirates-the-alabama-georgia -and-the-tuscaloosa-at-the.html.

13 Sinclair, *Two Years on the* Alabama, 154–55.

14 For more details on the local population's response to the arrival of the *Alabama* in Cape Town, see the August 8, 1863, edition of the *Cape Argus*.

15 From "Rebel Pirates" in the *New York Times* of October 8, https://www. nytimes.com/1863/10/08/archives/the-rebel-pirates-the-alabama -georgia-and-the-tuscaloosa-at-the.html:

> The Captain's cabin is in the very stern of the ship, and in shape just a half moon. It is very small, and plainly furnished. A horse-hair sofa runs round the little horse-shoe table in the centre. There is only room besides for two or three chairs, and a little sideboard or buffet opening into the steward's pantry as well as the cabin. On the ledge, or shelf running round the back of the sofa, are ranged between fifty and sixty chronometers, taken out of the different ships captured and destroyed by the Alabama. Her Captain's charts and those taken from her prizes are stowed away in great profusion behind the chronometers, against the bulk-heads and cross-beams, or litter the floor, sofa, table, and chairs. A colored engraving of the Alabama, and small photographic portraits of DAVIS, LEE, and two or three other Confederate celebrities, hang against the panels. A door at one side opens into the Captain's sleeping apartment, in which, beside the narrow bunk with drawers beneath, there is barely room for a strong box, chair, and wash-stand.

16 Semmes, *Memoirs of Service Afloat*, 653.

17 Interestingly, Fox points out that the Afrikaner newspaper *Het Volksblad*, perhaps chafing at all this British enthusiasm, dismissed the vessel as "nothing more than a well-equipped pirate." See Fox, *Wolf of the Deep*, 163.

CHAPTER 18. SIMON'S TOWN

1 Raphael Semmes, *Service Afloat; Or, the Remarkable Career of the Confederate Cruisers* Sumter *and* Alabama, *during the War between the States: Memoirs of Service Afloat during the War between the States* (Baltimore: Baltimore Publishing Company, 1887), 660–61.

2 Semmes, *Alabama* Log, entry for August 23, 1863, Semmes Family Papers.

3 Fox, *Wolf of the Deep*, 157. See also Symonds, *Civil War at Sea*, 97.

4 Melville, *White Jacket*, 4–5.

5 Listed by name in Summersell, *Journal of George Townley Fullam*, 137.

6 Mr. Graham to Mr. Adams, Dispatch, Accompanying the Annual Message of the President to the 1st sess., 38th Congress, Part 1, No. 530, United States Department of State, Papers Relating to Foreign Affairs, Document 655, Office of the Historian, Foreign Service Institute, https://history.state.gov/historicaldocuments/frus1863p1/d655.

7 Sinclair, *Two Years on the* Alabama, 344–32.

8 Bowcock, *Anatomy of a Confederate Raider*, 51.

CHAPTER 19. THE INDIAN OCEAN

1 According to Fullam, by the end of August, the condenser was failing. Summersell, *Journal of George Townley Fullam*, 143.

2 Semmes, *Alabama* Log, entry for Wednesday, October 14, 1863, Semmes Family Papers.

3 Debby Applegate, *The Most Famous Man in America: The Biography of Henry Ward Beecher* (New York: Three Leaves Press, 2006).

4 Great Meeting in the Philharmonic Hall, Liverpool, October 16, 1863, in Henry Ward Beecher, *American Rebellion Report of the Speeches of the Rev. Henry Ward Beecher, Delivered at Public Meetings in Manchester, Glasgow, Edinburgh, Liverpool, and London; and at The Farewell Breakfasts in London, Manchester, and Liverpool* (Manchester: Union and Emancipation Society, 1864), 62–84.

5 "The Black Man's Organ on Mr. Beecher," *Brooklyn Daily Eagle*, December 8, 1862, 1.

6 Sinclair, *Two Years on the* Alabama, 189.

7 Sinclair, 189.

8   Semmes, *Memoirs of Service Afloat*, 695.

9   "Franklin's Lost Expedition," Wikipedia, accessed December 13, 2023, https://en.wikipedia.org/wiki/Franklin%27s_lost_expedition.

10 Semmes, *Memoirs of Service Afloat*, 453.

11 Larrabee, quoted in Fox, *Wolf of the Deep*, 180.

12 Cumming, quoted in Fox, 180.

13 Copy of statement of James D. Babcock, of New Bedford. *O.R. Navy* (1895), Ser. I: Vol 2, 562.

.14 William Nevius to Peter Nevius, December 11, 1863, Nevius Family File, New-York Historical Society Museum and Library, New York.

15 Semmes, *Alabama* Log, entry for Friday November 13, 1863, 42, Semmes Family Papers.

16 Semmes, *Alabama* Log, entry for Monday, November 16, 1863, Semmes Family Papers.

17 Fullam, in Summersell, *Journal of George Townley Fullam*, 160. See also Norman C. Delaney, "The Alabama's 'Bold and Determined Man,'" *Naval History Magazine* 25, no. 4 (July 2011), https://www.usni.org/magazines/naval-history-magazine/2011/july/alabamas-bold-and-determined-man.

18 Fox, *Wolf of the Deep*, 191.

19 Fox, 193.

20 Stobb to Seward, December 22, 1863, and January, 8, 1864, United States Consular Despatches, Records of the Foreign Service Posts of the Department of State, 1788–1990 (Record Group 84), National Archives. See also Frenise A. Logan, "Activities of the *Alabama* in Asian Waters," *Pacific Historical Review* 31, no. 2 (1962): 146, https://doi.org/10.2307/3636572.

21 See Delaney, *John McIntosh Kell*, 155; and Fox, *Wolf of the Deep*, 187. See also John Cameron, *Our Tropical Possessions in Malayan India: Being a Descriptive Account of Singapore, Penang, Province Wellesley, and Malacca; Their Peoples, Products, Commerce, and Government* (London: Smith and Elder, 1865).

22 "Captain, I Am Going to Burn Your Ship," *Times of India*, February 4, 1864.

23 *Bombay Gazette*, February 24, 1864. See also Logan, "Activities of the *Alabama*."

24   Semmes, *Alabama* Log, entry for Monday, December 7, 1863, 52, Semmes Family Papers.

25   Semmes, *Alabama* Log, entry for Saturday, February 13, 1864, 81–82, Semmes Family Papers.

26   Semmes, *Alabama* Log, entry for Sunday, February 14, 1864, 82, Semmes Family Papers.

27   Marvel, *The* Alabama *and the* Kearsarge, 228.

28   Porter, *Naval History of the Civil War*, 649.

29   Semmes, *Memoirs of Service Afloat*, 750.

30   Porter, *Naval History of the Civil War*, 649; George Gordon Byron, *The Corsair: A Tale* (London: John Murray, 1814), canto III, ch. XXIV.

CHAPTER 20. THE LOOMING BATTLE

1   Juliet Wilson-Bareau and David Degener, *Manet and the American Civil War: The Battle of the U.S.S. Kearsarge and C.S.S. Alabama* (New York: Metropolitan Museum of Art, 2003). See also Norman C. Delaney, "Monsieur Rondin's Fake Photo: A Scam That Failed," *Military Image* 19, no. 4 (1998): 30–32.

2   Refusal to admit defeat among Confederate veterans is discussed more broadly by Janney, *Remembering the Civil War*, 54.

3   W. E. B. Du Bois, "The American Negro in My Time," *Masses and Mainstream* 9, no. 2 (1956): 1–9.

4   Quoted in Ellicott, *Life of John Ancrum Winslow*, 86.

5   Jim Dan Hill, *Sea Dogs of the Sixties: Farragut and Seven Contemporaries* (Minneapolis: University of Minnesota Press, 1935), 204–5.

6   Hill, 204.

7   Winslow to Welles, October 4, 1862, quoted in Ellicott, *Life of John Ancrum Winslow*, 91.

8   Ellicott, *Life of John Ancrum Winslow*, 88.

9   Nor was abolitionism synonymous with a commitment to equality and justice, as reflected in the many divisions between white and Black abolitionists.

10   For a detailed description of the chain armor and its effect, see Frederick Milnes Edge, *An Englishman's View of the Battle between the* Alabama *and the* Kearsarge: *An Account of the Naval Engagement in the*

British Channel, on Sunday June 19th, 1864 (New York: A. D. F. Randolph, 1864).

11   Semmes, *Memoirs of Service Afloat*, 753–54.

12   See Robinson, *Shark of the Confederacy*, 147.

13   Sinclair, *Two Years on the* Alabama, 259. See also Ellicott, *Life of John Ancrum Winslow*, 185.

14   Ellicott, *Life of John Ancrum Winslow*, 17.

15   Poole, quoted in Marvel, *The* Alabama *and the* Kearsarge, 212.

16   Poole, quoted in Marvel, *The Alabama and the* Kearsarge, 242.

17   See William Wainwright, "Ms. Journal Kept by William Wainwright on Board the U.S.S. *Kearsarge*, Captain Pickering, and Later Captain John A. Winslow, Commanding for a Naval Cruise. A Detailed Descriptive Journal, Including Details of Burial at Sea," 300, Log 429, Manuscripts Collection, G. W. Blunt White Library, Mystic Seaport Museum, Mystic, CT.

18   It isn't clear why Winslow didn't just respond to Dayton, but it has been suggested that he didn't trust the telegraph system in France. See Wilson-Bareau and Degener, *Manet and the American Civil War*, 28.

19   Delaney, *John McIntosh Kell*, 159.

20   Semmes to Ad. Bonfils, Esq., Cherbourg, June 14, 1864, 181, *O.R. Navy*, Ser. I: Vol. 3, 648.

21   Wainwright, "Ms. Journal Kept by William Wainwright," 304.

22   Wainwright, 305.

Chapter 21. The Battle of Cherbourg

1   See also Francis Boardman Crowninshield Bradlee and James Magee, *The* Kearsarge-Alabama *Battle, the Story as Told to the Writer by James Magee of Marblehead, Seaman on the Kearsarge* (Salem, MA: Essex Institute, 1921), 5.

2   John Lancaster, "The *Deerhound*, The *Alabama*, and the *Kearsarge*." *London Daily News*, June 29, 1864, Letters, 5.

3   Fox, *Wolf of the Deep*, 226–27.

4   Sinclair, *Two Years on the* Alabama, 263.

5   Starting that weekend, for 16 francs (12 francs third class), Parisians

could board an overnight train on Friday and arrive at Cherbourg Saturday morning. See Marvel, *The* Alabama *and the* Kearsarge, 249.

6   Marvel, *The* Alabama *and the* Kearsarge, 250.

7   Semmes, *Memoirs of Service Afloat*, 756.

8   James R. Wheeler, Acting Master, Log of the USS *Kearsarge*, entry for July 19 1864, Records of the Bureau of Naval Personnel (Record Group 24), 1862–1864, National Archives.

9   Boykin, *Ghost Ship of the Confederacy*, 363.

10 Edge, *An Englishman's View.*

CHAPTER 22. DEMISE

1   Like every other claim about the battle, this assertion, made many years later by John Fairfield Bickford, first loader of the *Kearsarge*'s forward pivot gun, was questioned, but this one was found to be largely plausible. See Norman C. Delaney, "I Didn't Feel Excited a Mite," *Naval History Magazine* 24, no. 6 (December 2010), https://www.usni.org/magazines/naval-history-magazine/2010/december/i-didnt-feel-excited-mite.

2   Irvine Bulloch, quoted in Delaney, *John McIntosh Kell*, 168.

3   Kell himself acknowledged this. Delaney, 169.

4   Boykin, *Ghost Ship of the Confederacy*, 366.

5   Sinclair, *Two Years on the* Alabama, 285.

6   Kell, *1886 Cruise and Combats*, 918.

7   Kell, *Recollections of a Naval Life*, 249.

8   Kell, *Recollections of a Naval Life*, 249.

9   Kell, *1886 Cruise and Combats*, 920.

10 Boykin, *Ghost Ship of the Confederacy*, 373. Marvel also placed White at the stern with Semmes, Kell, and Bartelli. *The* Alabama *and the* Kearsarge, 256. Kell mentions Bartelli at the stern, but not White. *Recollections of a Naval Life*, 249.

11 Dalzell, *Flight from the Flag*, 50.

12 Sinclair, *Two Years on the* Alabama, 278.

13 The exact circumstances of the surrender remain controversial but do not pertain to White's experience.

14   See John M. Browne to Surgeon W. Whelan, July 23, 1864 in *O.R. Navy* Ser. I, Vol. 3, Sec. 6, 70. Regarding the treatment of those wounded in the engagement between that vessel and the CSS *Alabama*, see Report of John M. Browne, U.S. Navy, U.S.S. *Kearsarge*, ibid.

15   "The Surgeon of the Alabama," *Illustrated London News*, supplement. July 9, 1864, 41.

16   John M. Browne, "The Duel between the *Alabama* and the *Kearsarge*," *Century Magazine* 31 (April 1886): 928.

17   "The Alabama: Official Report of Captain Semmes," *London Morning Post*, June 24, 1864, 7; Kell, *Recollections of a Naval Life*, 200.

18   Lancaster, "The *Deerhound*, the *Alabama*, and the *Kearsarge*," 5.

19   Browne, "The Duel Between the *Alabama* and the *Kearsarge*."

20   John Lancaster, "The Fight Between the *Alabama* and the *Kearsarge*," *Illustrated London News*, July 2, 1864, Letters, 2.

21   Kell, *1886 Cruise and Combats*, 613.

22   Keith and Clavin, *To the Uttermost Ends of the Earth*, 257.

23   See Captain Jones's statement, in Sinclair, *Two Years on the Alabama*, 290.

24   Kell, *Recollections of a Naval Life*, 253.

25   John A. Winslow, "Additional Report of Captain Winslow, US Navy commanding USS *Kearsarge* regarding the engagement of that vessel with the CSS *Alabama*," Cherbourg, France, June 21, 1864, 61–62, in *O.R. Navy*, Ser. I: Vol. 3, Sec. 6.

26   Bradlee, Kearsarge-Alabama *Battle*, 4.

27   Winslow to Welles, July 30, 1864, in "Report of Captain Winslow, US Navy Commanding the USS *Kearsarge*, given the Crew and Armament of the CSS *Alabama*," 77, in *O.R. Navy*, Ser. I: Vol. 3, Sec. 6.

28   Porter, *Naval History of the Civil War*, 653.

29   Bradlee, Kearsarge-Alabama *Battle*, 4.

30   "The Alabama: Official Report of Captain Semmes," 7.

31   "The Destruction of the *Alabama*: Official List of Killed, Wounded, Captured, and Saved," *Liverpool Mercury*, June 27, 1864, 5.

32   "As soon as the Kearsarge ceased firing," Kell recalled in an interview in 1883, "I went over the decks and ordered every man to secure what

he could cling to and . . . jump overboard. This order was issued to prevent any of the crew being carried down in the vortex made by the sinking ship. But two men went down with her. One was a man who had deserted from a Yankee vessel, and the other was a carpenter, who, poor fellow, could not swim." Alfred Iverson Branham, *Story of the Sinking of the Alabama "290": Interview with Captain John McIntosh Kell, Executive Officer of the Alabama, Given to Alfred Iverson Branham, Forty-Six Years Ago, June, 1883* (Atlanta: Cornell Press, 1930). White is also omitted in the list of casualties in Edge, *An Englishman's View.*

CHAPTER 23. ACCOUNTS

1   Semmes, *Alabama* Log, entry for October 9, 1862, Semmes Family Papers.

2   Semmes, *Memoirs of Service Afloat,* 466.

3   Sinclair, *Two Years on the* Alabama, 37.

4   Kevin M. Levin, *Searching for Black Confederates: The Civil War's Most Persistent Myth* (Chapel Hill: University of North Carolina Press, 2019), 4.

5   See "Citizens of Delaware Who Saved the Confederacy," Sons of Confederate Veterans Camp #2068: Delaware Grays, accessed December 17, 2023, https://www.descv.org/DelawareConfederates. html.

6   See, for example, Symonds, *Civil War at Sea,* and McPherson, *War on the Waters.*

7   Among the published accounts of White, the following are notable:

Dalzell, *Flight from the Flag,* 139. Perhaps because he was writing closest in time to the events, Dalzell was the most cautious, referring only to "Dave, a seventeen-year-old black boy from the Northern slave state of Delaware." But Dalzell, like all the subsequent writers, accepts without evidence that White refused to accept the liberty offered him by various US consuls.

Boykin, in *Ghost Ship of the Confederacy,* refers to "Dave . . . a likely negro lad of seventeen, a slave from Delaware, traveling with his master on the prize Tonawanda" (214).

Edna Bradlow and Frank Bradlow, in *Here Comes the* Alabama: *The Career of a Confederate Raider* (Cape Town: A. A. Balkema, 1958), refer to the relationship that "existed between Dr. Galt, the *Alabama*'s surgeon, and David White, a slave boy. White who was travelling from Delaware to Europe with his master on board the *Tonawanda*" (28).

Hoole, in *Four Years in the Confederate Navy*, mentions "David White, a young Negro slave boy" (63).

Summersell, in *Journal of George Townley Fullam*, wrote of "David White, a 17-year-old slave who was traveling in the company with his master en route to Europe" (35).

Summersell, in *CSS* Alabama, explained: "A young slave named David White was traveling with his master on the *Tonawanda*, and Semmes took him aboard *Alabama* as a mess steward. He was in effect emancipated by the raider because he was enemy property. David became attached to Dr. Galt and never tried to escape." A caption to a figure depicting the *Tonawanda*'s capture reads: "Alabama captures the grain ship Tonawanda. She was released on ransom bond. A slave aboard, David White, was emancipated by Semmes and added to the Alabama's crew" (40).

Taylor, in *Confederate Raider*, relates that "the Alabama enlisted . . . none other than a slave, David White, who had been on his way to Europe with his master" (123).

Robinson, in *Shark of the Confederacy*, wrote:

One person remained behind, however, David White, a black slave from Delaware, who was about seventeen years old. Under the laws of that state, he remained a slave until he was twenty-one and was therefore legally confiscated enemy property. He was assigned to serve as a steward in the wardroom, where he struck up a friendship with the officers and the other stewards. His name was entered on the rolls of the ship with pay as a mess steward. White became very attached to Dr. Galt and served him in the same capacity that Bartelli served Semmes. Although various U.S. consuls tried to entice him away in liberty ports, he always returned to the Alabama and died with the ship off Cherbourg. (51)

Marvel, in *The* Alabama *and the* Kearsarge, is more careful, relating Semmes's story but hedging: "The returning boat did bring aboard the *Tonawanda*'s black cook, a boy of about seventeen named David Henry White. David hailed from the slave state of Delaware, according to the captain of the passenger vessel; he carried no manumission papers, and in Semmes's eyes that made him contraband of war" (75). Later in his book, Marvel refers to "the erstwhile slave" (106), then "the suspected slave" (259).

Spencer, in *Raphael Semmes*, writes: "One of the passengers had with him a 'likely negro lad (named David) of about seventeen years of age—a slave until he was twenty-one under the laws of Delaware'" (146).

James Tertius deKay, in *The Rebel Raiders: The Astonishing History of the Confederacy's Secret Navy* (New York: Ballantine Books, 2002), even embellishes the claim about the mystery master:

> His newest hand was a seventeen-year-old-black slave named David White. White was the property of a citizen of Delaware, a young man who was on his way to Europe to escape the Federal Army draft. Semmes, the consummate Southern gentleman, was amused at the idea of taking as lawful prize a slave . . . and appointed him a wardroom orderly. David White's name was duly entered on the books of the Alabama as a member of the crew, and he was paid at the same rate as others of his grade. (106–7)

Fox, in *Wolf of the Deep*, is initially cautious: "The captured *Tonawanda* yielded . . . a black youth from the slave state of Delaware. David Henry White, about seventeen years old, was taken despite protests." Fox comes close to getting the point when he cites the *New York Herald* headline "The Pirate Steals a Colored Boy From the *Tonawanda* (202), but later in his narrative, he refers to "the wardroom waiter, the black slave David White" (215) and "the slave waiter" (227).

Tomblin, in *Life in Jefferson Davis' Navy*, writes: "A notable addition was David White, a seventeen-year-old lad who was a slave traveling with his master to Europe. White became a wardroom mess steward and servant of Dr. Francis Galt, the Alabama's surgeon" (167).

Keith and Clavin, in *Uttermost Ends of the Earth*, more recently identify White as a slave and uncritically accept Semmes's story that

> one of the passengers had brought with him his slave, a man called David White. Of course, a major reason why the Confederate States of America, which Semmes represented on the ocean, existed was to preserve the right to own slaves. But the captain thought it hypocritical that a passenger from the North, which sought to take that right away, could legally own a slave. On the *Alabama* there was no higher law than Semmes. He declared that David White was free and signed him up as a member of the crew. In a short time, he became an assistant to the ship's surgeon, Dr. Galt. (151)

CHAPTER 24. AN OCEAN OF LIES

1 In the twenty-first century, we have a word for politically inspired lies propagated through the news media: *disinformation*.

2 "An Act for the Better Regulation of Servants and Slaves within this Government" (1797).

3 Randy J. Holland, personal communication, August 10, 2021.

4 Stobb to Seward, December 22, 1863, United States Consular Despatches.

CHAPTER 25. *AIDE TOI ET DIEU T'AIDERA*

1 See Aesop fable "Hercules and the Wagoneer."

2 "A warm, informal, personal way of enlisting God's attention, not invoking His aid." Leo Rosten, *The New Joys of Yiddish* (New York: Three Rivers Press, 2001), 131.

3 Clarence L. Haynes Jr., "Why 'God Helps Those Who Help Themselves' Is Presumed to Be Biblical," Christianity.com, July 7, 2020, https://www.christianity.com/wiki/christian-life/why-god-helps-those-who-help-themselves-is-presumed-to-be-biblical.html.

4 Isaiah 25:4 (King James Version). See also "God Helps Those Who Help Themselves—Is It in the Bible?" Got Questions—Your Questions, Biblical Answers, accessed December 18, 2023, https://www.gotquestions.org/God-help-themselves.html.

5 Indeed, William Jennings Bryan famously objected to evolution: "The Darwinian theory represents man as reaching his present perfection by the operation of the law of hate," Bryan said. "Evolution is the merciless law by which the strong crowd out and kill off the weak." Quoted in "*Monkey Trial*—Article: William Jennings Bryan," *American Experience*, accessed December 18, 2023, https://www.pbs.org/wgbh/americanexperience/features/monkeytrial-william-jennings-bryan.

6 William Irvine, *Apes, Angels, and Victorians: The Story of Darwin, Huxley, and Evolution* (New York: McGraw-Hill, 1955), 6.

Bibliography

⤫

ARCHIVES AND MANUSCRIPT COLLECTIONS

Avil Family Papers. Courtesy of Avil family.

Confederate States Navy Misc. Manuscripts, 1885–2001, Museum of the Confederacy. Mss3 M9722 f 265–269.

Conner, David, Papers. Manuscripts and Archives Division. Astor, Lenox, and Tilden Foundations. New York Public Library.

Cope Family Papers. Collection 1486. Historical Society of Pennsylvania, Philadelphia.

Galt, Francis L., Papers. Manuscript Division, Library of Congress.

Maritime Records, Phila. V. Masters, Crews, Ships. Vols. 73–75, 1862–1863. Independence Seaport Museum, Philadelphia.

Mystic Seaport Museum, Mystic, CT
>	Correspondence and Reports, 1864–1868. Manuscript Collection, Maritime Historical Association, Inc. American Seamen's Friend Society.
>	Wainwright, William. "Ms. Journal Kept by William Wainwright on Board the U.S.S. Kearsarge, Captain Pickering, and Later Captain John A. Winslow, Commanding for a Naval Cruise. A Detailed a Descriptive Journal, Including Details of Burial at Sea." G.W. Blunt White Library, Log 429, Manuscripts Collection.
>	Letters from the Colored Sailor's Home in the Mid-19th Century. https://www.mysticseaport.org/news/letters-from-the-colored-sailors-home/.

National Archives and Records Administration, Washington, DC.
>	Naval Records Collection of the Office of Naval Records and Library, Record Group 45.

Records of General Courts Martial and Courts of Enquiry of the
    Navy Department, 1799–1867, Record Group 125.
Records of the Bureau of Naval Personnel, Record Group 24.
Records of the Foreign Service Posts of the Department of State,
    1788–1990, Record Group 84.
National Archives, Kew. London.
    "Captain's Logs Including Endymion, 6 November 1840 to 18 January
    1848." ADM 51/3603.
National Museums Liverpool, Archives Center. Maritime Museum,
    Liverpool, UK.
Naval History and Heritage Command. https://www.history.navy.mil
    /research/underwater-archaeology/conservation-and-curation
    /ua-artifact-collections/css-alabama-artifact-collection/css-alabama
    -artifact-photo-collection/css-alabama-davenport-dinnerware.html.
Nevius Family File. New-York Historical Society Museum and Library,
    New York.
Semmes Family Papers. Alabama Department of Archives and History,
    Montgomery.

GOVERNMENT DOCUMENTS

An Act in Relation to Free Negroes and Mulattoes. 305 *Del. Laws* 330
    (1863).
An Act for the Better Regulation of Free Negroes and Free Mulattoes.
    42 *Del. Laws* 108 (1807).
An Act for the Better Regulation of Servants and Slaves within this
    Government." 77 *Del. Laws* 214 (1797).
An Additional Supplement to the Act Entitled: An Act to Prohibit the
    Emigration of Free Negroes or Mulattoes into this State, and for Other
    Purposes. 324 *Del. Laws* 319 (1845).
Consular Despatches, Records of the Foreign Service Posts of the Department
    of State, 1788–1990 (Record Group 84), National Archives.
*Correspondence Concerning Claims against Great Britain, Transmitted to the Senate
    of the United States in Answer to the Resolutions of December 4 and 10, 1867,
    and of May 27, 1868*, Vol. 3: *Rebel Cruisers*. Washington, DC: Government
    Printing Office, 1870.
Federal Reserve Bulletin. Washington, DC: Government Printing Office, May
    1923.
Lewes & Rehoboth Hundred, Sussex County, Delaware, Assessment Office,
    Assessment Records, Tax, John White (1860), 314, Family History
    Library, Microfilm 105634372. http://www.familysearch.org.

Mason, J. Y. Report of the Secretary of the Navy in Answer to a Resolution of the Senate Calling for Information in Relation to the Loss of the United States Brig *Somers*, and to the Assistance Rendered by the Officers and Crews of the French, Spanish, and British Ships-of-War Lying off Vera Cruz, in the Rescue of the Officers and Crew of the Somers. 29th Cong., 2d sess., no. 43 (January 7, 1847).

Official Records of the Union and Confederate Navies in the War of the Rebellion. Series I: Volume 2, No. 3. Washington, DC: US Government Printing Office, 1895.

Official Records of the Union and Confederate Navies in the War of the Rebellion. Series I: Volume 3. Washington, DC: US Government Printing Office, 1896.

Official Records of the Union and Confederate Navies in the War of the Rebellion. Series I: Volume 16. Washington, DC: US Government Printing Office, 1903.

Records of Deeds. Deeds Registry, ACH #123: 393. Philadelphia Department of Archives, Philadelphia, PA.

Second Confiscation Act (1863). *US Statutes at Large, Treaties, and Proclamations of the United States of America*, vol. 12, 589–92. Freedmen and Southern Society Project. Accessed December 10, 2023, http://www.freedmen.umd.edu/conact2.htm.

US Census Bureau. Lewes and Rehoboth Hundred, Sussex County, Delaware. Dwelling 875, Family 875, John White household (1850), 116. http://www.ancestry.com.

US Census Bureau. Lewes and Rehoboth Hundred, Sussex County, Delaware. Dwelling 174, Family 167, John White household (1860), 26. http://www.ancestry.com.

US Census Bureau. Lewes and Rehoboth Hundred, Sussex County, Delaware. Dwelling 195, Family 187, Edward Watson household (1860), 29. http://www.ancestry.com.

US Department of State. Office of the Historian, Foreign Service Institute. Papers Relating to Foreign Affairs. https://history.state.gov/historicaldocuments.

NEWSPAPERS

Bombay Gazette
Brooklyn Daily Eagle
Cape Argus
Cape Gazette
Daily National Intelligencer

Delaware Tribune
Georgetown Messenger
Illustrated London News
Liverpool Daily Post
Liverpool Mercury
London Daily News
London Morning Post
National Anti-Slavery Standard
New York Daily Herald
New York Daily Times
New York Times
Philadelphia Inquirer
Philadelphia Public Ledger
Times of India
Vineyard Gazette
Washington Post

Books, Articles, and Theses

"The Agriculture of the United States." *Delaware Journal* 1, no 2 (April 27, 1827).

Applegate, Debby. *The Most Famous Man in America: The Biography of Henry Ward Beecher.* New York: Three Leaves Press, 2006.

Beecher, Henry Ward. *American Rebellion Report of the Speeches of the Rev. Henry Ward Beecher, Delivered at Public Meetings in Manchester, Glasgow, Edinburgh, Liverpool, and London; and at The Farewell Breakfasts in London, Manchester, and Liverpool.* Manchester: Union and Emancipation Society, 1864.

———. *Evolution and Religion*, Part I: *Eight Sermons, Discussing the Bearing of the Evolutionary Philosophy on the Fundamental Doctrines of Evangelical Christianity.* New York: Fords, Howard and Hulbert, 1885.

Benjamin, Park. *United States Naval Academy, Being the Yarn of the American Midshipman.* New York: G. P. Putnam's Sons, 1900.

Beukes, Lauren, and Nechama Brodie. *Maverick: Extraordinary Women from South Africa's Past.* Century City, South Africa: Umuzi, 2015.

Biko, Hlumelo. *The Great African Society: A Plan for a Nation Gone Astray.* Johannesburg: Jonathan Ball, 2013.

Biko, Steve. *I Write What I Like: Selected Writings.* Foreword by Lewis R. Gordon. Chicago: University of Chicago Press, 1978.

Blight, David W. "Europe in 1989, America in 2020, and the Death of the Lost Cause." *New Yorker,* July 1, 2020. https://www.newyorker.com

/culture/cultural-comment/europe-in-1989-america-in-2020-and-the
-death-of-the-lost-cause.

Bolster, Jeffrey W. *Black Jacks: African American Seamen in the Age of Sail.*
Cambridge, MA: Harvard University Press, 1997.

Bowcock, Andrew. *CSS* Alabama*: Anatomy of a Confederate Raider.* Annapolis,
MD: Naval Institute Press, 2002.

Boykin, Edward. *Ghost Ship of the Confederacy.* New York: Funk and Wagnalls,
1957.

Bracher, Nathan. "Introduction: Writing History and the Social Sciences
with Ivan Jablonka." *French Politics, Culture, and Society* 36, no. 3 (December
1, 2018): 1–13. https://doi.org/.doi:10.3167/fpcs.2018.360301.

Bradlee, Francis Boardman Crowninshield, and James Magee. *The*
Kearsarge-Alabama *Battle, the Story as Told to the Writer by James Magee of
Marblehead, Seaman on the Kearsarge.* Salem, MA: Essex Institute, 1921.

Bradlow, Edna, and Frank Bradlow. *Here Comes the* Alabama*: The Career of a
Confederate Raider.* Cape Town: A. A. Balkema, 1958.

Branham, Alfred Iverson. *Story of the Sinking of the Alabama "290": Interview
with Captain John McIntosh Kell, Executive Officer of the Alabama, Given to
Alfred Iverson Branham, Forty-Six Years Ago, June, 1883.* Atlanta: Cornell
Press, 1930.

Browne, John M. "The Duel Between the Alabama and the Kearsarge."
Century Magazine 31 (1886): 923–34.

Bryan, E. D. "The Confederate Raider *Alabama*: A Lewes Connection."
Journal of the Lewes Historical Society 4 (2001): 45–56.

Buker, George E. *Swamp Sailors in the Second Seminole War.* Gainesville:
Library Press at University of Florida, 1997.

Burrows, Edwin G., and Mike Wallace. *Gotham: A History of New York City to
1898.* New York: Oxford University Press, 1999.

Burrows, Tracy. "JSE Creates Social Responsibility Index." ITWeb, May 19,
2004. https://www.itweb.co.za/content/G98YdMLxl1yMX2PD.

Byron, George Gordon. *The Corsair: A Tale.* London: John Murray, 1814.

Calland, Richard. *The Zuma Years: South Africa's Changing Face of Power.*
Johannesburg: Random House Struik, 2013.

Cameron, Christopher. "The Puritan Origins of Black Abolitionism in
Massachusetts." *Historical Journal of Massachusetts* 39, nos. 1–2 (Summer
2011): 78–107. https://www.westfield.ma.edu/historical-journal/wp
-content/uploads/2018/06/Puritan-Origins-of-Black-Abolitionism.pdf.

Cameron, John. *Our Tropical Possessions in Malayan India: Being a Descriptive
Account of Singapore, Penang, Province Wellesley, and Malacca; Their Peoples,
Products, Commerce, and Government.* London: Smith and Elder, 1865.

Campbell, Joseph. *The Hero with a Thousand Faces*. New York: Pantheon Books, 1949.

Carriage of Passengers Act of March 3, 1855. Wikipedia, updated February 7, 2023. https://en.wikipedia.org/wiki/Carriage_of_Passengers_Act _of_1855.

Chaffin, Tom. *Sea of Gray: The Around-the-World Odyssey of the Confederate raider Shenandoah*. New York: Hill and Wang, 2007.

"Citizens of Delaware who Saved the Confederacy." Sons of Confederate Veterans Camp #2068: Delaware Grays. Accessed December 17, 2023, https://www.descv.org/DelawareConfederates.html.

Clark, Kenneth B. "Segregated Schools in New York City." *Journal of Educational Sociology* 36, no. 6 (1963): 245–49.

Coetzee, John Maxwell. *Dusklands*. New York: Penguin Books, 1974.

Costello, Ray. *Black Salt: Seafarers of African descent on British ships*. Liverpool, UK: Liverpool University Press, 2012.

Cross, William R. *Winslow Homer: American Passage*. New York: Farrar, Straus and Giroux, 2022.

Dalzell, George W. *The Flight from the Flag: The Continuing Effect of the Civil War upon the American Carrying Trade*. Chapel Hill: University of North Carolina Press, 1940.

Dana, Richard Henry, Jr. *Two Years Before the Mast: A Personal Narrative of Life at Sea*. New York: Harper and Brothers, 1840.

Dass, Sherylle, Zimkhitha Mhlahlo, and Tsukudu Moroeng. "Broken Promises: Is South Africa on the Verge of Being a Failed State?" Friends of the LRC, Occasional Paper, 2001.

Davidson, Shayne. *Civil War Soldiers: Discovering the Men of the 25th United States Colored Troops*. Charleston: CreateSpace, 2013.

Deetz, James. *In Small Things Forgotten: The Archaeology of Early American Life*. New York: Anchor Press, 1977.

DeKay, James Tertius. *The Rebel Raiders: The Astonishing History of the Confederacy's Secret Navy*. New York: Ballantine Books, 2002.

Delaney, Norman C. "The *Alabama*'s 'Bold and Determined Man.'" *Naval History Magazine* 25, no. 4 (July 2011). https://www.usni.org/magazines /naval-history-magazine/2011/july/alabamas-bold-and-determined -man.

———. "I Didn't Feel Excited A Mite." *Naval History Magazine* 24, no. 6 (December 2010). https://www.usni.org/magazines/naval-history -magazine/2010/december/i-didnt-feel-excited-mite.

———. *John McIntosh Kell of the Raider* Alabama. Tuscaloosa: University of Alabama Press, 1973.

———. "Monsieur Rondin's Fake Photo: A Scam That Failed." *Military Image* 19, no. 4 (1998): 30–32.

Domby, Adam H. *The False Cause: Fraud, Fabrication, and White Supremacy in Confederate Memory.* Charlottesville: University of Virginia Press, 2020.

Donnelly, James S., Jr. *The Great Irish Potato Famine.* Stroud, UK: History Press, 2001.

Douglass, Frederick. *Narrative of the Life of Frederick Douglass, an American Slave.* Boston: Anti-Slavery Office, 1845.

Du Bois, W. E. B. "The American Negro in My Time." *Masses and Mainstream* 9, no. 2 (1956): 1–9.

———. "Strivings of the Negro People." *The Atlantic*, August 1897. https://www.theatlantic.com/magazine/archive/1897/08/strivings-of-the-negro-people/305446/.

Dudley, William S. *Going South: U.S. Navy Officer Resignations and Dismissals on the Eve of the Civil War.* Washington, DC: Naval Historical Foundation, 1981.

Du Moulin, Richard. "Video: Maritime History, Technology, and Seamanship." gCaptain, May 6, 2018. https://gcaptain.com/maritime-history-technology-seamanship/.

Edge, Frederick Milnes. *An Englishman's View of the Battle between the* Alabama *and the* Kearsarge: *An Account of the Naval Engagement in the British Channel, on Sunday June 19th, 1864.* New York: A. D. F. Randolph, 1864.

Ellicott, John M. *The Life of John Ancrum Winslow: Rear-Admiral, United States Navy, who Commanded the U.S. steamer "Kearsarge" in her Action with the Confederate Cruiser "Alabama."* New York: G. P. Putnam's Sons, 1902.

Essah, Patience. *A House Divided: Slavery and Emancipation in Delaware, 1538–1865.* Carter G. Woodson Institute Series: Black Studies at Work in the World. Charlottesville: University Press of Virginia, 1997.

Falconer, William. *Shipwreck: A Sentimental and Descriptive Poem, in Three Cantos.* 1762. Online at Evans Early American Imprint Collection. Accessed December 10, 2023, https://quod.lib.umich.edu/e/evans/N16417.0001.001/1:3?rgn=div1;view=fulltext.

Farnum, George R. "Raphael Semmes: Lawyer and Falcon of the Seas." *American Bar Association Journal* 30, no. 11 (1944): 363–69, 665–66.

Farragut, Loyall. *The Life of David Glasgow Farragut, First Admiral of the United States Navy, Embodying his Journal and Letters.* New York: D. Appleton and Company, 1882.

Feinstein, Andrew. *After the Party: A Personal and Political Journey inside the ANC.* Johannesburg: Jonathan Ball, 2007.

Fernandez-Partagas, Jose J. "Year 1862." In "Storms of 1858–1864." Atlantic

Oceanographic and Meteorological Laboratory, National Oceanic and Atmospheric Administration. Accessed December 10, 2023, https://www.aoml.noaa.gov/hrd/Landsea/Partagas/1858–1864/1862.pdf.

Fields, Barbara Jeanne. *Slavery and Freedom on the Middle Ground: Maryland during the Nineteenth Century.* New Haven, CT: Yale University Press, 1985.

"Flamstead, Jamacia, Port Royal." Centre for the Study of the Legacies of British Slavery, University College London. Accessed December 12, 2023. https://www.ucl.ac.uk/lbs/estate/view/2965.

Foner, Philip Sheldon. "William P. Powell: Militant Champion of Black Seamen." In *Essays in Afro-American History.* Philadelphia: Temple University Press, 1978.

Foote, Shelby. *The Civil War, a Narrative.* Volume 1: *Fort Sumter to Perryville.* New York: Vintage Books, 1958.

Foreman, Amanda. *A World on Fire: Britain's Crucial Role in the American Civil War.* New York: Random House, 2010.

Foster, Gaines M. *Ghosts of the Confederacy: Defeat, the Lost Cause, and the Emergence of the New South.* New York: Oxford University Press, 1987.

Fox, Stephen R. *Wolf of the Deep: Raphael Semmes and the Notorious Confederate Raider CSS* Alabama. New York: Vintage Books, 2007.

Franklin, John Hope. *The Emancipation Proclamation.* Garden City: Doubleday, 1963.

"Franklin's Lost Expedition." Wikipedia. Accessed December 13, 2023, https://en.wikipedia.org/wiki/Franklin%27s_lost_expedition.

Frykman, Niklas. "Seamen on Late-Eighteenth-Century European Warships." *International Review of Social History* 54, no. 1 (2009): 67–93. https://doi.org/10.1017/s0020859009000030.

Fuentes, Marisa J. *Dispossessed Lives: Enslaved Women, Violence, and the Archive.* Philadelphia: University of Pennsylvania Press, 2016.

Great Britain Historical GIS Project. "Liverpool District" (population statistics, total population). A Vision of Britain through Time, University of Portsmouth. https://www.visionofbritain.org.uk/unit/10105821/cube/TOT_POP.

"God Helps Those Who Help Themselves. Is It in the Bible?" Got Questions—Your Questions, Biblical Answers. Accessed December 18, 2023, https://www.gotquestions.org/God-help-themselves.html.

Gomez, Michael. *Reversing Sail: A History of the African Diaspora.* Cambridge: Cambridge University Press, 2005.

Gonzalez, Anita. "Maritime Migrations: Stewards of the African Grove." *Theatre Research International* 44, no. 1 (2019): 64–70. https://doi.org/10.1017/s0307883318000962.

Gordon, Lewis R. Foreword to *I Write What I Like*, by Steve Biko, vii–xiii. Chicago: University of Chicago Press, 2002.

Hancock, Harold B. "William Yates' Letter of 1837: Slavery and Colored People in Delaware." *Delaware History* 14, no. 3 (April 1971): 205–16.

———, ed. *The History of Sussex County*. Rehoboth, DE: Sussex County Bicentennial Committee, 1976.

Hanna-Jones, Nikole. *The 1619 Project: A New Origin Story*. New York: One World, 2021.

Harper, Douglas. "Slavery in Delaware." Slavery in the North, 2003. Accessed November 15, 2023. http://slavenorth.com/delaware.htm.

Hartman, Saidiya V. *Scenes of Subjection: Terror, Slavery, and Self-Making in Nineteenth-Century America*. Oxford: Oxford University Press. 1997.

Haynes, Clarence L. "Why 'God Helps Those Who Help Themselves' Is Presumed to Be Biblical." Christianity.com, July 7, 2020. https://www. christianity.com/wiki/christian-life/why-god-helps-those-who-help -themselves-is-presumed-to-be-biblical.html.

Hazzard, Robert. "The History of Seaford." In *The History of Sussex County*, edited by Harold B. Hancock. Rehoboth, DE: Sussex County Bicentennial Committee, 1976.

Headley, Joel Lewis. *Farragut and Our Naval Commanders*. New York: E. B. Treat and Co., 1867.

Hill, Jim Dan. *Sea Dogs of the Sixties: Farragut and Seven Contemporaries*. Minneapolis: University of Minnesota Press, 1935.

Hoole, William Stanley. *Four Years in the Confederate Navy: The Career of Captain John Low on the C.S.S. Fingal, Florida, Alabama, Tuscaloosa, and Ajax*. Athens: University of Georgia Press, 1964.

Irvine, William. *Apes, Angels, and Victorians: The Story of Darwin, Huxley, and Evolution*. New York: McGraw-Hill, 1955.

Jablonka, Ivan. *History Is A Contemporary Literature: Manifesto for the Social Sciences*. Translated by Nathan J. Bracher. Ithaca, NY: Cornell University Press; 2018.

———. "Historical Fiction and Intertextuality." Presentation in panel discussion "Narrating the Past: Innovative Strategies for Writing History." La Maison Française, New York University, New York, February 26, 2020.

James, Lawrence. *Raj: The Making and Unmaking of British India*. London: Abacus, 1997.

Janney, Caroline E. *Remembering the Civil War: Reunion and the Limits of Reconciliation*. Chapel Hill: University of North Carolina Press, 2013.

Johnston, Paul F. "The Smithsonian and the 19th Century Guano Trade:

This Poop Is Crap." National Museum of American History, May 31,
    2017. https://americanhistory.si.edu/blog/smithsonian-and-guano.
Karsten, Peter. *The Naval Aristocracy: The Golden Age of Annapolis and the
    Emergence of Modern American Navalism.* Annapolis, MD: Naval Institute
    Press, 1972.
Keith, Philip A., and Tom Clavin. *To the Uttermost Ends of the Earth: The Epic
    Hunt for the South's Most Feared Ship—And the Greatest Sea Battle of the Civil
    War.* Toronto: Hanover Square Press, 2022.
Kell, John McIntosh. *1886 Cruise and Combats of the "Alabama"* 31 (April 1886):
    911–22.
———. *Recollections of a Naval Life—As Executive Officer of the CSS Warships
    Sumter and Alabama.* Washington, DC: Neale Company, 1900.
Killick, John. "An Early Nineteenth-Century Shipping Line: The Cope
    Line of Philadelphia and Liverpool Packets, 1822–1872." *International
    Journal of Maritime History* 12, no. 1 (2000): 61–87. https://doi.org
    /10.1177/084387140001200104.
Kinnaman, Stephen Chapin. *The Most Perfect Cruiser: How James Dunwoody
    Bulloch Constructed and Equipped the Confederate States Steamer Alabama—A
    Work of History.* Indianapolis: Dog Ear, 2009.
Koenig, Stephanie K. "Common Men in Uncommon Times: Analyzing the
    Daily Lives of American Civil War Sailors Using Personal Narratives."
    MA thesis, Texas A&M University, 2016.
Kolchin, Peter. *American Slavery, 1619–1877.* London: Penguin Books, 1993.
Krog, Antjie. *Country of My Skull: Guilt, Sorrow and the Limits of Forgiveness in
    the New South Africa.* New York: Three Rivers Press, 1999.
Langley, Harold D. *Social Reform in the United States Navy, 1798–1862.*
    Annapolis, MD: Naval Institute Press, 1967.
Levin, Aaron. "Tutu Praises Healing Power of Forgiveness." *Psychiatric
    News* 46, no. 12 (2011): 6–33. https://doi.org/10.1176/pn.46.12.
    psychnews_46_12_6.
Levin, Kevin M. *Searching for Black Confederates: The Civil War's Most Persistent
    Myth.* Chapel Hill: University of North Carolina Press, 2019.
Lewes & Rehoboth Hundred, Sussex County, Delaware, Assessment Office,
    Assessment Records, Tax, John White (1860), 314, Family History
    Library, Microfilm 105634372. http://www.familysearch.org.
Lieberman, Evan. *Until We Have Won Our Liberty: South Africa after Apartheid.*
    Princeton, NJ: Princeton University Press, 2022.
Lieberman, Mark. "Egg Corns: Folk Etymology, Malapropism,
    Mondegreen, ???" *Language Log* (blog), April 4, 2004. http://itre.cis.upenn.
    edu/~myl/languagelog/archives/000018.html.

Lineberry, Cate. *Be Free or Die: The Amazing Story of Robert Smalls' Escape from Slavery to Union Hero*. New York: St. Martin's Press, 2017.

Livermore, Abiel Abbot. *The War with Mexico Reviewed*. Boston: American Peace Society, 1850.

"Liverpool and the American Civil War." Information Sheet 59. National Museums Liverpool, Archives Center. Maritime Museum, Liverpool, UK. Accessed November 25, 2023, https://www.liverpoolmuseums.org.uk/archivesheet59.

Logan, Frenise A. "Activities of the *Alabama* in Asian Waters." *Pacific Historical Review* 31, no. 2 (1962): 143–50. https://doi.org/10.2307/3636572.

Luraghi, Raimondo. "Background." In Still, *Confederate Navy*, 1–15.

Mandela, Nelson R. *Long Walk to Freedom: The Autobiography of Nelson Mandela*. New York: Little, Brown, 1994.

Marcellinus, Ammianus. Essay. In *The Roman History of Ammianus Marcellinus During the Reigns of The Emperors Constantius, Julian, Jovianus, Valentinian, and Valens*, translated by C. D. Younge, Volume 31: *Roman History*, II.22:582–82. London: G. Bell and Sons, 1911.

Marks, Carole C. *A History of African Americans of Delaware and Maryland's Eastern Shore*. Wilmington: Delaware Heritage Commission, 1996.

Marvel, William. *The* Alabama *and the* Kearsarge—*The Sailor's Civil War*. Chapel Hill: University of North Carolina Press, 1996.

McKee, Christopher. *A Gentlemanly and Honorable Profession: The Creation of the U.S. Naval Officer Corps, 1794–1815*. Annapolis, MD: Naval Institute Press, 1991.

McPherson, James M. *For Cause and Comrades: Why Men Fought in the Civil War*. New York: Oxford University Press, 1997.

———. *War on the Waters: The Union and Confederate Navies, 1861–1865*. Chapel Hill: University of North Carolina Press, 2012.

Mda, Zakes. "BIKO: The Quest for a True Humanity." Paper presented at the Steve Biko Memorial Lecture, 2001. https://www.apartheidmuseum.org/exhibitions/biko-the-quest-for-a-true-humanity.

Melville, Herman. *Redburn: His First Voyage; Being the Sailor-Boy Confessions and Reminiscences of the Son-of-a-Gentleman, in the Merchant Service*. New York: Harper and Brothers, 1849.

———. *White Jacket; Or, the World of a Man-of-War*. London: Richard Bentley, 1850.

"Metastability." Wikipedia, October 5, 2022. https://en.wikipedia.org/wiki/Metastability.

Miggs, C. D. Untitled essay. In *Summary of the Transactions of the College of*

Physicians of Philadelphia, Volume 2: *New Series,* 280. Philadelphia: J. B. Lippincott & Co., 1856.

Mintz, Steven, ed. *African American Voices: A Documentary Reader, 1619–1877.* Oxford: Wiley-Blackwell, 2009.

Monkey Trial: William Jennings Bryan (video). *American Experience.* PBS, aired February 17, 2002. https://www.pbs.org/wgbh/americanexperience /features/monkeytrial-william-jennings-bryan/.

Morgan, James M. *Recollections of a Rebel Reefer.* Boston: Houghton Mifflin Company, 1917.

Morison, Samuel Eliot. *The Oxford History of the American People.* New York: Oxford University Press, 1965.

Morris, Alan G. "Trophy Skulls, Museums, and the San." In *Miscast: Negotiating the Presence of the Bushmen,* edited by Pippa Skotnes, 67–80. Cape Town: University of Cape Town Press, 1996.

Mueller, Jean West, and Wynell B. Schamel. "Lincoln's Spot Resolutions." *Social Education* 52, no. 6 (October 1988): 455–57, 466. Online at "Educator Resources: Lincoln's Spot Resolutions." National Archives. Accessed November 27, 2023, https://www.archives.gov/education /lessons/lincoln-resolutions.

Nash, Gary B. *Forging Freedom: The Formation of Philadelphia's Black Community, 1720–1840.* Cambridge, MA: Harvard University Press, 1998.

Newmark, Jill L. "Face to Face with History." *Prologue Magazine* 41, no. 3 (Fall 2009). https://www.archives.gov/publications/prologue/2009/fall /face.html.

"The Norie Marin Atlas and the Guano Trade." National Museum of American History. Exhibition, February 16, 2016–January 29, 2017. Preserved online at Archive-It, https://wayback.archive-it. org/3340/20231013213836/https://americanhistory.si.edu/norie-atlas/.

Northup, Solomon. *Twelve Years a Slave.* Edited by Kevin M. Burke and Henry Louis Gates Jr. Norton Critical Edition. New York: W. W. Norton, 2016.

Norwood, Hilda Belltown. "A Recollection." *Journal of the Lewes Historical Society* 4 (2001): 21–30.

Nwaubani, Adaobi Tricia, "My Nigerian Great-Grandfather Sold Slaves." *BBC News,* July 19, 2020. https://www.bbc.co.uk/news/world -africa-53444752.

Oblack, Rachel. "How to Read a Barometer: Use Rising and Falling Air Pressure to Predict the Weather." *ThoughtCo.,* updated March 4, 2020. https://www.thoughtco.com/how-to-read-a-barometer-3444043.

O'Sullivan, John. "Annexation." *United States Magazine and Democratic Review* 17 (1845): 5–6, 9–10.

"Our Relations with Great Britain." *Harper's Weekly* 7, no. 330 (April 25, 1863): 283. Online at Daily Observations from the Civil War, March 27, 2013. https://dotcw.com/our-relations-with-great-britain/.

Parker, William H. *Recollections of a Naval Officer, 1841–1865.* New York: Charles Scribner's Sons, 1883.

Perl-Rosenthal, Nathan. *Citizen Sailors: Becoming American in the Age of Revolution.* Cambridge, MA: Belknap Press of Harvard University Press, 2015.

Pollard, Edward A. *The Lost Cause; A New Southern History of the War of the Confederates.: Comprising a Full and Authentic Account of the Rise and Progress of the Late Southern Confederacy—The Campaigns, Battles, Incidents, and Adventures of the Most Gigantic Struggle of the World's History: Drawn from Official Sources, and Approved by the Most Distinguished Confederate Leaders.* New York: E. B. Treat & Co., 1866.

Porter, David D. *The Naval History of the Civil War.* New York: Sherman Publishing Company, 1886.

Quarstein, John V. "Mutiny at Sea: Death and Destruction on USS Somers." Mariners' Museum and Park (Newport News, VA), December 15, 2022. https://www.marinersmuseum.org/2022/12/mutiny-at-sea-death-and -destruction-on-uss-somers/.

Quigley, Paul. *Shifting Grounds: Nationalism and the American South, 1848–1865.* New York: Oxford University Press, 2012.

Ramold, Steven J. *Slaves, Sailors, Citizens: African Americans in the Union Navy.* DeKalb: Northern Illinois University Press, 2002.

Ramphele, Mamphela. *A Life.* Cape Town: David Philip, 1995.

———. *Dreams, Betrayal and Hope.* Cape Town: Penguin Random House, 2017.

Rathbun, G. "The Wilmot Proviso; Speech of Mr. G. Rathbun of New York in the House of Representatives, February 9, 1847." Cong. Globe, 29th Cong., 2d Sess., New Series, no. 12, 179. Available online at American Memory, Library of Congress, https://memory.loc.gov/cgi-bin /ampage?collId=llcg&fileName=018/llcg018.db&recNum =786.

"Report of the Secretary of the Navy." *Sailor's Magazine and Seamen's Friend* 35 (January 1863). https://babel.hathitrust.org/cgi/pt?id=hvd. ah6ggc&seq=7.

Ripley, Peter C., Jeffrey S. Rossbach, Roy E. Finkenbine, Fiona E. Spiers, and Debra Sussie, eds. *The Black Abolitionist Papers*, Volume 1: *The British Isles 1830–1865.* Chapel Hill: University of North Carolina Press, 1985.

Robinson, Charles M. *Shark of the Confederacy: The Story of the CSS Alabama.* London: Leo Cooper, 1995.

Robinson, William M. *The* Alabama-Kearsarge *Battle: A Study in Original Sources.* Salem, MA: Essex Institute, 1924.

Rose, Alexander. *The Lion and the Fox: Two Rival Spies and the Secret Plot to Build a Confederate Navy.* New York: W. W. Norton, 2023.

Rosten, Leo. *The New Joys of Yiddish.* New York: Three Rivers Press, 2001.

Salthe, Stanley N. "Analysis and Critique of the Concept of Natural Selection (and of the NeoDarwinian Theory of Evolution) in Respect (Part 1) to Its Suitability as Part of Modernism's Origination Myth, as Well as (Part 2) of Its Ability to Explain Organic Evolution." Niels Bohr Institute, updated 2006. https://www.nbi.dk/~natphil/salthe/Critique_of_Natural_Select_.pdf.

Sandburg, Carl. *Abraham Lincoln: The Prairie Years and the War Years.* New York: Harcourt Inc., 1954.

Schreffler, Gibb. *Boxing the Compass: A Century and a Half of Discourse about Sailor's Chanties.* Occasional Papers in Folklore 6. Lansdale, PA: Loomis House Press, 2018.

Schrire, Carmel. *Digging through Darkness: Chronicles of an Archaeologist.* Charlottesville: University Press of Virginia, 1995.

———. *Tigers in Africa: Stalking the Past at the Cape of Good Hope.* Charlottesville: University of Virginia Press, 2002.

Schwartz, Marcie. "Children of the Civil War: On the Battlefield—Youth in Wartime." American Battlefield Trust, April 6, 2017. https://www.battlefields.org/learn/articles/children-civil-war-battlefield.

Schwartz, Stuart B. *Sea of Storms: A History of Hurricanes in the Greater Caribbean from Columbus to Katrina.* Lawrence Stone Lectures 6. Princeton, NJ: Princeton University Press, 2015.

Semmes, Raphael. *Memoirs of Service Afloat During the War Between the States.* Baltimore: Kelly, Piet and Co., 1869.

———. *Service Afloat and Ashore during the Mexican War.* Cincinnati: Wm. H. Moore and Co., 1851.

———. *Service Afloat; or the Remarkable Career of the Confederate Cruisers* Sumter *and* Alabama, *during the War between the States: Memoirs of Service Afloat during the War between the States.* Baltimore: Baltimore Publishing Company, 1887.

Shapiro, Jonathan. *Zapiro: But Will It Stand Up in Court? Cartoons from* Mail & Guardian, Sunday Times, *and the* Times. Auckland Park, South Africa: Jacana, 2013.

Sheppard, Rebecca, and Kimberly Toney. *Reconstructing Delaware's Free Black Communities, 1800–1870.* Newark: University of Delaware Press, 2010.

Shingleton, Royce. "Seamen, Landsmen, Firemen and Coal Heavers." In Still, *The Confederate Navy*, 133–44.

Silbey, Joel H. *Storm over Texas: The Annexation Controversy and the Road to Civil War.* New York: Oxford University Press, 2007.

Sillen, Andrew. "The Cope Line Voyages of David Henry White; Evidence from the Cope Family Archive." *Pennsylvania Magazine of History and Biography* 148 (January 2024).

Simmons, Sellano L. "Count Them Too: African Americans from Delaware and the United States Civil War Navy, 1861–1865." *Journal of Negro History* 85, no. 3 (2000): 183–90. https://doi.org/10.2307/2649075.

Sinclair, Arthur. *Two Years on the Alabama.* Boston: Lee and Shepard, 1895.

Skotnes, Pippa. *Claim to the Country: The Archive of Lucy Lloyd and Wilhelm Bleek.* Johannesburg: Jacana, 2007.

———, ed. *Miscast: Negotiating the Presence of the Bushmen.* Cape Town: University of Cape Town Press, 1996.

Slade, Rachel. *Into the Raging Sea: Thirty-Three Mariners, One Megastorm, and the Sinking of the* El Faro. New York: Harper Collins, 2018.

Sobel, Dava. *Longitude: The True Story of a Lone Genius Who Solved the Greatest Scientific Problem of His Time.* London: Fourth Estate, 1998.

Sokolow, Michael. *Charles Benson: Mariner of Color in the Age of Sail.* Amherst: University of Massachusetts Press, 2003.

Spencer, Herbert. *Social Statics; Or, The Conditions Essential to Human Happiness Specified, and the First of Them Delivered.* London: John Chapman, 1851.

Spencer, Warren, F. *The Confederate Navy in Europe.* Tuscaloosa: University of Alabama Press, 1983.

———. *Raphael Semmes: The Philosophical Mariner.* Tuscaloosa: University of Alabama Press, 1997.

Spillman, Rick. "Are Modern Ships Slower than Sailing Ships? Probably Not." *The Old Salt Blog,* September 17, 2012. https://www.oldsaltblog. com/2012/09/are-modern-ships-slower-than-sailing-ships-probably -not/.

Stanton, Zack. "How Trumpism Is Becoming America's New 'Lost Cause.'" *Politico,* December 1, 2021. https://www.politico.com/news /magazine/2021/01/21/trump-civil-war-reconstruction-biden-lost -cause-461161.

Stephens, Alexander H. *Constitutional View of the Late War between the States.* New York: National Publishing Company, 1870.

Still, William N., ed. *The Confederate Navy: The Ships, Men, and Organization, 1861–65.* Annapolis, MA: Naval Institute Press, 1997.

Summersell, Charles Grayson. "The Career of Raphael Semmes Prior to the Cruise of the Alabama," PhD dissertation, Vanderbilt University, Nashville, TN, 1940.

———. *CSS* Alabama*: Builder, Captain, and Plans.* Tuscaloosa: University of Alabama Press, 1985.

———, ed. *The Journal of George Townley Fullam: Boarding Officer of the Confederate Sea Raider* Alabama. Tuscaloosa: University of Alabama Press, 1973.

Swisshelm, Jane Grey. *Crusader and Feminist: Letters of Jane Grey Swisshelm 1858–1865.* Edited, with an introduction and notes, by Arthur J. Larsen. St. Paul: Minnesota Historical Society, 1934.

———. *Half a Century.* 3rd edition. Chicago: Jansen, McClurg and Co., 1880.

Symonds, Craig L. *The Civil War at Sea.* New York: Oxford University Press, 2009.

Tadman, Michael "The Interregional Slave Trade in the History and Myth-Making of the U.S. South." In *The Chattel Principle: Internal Slave Trades in the Americas,* edited by Walter Johnson, 117–64. New Haven, CT: Yale University Press, 2004.

Taylor, Frank H. *Philadelphia in the Civil War, 1861–1865: A Complete History Illustrated with Contemporary Prints and Photographs and from Drawings by the Author.* Philadelphia: Published by the City, 1913.

Taylor, John M. *Confederate Raider: Raphael Semmes of the* Alabama. Washington, DC: Brassey's, 1994.

Thibert, Keshler. "On the Waterfront: Chronicling the Lives of Philly's Black Seamen." *Hidden City: Exploring Philadelphia's Landscape,* July 22, 2022. https://hiddencityphila.org/2022/07/on-the-waterfront-chronicling-the-lives-of-phillys-black-seamen/.

Thirty-Sixth Annual Report of the American Seaman's Friend Society. New York: S. Halle, Book and Job Printer, 1864.

Thoreau, Henry David. *Walden and Civil Disobedience: Complete Texts with Introduction, Historical Contexts, Critical Essays.* Edited by Paul Lauter. Boston: Houghton Mifflin, 2000.

Toll, Ian W. *Six Frigates: The Epic History of the Founding of the U.S. Navy.* New York: W. W. Norton, 2006.

Tomblin, Barbara Brooks. *Life in Jefferson Davis' Navy.* Annapolis, MD: Naval Institute Press, 2019.

Townley, John. "Music in the Confederate Navy." *Confederate Naval Historical Society Newsletter,* no. 5 (October 5, 1990): 3–5.

Turner, Victor. *The Ritual Process: Structure and Anti-structure.* London: Aldine, 1969.

"USS Chesapeake–HMS Leopard Affair." Naval History and Heritage

Command. Accessed December 21, 2023, https://www.history.navy.mil /content/history/nhhc/our-collections/art/exhibits/conflicts-and -operations/the-war-of-1812/uss-chesapeake--hms-leopard-affair.html.

US Work Projects Administration. *Slave Narratives: A Folk History of Slavery in the United States from Interviews with Former Slaves.* Volume 14, *South Carolina Narratives*, Part 3. Washington, DC: Federal Writers' Project, 1941.

Vogler, Christopher. *The Writer's Journey: Mythic Structure for Writers.* 3rd edition. Studio City, CA: Michael Wiese Productions, 2007.

Wallace, Anthony F. C. "Revitalization Movements." *American Anthropologist* 58, no. 2 (April 1956). https://anthrosource.onlinelibrary.wiley.com/doi /epdf/10.1525/aa.1956.58.2.02a00040.

Wallace, Sarah Agnes, and Frances Elma Gillespie, eds. *The Journal of Benjamin Moran 1857–1865*, Volume 2. Chicago: University of Chicago Press, 1949.

"The War Turns Serious—1862." *Civil War Monitor* 2, no 2 (Summer 2012): 1–80.

Weeks, John W. Address. In *Record of the Dedication of the Statue of Rear Admiral John Ancrum Winslow: May 8, 1909 . . .*, 25–59. Boston: State Printers, 1909.

Welch, Mary Parker, George Theodore Welch, and Dorothy Welch White. *Memoirs of Mary Parker Welch, 1818–1912.* Brooklyn, NY: privately printed, 1947.

Welles, Gideon. *Diary of Gideon Welles*, Vol. 2, *1864–1866.* New York: Houghton Mifflin, 1909.

Werz, Bruno. *The Shipwrecks of the* Oosterland *and* Waddinxveen, *1697, Table Bay.* Johannesburg: Zulu Planet, 2009.

"Wesley to Wilberforce; John Wesley's Last Letter from His Deathbed." *Christianity Today.* Accessed November 15, 2023, https://www. christianitytoday.com/history/issues/issue-2/wesley-to-wilberforce. html.

West, Emily. *Family or Freedom: People of Color in the Antebellum South.* Lexington: University Press of Kentucky, 2012.

Wetta, Frank J., and Martin A. Novelli. *The Long Reconstruction: The Post–Civil War South in History, Film, and Memory.* New York: Routledge, 2014.

Williams, Jennie K. "Oceans of Kinfolk; The Coastwise Traffic of Enslaved People to New Orleans, 1820–1860." PhD dissertation, John Hopkins University, 2020.

Williams, William Henry. *Slavery and Freedom in Delaware, 1639–1865.* Wilmington, DE: SR Books, 1996.

Wilson, Carol. *Freedom at Risk: The Kidnapping of Free Blacks in America, 1780–1865.* Lexington: University Press of Kentucky, 1994.

Wilson-Bareau, Juliet, and David Degener. *Manet and the American Civil War: The Battle of the U.S.S. Kearsarge and C.S.S. Alabama*. New York: Metropolitan Museum of Art, 2003.

Wood, Peter W. *1620: A Critical Response to the 1619 Project*. New York: Encounter Books, 2022.

Zinn, Howard. *A People's History of the United States, 1492–2001*. New York: HarperCollins, 1999.

Index

❧

Page numbers in *italics* refer to figures and tables

Butler, Benjamin, 115
Byron, George Gordon, 199

Calhoun, John C., 61
Call, Richard K., 58–59
Calvert, Leonard, 54
Camps, John W., 154, 238
Cannon, Patty, 27
Cannon, William H., *40*, 40–41, 42–43, 45,
  51, *51*, 112, 118
cannons, 87, 197–98, 212, 217
Cape Town, South Africa: as port, 172–73,
  174–75; removal of statues, xiv; and *Sea
  Bride* capture, xi–xii, 174, 176; stopover
  (1863), 172–78; stopover (1864), 197;
  sympathy for Confederacy in, 174
Carpenter, Edward W., 275n34
Carriage of Passengers Act, 39
cats, 144–46
census of 1850, 5, 22, *30*, 30–33, *31*, *33*, 235
census of 1860, 30–32, *31*, *33*, 235
Certificate of Protection, 50–51, 112,
  131–32
Chaffin, Tom, 120
Charles Hill, 163
Chasseloup-Laubat, Prosper de, 206
Chastelaine, 156
Cherbourg, France: *Alabama* arrival, 205–7;
  harbor, *205*; *Kearsarge* voyage to, 204–7.
  See also *Kearsarge* battle
Chesapeake, 74–75, 132
Chilton, Mary, 71
cholera, 49
chronometers, 47, 103–4, 162, 209, 295n15
churches, 27, 30
cigar-box mutiny, 194
Circe, 241
Civil War: activity in Sept 1862, 48–49;
  Black soldiers and sailors in, 28–29, 115;
  and escaped slaves, 115; events leading
  to secession, 76–77; fears of in Delaware
  area, 35–36; and naval blockade, 77, 79–
  80, 136, 189; and raider construction,
  80–85; role of raiders in, 4–5, 78–80.
  See also *Kearsarge* battle; Lost Cause
  literature; neutrality; *and specific battles*

Claiborne, G. L., 67, 69, 73
Clarke, Frances J., 68, 69, 73, 94
Clavin, Tom, 304n7
Coetzee, J. M., xv
Collier, Robert P., 84
colonialism: and cultural context of 1840s,
  15–16; in Delaware history, 20–21; and
  illiteracy, 10–11; removal of statues, xiv
Colored Seamen's Homes, 42
Comoros Islands stopover (1864), 196–97
Condore Island stopover (1863), 196
Confederacy: Black support for, 232–33;
  Confederate ensign on *Alabama*, 100;
  formation of and secession, 76–77; and
  honor, 7–8, 82; Kell's enlistment in, 94;
  lack of ships, 77; and liberty language,
  10; motivations for joining, 82; mottoes,
  87, 241–43; removal of statues, xiv; role
  of raiders in, 4–5, 78–80; Semmes's
  joining of, 77; and slaves of officers, 77;
  sympathy for in Britain, 46, 81, 83, 85,
  152–53, 189; sympathy for in Europe,
  189, 197, 198, 205–6; sympathy for in
  South Africa, 174. *See also* Lost Cause
  literature
Confiscation Acts, 115
Conner, David, 64
Conrad, *167*. See also *Tuscaloosa*
conscription. *See* Enrollment Act
Constellation, 56, 148
Constitutional View of the Late War
  (Stephens), 8
Contest, 190, *191*
cooks: duties of, 41–42, 45; White as,
  38–48, 51–52, 237
Cope, Thomas P., 38, 40
Cope Line: and abolition, 40, 43, 235; and
  disease controls, 49; *Wyoming*, 38–48.
  See also *Tonawanda*
copper sheathing, 87, 198
Corsair (Byron), 199
cotton, 19–20, 189, 196
Courser, *106*
court martials, 59, 67, 94, 194
Crenshaw, *135*
Creole, 67–68